The Sunday Times

"Everywhere across Malawi, children sit by the roadside, waiting for something terrible. Here, they run up to you, each more charming, clever, funny and take-home-able than the last"

The *Guardian*

"I can't stop talking about Kondanani. There is no place like it!"

Guy Ritchie

"Kondanani is a five-star orphanage. What they are doing is extraordinary. It's a centre of excellence. A fantastic level of care is being given to these children"

Jacques Peretti, Channel 4

Annie Chikhwaza was brutally attacked and left for dead.

She overcame hatred with love, and the result is Kondanani Children's Village – an "oasis of love" that she and her late husband, Lewis, founded in Malawi in 1998. Since then, hundreds of lives have been saved in this nation with a million orphans, and Kondanani continues to offer hope to a new generation of African leaders.

Annie has been interviewed by major TV networks and Kondanani has been recognized in the media as an example of good aid to Africa. When American celebrity Madonna went to Malawi to adopt a baby in 2008 the orphanage became a focus of global attention, and a Dutch network produced a documentary on Annie entitled *Mother of Malawi*.

"Kondanani" means "Love one another", and Annie lives this out daily. Her story is one of victory over defeat and forgiveness over injustice. Suffering has been no stranger to her. She knows the pain of abuse, self-harm, and depression. Her first husband mistreated her and she survived the trauma of divorce. She knows the threat of having children removed and the anguish of dealing with abortion. Lewis's family rejected her, she was falsely accused and attacked, and her life hung in the balance. It took months for her to heal, but she knew the power of forgiveness. Throughout her life Annie has reached out from her own pain to comfort others. Now a widow, she continues to build a brighter future for the children in her care.

www.motherofmalawi.com

Mother of Malawi

The story of Annie Chikhwaza,
who created an oasis of love in a country
of orphans

As told to

Al Gibson

MONARCH
BOOKS

Oxford, UK & Grand Rapids, Michigan, USA

Published by Monarch Books
an imprint of
Lion Hudson plc
Wilkinson House, Jordan Hill Road,
Oxford OX2 8DR, England
E-mail: monarch@lionhudson.com
www.lionhudson.com/monarch

ISBN 978 0 85721 375 4
e-ISBN 978 0 85721 465 2

First edition 2013

Acknowledgments

Unless otherwise stated Scripture is taken from the New King
James Version. Copyright © 1982 by Thomas Nelson, Inc. Used by
permission. All right reserved. Scripture quotations marked NIV
taken from the Holy Bible, New International Version, copyright ©
1973, 1978, 1984 International Bible Society. Used by permission of
Hodder & Stoughton, a member of the Hodder Headline Group. All
rights reserved. 'NIV' is a trademark of International Bible Society.
UK trademark number 1448790. Scripture quotations marked NLT
are taken from the Holy Bible, New Living Translation, copyright ©
1996, 2004, 2007 by Tyndale House Foundation. Used by permission
of Tyndale House Publishers, Inc., Carol Stream, Illinois 60188. All
rights reserved.

p. 10: Map adapted with permission of Jean Gibson.

A catalogue record for this book is available from the British Library

Printed and bound in the UK, March 2013, LH26

Dedication

This book is dedicated to my wonderful late
husband, Lewis Chikhwaza, who gave me so much
support throughout our marriage in spite of the pain
he suffered as a result of the attack on my life; to my
dear children – Samuel, Rebekah, Paul, and Esther
– who are so very precious to me; and to each of the
children of Kondanani, as together we build a new
generation of leaders in Malawi.

Antje Saakje Chikhwaza

About the author

Al Gibson was born in Zimbabwe and graduated with a degree in journalism from Rhodes University in 1984. He attended Rhema Bible Training Centre and spent seventeen years working as a journalist in South Africa. He now lives in the UK, where he has been with GOD TV (www.god.tv) since 2001 as Communications Officer and Editor of the global television network's publications.

In close on thirty years in media, Al has interviewed many inspirational leaders. As an author, his passion is to inspire readers with true-life stories of those who have overcome impossible obstacles. His first book, *Life on the Line*, focused on Des Sinclair, who was kicked out of his home as a boy and met God on a rubbish dump! This was the start of an amazing journey on which Des was left for dead several times, yet he miraculously survived and now encourages people to become a lifeline to others.

Al met Annie Chikhwaza through GOD TV and travelled to Malawi to visit the Kondanani Orphanage. He was amazed to see all Annie has accomplished and counts it a privilege to share her extraordinary story.

Visit www.kondanani.org to find out more about the orphanage and www.halloffaithbooks.com for the latest news about Al's books.

Contents

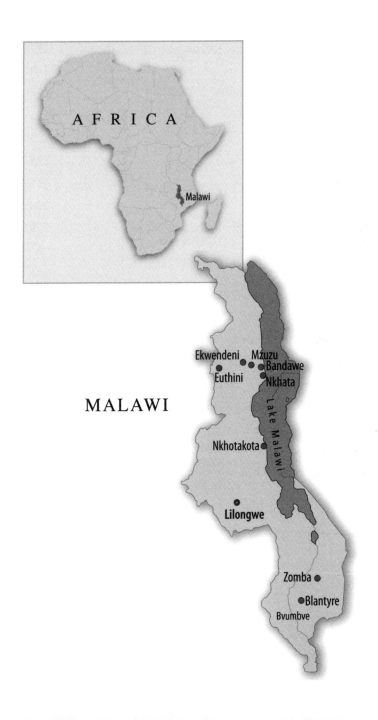

Foreword

RORY ALEC

RELIGION THAT GOD OUR FATHER

ACCEPTS AS PURE AND FAULTLESS IS

THIS: TO LOOK AFTER ORPHANS AND

WIDOWS IN THEIR DISTRESS...

(James 1:27, NIV)

Having a true faith in God includes caring for widows and orphans and helping the helpless. This is the heart of the work of Kondanani and of GOD TV, and we're privileged to be a part of what God is doing through the far-reaching ministry of Annie Chikhwaza to help the children of Africa.

Annie has very nearly lost her life on several occasions and it's a complete miracle that she is alive today! She is a woman of tremendous faith and an inspiration to people worldwide. You'll be challenged as you read this extraordinary story of God's faithfulness, protection, and provision.

It's amazing to think that a woman born in the Netherlands went to England, to South Africa, and then to Malawi, where she married a wonderful man, her late husband, Lewis Chikhwaza, and where God used them both to establish a ministry that is touching so many precious young lives today.

I believe that God's work through Kondanani is something profound and that it will have an impact on the entire continent of Africa. It has been my privilege to visit the Children's Village several times to film the fruit of this extraordinary ministry and to share this with GOD TV's viewers worldwide.

Kondanani truly is an oasis of tranquillity, education, and equipping. The babies are such bundles of joy and I'm sure that among these wonderful young men and women we will find future presidents, doctors, pastors, business people, and so on. I see phenomenal integrity, entrepreneurship, and the favour of God through the work of an amazing woman who has such a mother's heart for Africa.

I have known Annie for over twenty-five years and she has been a great blessing to my wife and me. In fact, she brought Wendy to the church where I was leading worship one Sunday morning, and that is how I got to meet my wife!

Wendy and I have seen many miracles of God's provision over the years and I want to tell you that, when we were first starting out, Annie and Lewis came to visit and gave us the first gift we received towards launching Europe's first daily Christian television network. We had nothing but faith, and Annie and Lewis didn't have much either, but we all knew how to trust God!

It amazes me today to look back and see what God has accomplished in our lives as we have stepped out in obedience and we're forever grateful to each person who has stood with us to reach the world through media including this dear pastor and his lovely wife.

We were pleased to bring Annie and Lewis to the UK in April 1996 when GOD TV was just a baby, broadcasting for only three hours a day. They came for the dedication service at Westminster Central Hall. A couple of years later, while I was praying one morning, God gave me a vision of Annie standing with HIV/AIDS orphans in Africa and He clearly instructed me to help her.

I'm thrilled that, by God's grace and the generosity of our

partners, GOD TV can now pour into the vision of Kondanani in a measure beyond what Wendy and I ever thought possible. It is wonderful to think that, as we do this, we are making a real difference in the lives of African children.

I'm reminded of the story of the starfish that were washed up on a beach and of the boy who threw them back into the sea because he knew that if he didn't they would die:

> **"Young man, don't you realize there are miles of beach and starfish all along it. You can't possibly make a difference!" an older man cautioned.**
>
> **The young man listened politely. Then he bent down, picked up another starfish, and threw it into the sea. "It made a difference for *that* one!" he exclaimed.**

Annie is an example of someone who is making a difference, and we can all make a difference as we are challenged by the plight of the individual.

Annie has always had a heart for the downcast. She was a successful businesswoman, but her ministry came first. I remember her days reaching out to help people in the violent township of Alexandra towards the end of the apartheid regime in South Africa. It was a squalid, overcrowded place, but God equipped Annie to reach out with His arms to people who were suffering. She was His hands, His feet, as the GOD TV family is called to be to a hurting world.

Now look what Annie is accomplishing in Malawi with such excellence. It's so exciting to see the fruit God is bringing forth in her life despite the barriers that have stood in her way. It was a privilege to have known Lewis; he was a real gentleman, a pastor to pastors, and he leaves behind a legacy of faithfulness: "What a *faith*-ful God!" I can still hear him say.

We believe God has called GOD TV, as a media mission ministry, to be a servant to those who minister to widows and orphans, and we rejoice that we have been able to stand alongside Annie Chikhwaza and the work of Kondanani from the start. As you read her story you will be faced with things that make your heart ache, but, as you see what God has done for her and for these precious children, you will be filled with hope and joy.

Every person who reads this book will be at a different stage of their walk with God. Some may not yet have experienced the love of God or the saving grace of our Lord Jesus Christ; if not, I am sure you will through this book. Others may have served God for years, but be looking to find a renewed vision and encouragement...

Wherever you are on your spiritual journey, I believe that as you turn the pages of *Mother of Malawi* you will be nurtured and changed. You'll also be inspired by Annie's tremendous faith and her selfless example. And you will take strength from the knowledge that what God can do for Rory and Wendy, what he can do for Annie Chikhwaza, He can do for you!

Rory Alec
GOD TV Co-founder and CEO

1

The day of my execution

"IT WASN'T THE END; IT WAS ONLY
THE BEGINNING!"

"Kill her... Kill her... *Kill her*!" screamed the crazed woman
leading the mob of African villagers as they rampaged towards
Annie and Lewis Chikhwaza's home. "*Pha... Pha... PHA ...*
('Kill')," she shouted in Chichewa, her mother tongue. Armed
with tribal weapons, "knobkerries", machetes, and large sticks
and stones, there was no telling what damage they might inflict
on the couple's property, let alone its occupants.

"Kill that white bitch!" Dorothy Chikhwaza ranted
with uncontrollable venom and a string of obscenities. "She
murdered my brother. She has stolen our inheritance!"
Common sense had long since given away to superstition and
false accusation, fuelling an intense hatred for her stepmother.

Ordinarily, the village of Bvumbwe, near Blantyre, the
former capital of Malawi, was a peaceful rural settlement.
Framed by clear blue skies, its dusty farm roads were lined
with green fields and shady trees, the hot African sun beating
down on the uneven thatched roofs of a myriad of brick
huts. The occupants were usually friendly and full of smiles,
their children waving, but not today. The tranquillity of the
Malawian countryside had been interrupted by maddened
cries for death and destruction.

Annie was shocked as she looked out of her front window to see a mob of two hundred armed villagers in the distance. She and her husband, Lewis, had received several death threats, but she had never expected this. The long-standing family feud had reached crisis point and she knew she was in grave danger. "This is the day of my execution" was her ominous evaluation of the developing crisis.

She hurriedly locked the doors of the house and ran to the bedroom she shared with Lewis, locking the door behind her and hiding under their bed. It was 30 September 1996 and Annie had lived in Malawi for barely three years. Already she had accomplished a lot to help alleviate the poverty of the local community, but her husband's children had never accepted her and now they wanted her dead.

"Is this the end for me?" Annie questioned as she heard gunshots. "Is this the way I'm going to finish up, even though God has called me to serve the people of Malawi?" she thought as she lay under the bed. "Who will help them now?" It was hurtful to think that the people she had tried to help the most had turned so violently against her.

"Annie, Annie?" she heard Lewis shouting, but she knew it was better not to answer because he would try to defend her and they would both be killed. So she kept silent, trying to be calm but praying under her breath beneath the mattress. She wondered whether the watchmen she and Lewis had employed would be able to stop the crowd, but she knew she could not rely entirely on them for her safety, or on the police. She had to trust God as never before.

Moments earlier, the crowd had been whipped into a frenzy by an altercation with the watchmen. The mob were throwing bricks and stones at the guards and hurling anything they could find as they surged forward, trying to grab a rifle.

The gang of villagers was soon out of control and, when

one of the watchmen tried to fire a warning shot, it only made things worse. In the confusion a young pregnant mother was tragically killed, along with her unborn baby, and four people were injured. This made the mob even wilder.

Dorothy instructed a young man to take an axe and kill her father, and the sixty-eight-year-old pastor had to run for his life. Annie had been unable to run away because her back had been broken in suspicious circumstances the year before, and hiding had seemed the safest option.

The Chikhwaza children were furious with their father and stepmother and had hired villagers to assist them in getting rid of the couple. The mob surged forward and surrounded Lewis's car as he dashed into the Bushveld, followed by the axe-wielding teenager.

The mob now started to attack his car. They smashed the windscreen and slashed the tyres, brandishing their pangas, a type of machete with a blade about forty centimetres in length.

Incensed by the death of the young mother-to-be, the crowd of villagers began to attack the house. They smashed the windows and broke down the doors, and eventually found their way to Annie's bedroom.

"Father, I commit my life into your hands," she cried out to God. "If I die today, then I know You have called me home. If I live through this, then I'll know it's Your will for me to continue with what You have called me to do."

Annie was pulled outside by her hair and thrown onto the ground, where her head was beaten and her body repeatedly kicked. Stones were thrown at her, bruising her all over, and her leg was stabbed by a panga, so that blood streamed down into the soil below.

Annie faded in and out of consciousness; her life was ebbing away and had it not been for the timely arrival of the police she would never have survived the ordeal. Even so, the mob had left her for dead as they quickly dispersed to avoid arrest.

One of Annie's employees, a tailor, had run all the way to the police station to alert them and thankfully two officers arrived just in time, but Annie still had to be rushed to the emergency room of the nearby Agricultural Research Institute. They saw that her life was hanging in the balance so she was quickly transferred to hospital in Blantyre.

Lewis had managed to get away from the young man who was pursuing him with an axe, and was reunited with his wife at the hospital. Annie believes an angel must have tripped the young man up, allowing her husband to escape into the bush.

Lewis would not leave Annie's bedside as the doctors struggled to save her life. It seemed that she had brain injuries, her body was battered and bruised, she had lost a lot of blood, and she was in danger of losing her leg.

"I didn't feel the agony of all this while it was happening," Annie remembers, "although recovery was a painful experience. At the time, it was as if God was cushioning me in His arms. I was in an awful situation, but my foundation was strong. I was able to abandon myself to the only one who could help me, my heavenly Father, because I had come to know Him so well."

Annie felt cocooned in God's love. As she lay in her hospital bed she remembered the silkworms her children had kept, and the protective coatings they had woven. Throughout the attack she had felt a sense of protection. "There was no fear; I was totally reliant on God!" she said.

"Thankfully, God wasn't finished with me. He sent two policemen on their bicycles to save my life. How could two policemen on bicycles think they could stand up to a mob of two hundred?"

When Annie saw those two hundred people surging towards her, she thought it was the end, but it wasn't the end; it was actually the beginning.

"We have to face difficult challenges like this in life because we are in an obstacle race. We can't just stop and give up; we have to jump over the obstacles and keep moving towards the finish line.

"An obstacle is there to be overcome. It is there to strengthen you, to bring out God's character in your life, so that you can continue to fight the good fight of faith."

> ...Chains and tribulations await me. But none of these things move me; nor do I count my life dear to myself, so that I may finish my race with joy, and the ministry which I received from the Lord Jesus, to testify to the gospel of the grace of God.
>
> (Acts 20:23–24)

"God is faithful and His word is true," Annie affirms. "When He tells you to do something, He will provide for you and protect you. So I was taken to hospital and all I could do was give glory to God. Although I did feel cocooned, there were still times of terrible pain, but I was filled with joy because I was alive!

"I also knew that God was going to do something extraordinary, that out of this near-death experience He would bring forth new life, that where my blood had been spilled on the ground something wonderful would grow out of my suffering.

"God later revealed to me that He would use the land where I had been left for dead to give life to others – that it would become a sanctuary for babies who had also been left for dead, for children who had been rejected. A place of hatred would become a place of love – Kondanani, which simply means 'Love one another'. He is the great restorer."

So how did Annie come to be in Malawi?

2

A good little Dutch Reformed girl

"WHO WOULD SHINE A LITTLE LIGHT IN THE DARKNESS?"

Annie was born in the Netherlands on 26 May 1944, during the Second World War. It was a dark time for Europe and for her parents, Harm and Maaike Terpstra, as they faced the uncertainty and danger of living under the Nazi occupation.

Annie's grandmother was Jewish, so her father had to lie low even though he considered himself a Christian. Everyday life was extremely difficult, with soldiers controlling the streets and food being constantly rationed. The newspapers were full of reports of cities being bombed and horrific stories of innocent lives lost, yet there were faint whispers of resistance.

Harm and Maaike started work at an early age, he delivering bread on his bicycle and she as a maid. He risked his life as part of the Dutch Resistance but after the war there were few career opportunities, especially in Friesland. Nevertheless he was able to take up carpentry and Maaike would soon become a full time mother.

Antje Saakje Terpstra was a lively baby with beautiful blue eyes and a bountiful mop of brown hair, and it was clear from the start that she was going to have enormous character. It wasn't long before she became affectionately known to everyone as "Annie".

While most people today consider Annie to be Dutch, she is actually from Friesland, a province in Northern Holland, and she grew up speaking *Fries*, which is as different from Dutch as English is from German!

Friesland is famous for its black and white cattle, but as much as the countryside was rich in beauty, Annie's family were poor. Cattle grazing in the fields, traditional windmills, and a network of canals made a picturesque landscape, but life was tough in this agricultural community.

Although her father worked hard as a carpenter, he earned little and her mother was kept busy enough caring for their children: Antje, Piet, Saakje, Geert and Douwe. Gifted at needlework, she sewed all their clothing, often working until late at night, and she knitted all their jerseys.

Annie's leadership abilities became obvious as soon as she started to help care for her younger brothers and sister. Her baby brother Douwe was born when Annie was eleven, and she recalls the day of his birth.

"I remember when my mother went into labour and my father took her to the hospital in Leeuwarden, a city about six miles from our town of Dronrijp. I was left to look after my three siblings and for the next ten days I had to run the household on my own and do all the washing by hand! When my dad came home and told us the baby was another boy, I wasn't impressed. I wanted another sister. I loved my little brother, though, and still do!"

Annie didn't get on quite so well with her eldest brother, Piet. "We were far from friends as children; we nearly killed each other. It must have been very difficult for our parents. One day Piet told me that he had just killed a mouse, describing how he had stood on it and how blood had sprayed out of its mouth. He knew I would be upset, and of course I cried for hours."

Despite Harm Terpstra's Jewish heritage, their home was typical of that of many a Dutch Reformed family at the time, with the Bible being read twice a day, providing a foundation for Annie's life; however, at that stage she knew little of the love of God.

She adored her father, although he was a stern disciplinarian and there was no shortage of hidings for the Terpstra children and especially for young Annie, who somehow managed to get the worst of his firm hand. Nevertheless, he was still *heit* ("dad" in *Fries*), and he could do no wrong in her eyes.

Annie's relationship with her mother was quite different. Maaike was a perfectionist and, despite her best efforts, Annie couldn't seem to please her. *Mem* was often impatient with her or too busy to be affectionate, and they were often at loggerheads.

"You'll never amount to anything," Maaike told her daughter in utter frustration – an erroneous evaluation that was repeated as Annie became a teenager. The words cut into her heart from the first time she heard them at the age of three, but Annie was a survivor, even then, and she was going to learn to rise above the criticism of others, even those close to her.

In this case, the oft-quoted saying "Mother knows best" didn't apply, and even though Annie couldn't see it at the time her heavenly Father was at work to disprove her mother's words.

Life was hard for the little *Fries* girl, growing up in the face of apparent rejection, but she wasn't going to wallow in self-pity. Instead, she became determined to reach out to others in the only way she knew how.

From an early age Annie had a passion for caring for people. She set up a pretend hospital in the attic of her parents' home: two chairs pulled together made an improvised hospital bed, and the children of the street became her "patients".

She never aspired to be a doctor; she only ever wanted to be a nurse. Dressed all in white, with a makeshift nurse's hat, she would enjoy taking her patients' temperature with a pencil acting as a thermometer. And, despite the lack of a mattress, she loved making her friends comfortable as they lay on the hard wooden chairs. She would cover them with her favourite blanket and let them share her only doll or teddy bear to make them feel special.

The world of make-believe nursing was fun, but it wasn't long before Annie realized there was no need to pretend. The desperate needs of people who were hurting in one way or another were a stark reality that lay all too close to her doorstep... especially the needs of those whom her community dismissed as "those dirty boat people".

"They live in such filth; I wonder how any of them can survive in that mess," Annie heard a neighbour remark as she and another woman gossiped in the street.

"They are not like us!" her friend replied. "I wouldn't be seen dead near them. I couldn't bear the smell. It's a shame what they've done to our canal."

"Neither would I, but it's not only the boat people, it's also the new immigrants... We need to keep our children away from them."

Given the way the Netherlands welcomes diversity today, it seems hard to believe that such prejudice abounded just sixty years ago, but in the town of Dronrijp, where everybody knew everybody else's business, this is how many people once felt.

The village folk were poor enough themselves, but it seemed there was always someone even poorer. Perhaps it made them feel better to tell tales about how others were worse off, or maybe it just distracted them from their own difficulties.

The Friesian homes were very clean and it was the new immigrants who were talked about most as they were considered "dirty". The Dutch colonies of Indonesia and Suriname had achieved independence yet there was an endless stream of immigrants from these countries coming into the Netherlands, all struggling to make a living in their new country. And, worst of all, there were "the dirty boat people", who lived on all kinds of floating contraptions. They looked bad enough from the outside; nobody would dare venture within.

Apart from Annie. From a young age, she had an understanding that all people were valuable to God, no matter who they were. And it wasn't as if her nose didn't work as well as everybody else's, or that her eyes were blind to the squalor. She was all too aware of it, but she was not going to allow this to stand in her way.

Who was going to step in and make a difference? Who would offer a glimpse of hope? Who could shine a bit of light in the darkness? These were some of the thoughts going round in her little head.

Annie's nose told her that something needed to be done, but nobody was doing anything. To her nine-year-old mind the solution was simple. If something was dirty, it needed to be cleaned! And so she would go round cleaning the homes and houseboats of the people society shunned.

"As a child I felt sorry for the people our community would have nothing to do with," Annie recalls today, "so obviously I was going to try to do something to help.

"We had a canal running through our town and boats would constantly pass by, loading and offloading goods. Sometimes the boats would be anchored for weeks; ablution facilities were limited and the boat people were considered 'dirty'.

"My parents forbade us to associate with them, but for me that was reason enough to seek them out! Besides, it reduced me to tears when these children came to my school and were ignored. Many of them were from Roma families, and I thought they were so beautiful."

Annie knew what it was like to feel put down and she was always the one playing with the children whom society was so quick to reject. Even then she was starting to follow her life's calling as a defender of the outcast.

"There was a family in our town with twelve children and nobody wanted to have anything to do with them," she remembers. "My brothers and sister and I were not allowed to speak to them either.

"I recall going into their home and many other homes of people whom the townsfolk would gossip about, and I would clean them. I was just a child, but there I was clearing up other people's messes and trying to make them feel accepted, hoping to encourage them by showing them that things could be different.

"Somehow, I would always be on the lookout for people in need. I didn't have any food to give them, as we were so poor ourselves, but I could at least show love and compassion by cleaning their homes!"

Years later, at her mother's funeral in 1997, Annie was reunited with an old lady who mentioned the time Annie had come to clean her house at the age of eleven and how wonderful it had made her feel, that someone really cared.

"She asked if I could recall that incident," Annie says. "What I remember most is that their house smelled so bad, but of course I didn't tell her that! It must have made an impression on her if she hadn't forgotten it after so many years.

"I was a good Dutch Reformed girl – although I scarcely had a personal relationship with God in those days, somehow I was an instrument of His love. What the people thought about my helping them, I don't know. I wasn't sharing the gospel with them in words, but in deeds."

3

Broken yet called by God

"YES, LORD, I'LL SERVE YOU ALL MY LIFE"

As a child, Annie had given hope to others, but her parents found her increasingly difficult to cope with. Nobody could understand why, and neither could Annie, though if she had really thought about it she would have known. Looking back now, it's obvious, but at the time she did everything she could to block out such a trauma. It was just too painful for a young girl to deal with.

It all started when she was just eight years old and a family friend stole her innocence. Her parents often struggled to make ends meet and during school holidays she and her siblings had to work for neighbouring farmers to earn extra money for the family.

Annie would plant cabbages and potatoes in the fields, help gather hay, and do whatever was needed on the farm. It was during this period that a particular farmer would find something "important" for her to do in the barn, away from the others.

This man was a friend of Annie's parents and she knew how much trouble it would cause if she said anything, never mind the fact that she would lose the little money she was able to contribute. Besides, what the farmer was doing to her was so confusing and embarrassing... and not something she could talk about.

"He would find a corner somewhere and he would abuse me," Annie confides. "He never penetrated, but the fondling was shameful enough. That's when the abuse started, and I was not able to tell anybody about it until years later."

Annie's sexuality had been awakened too early and during her teenage years she became cheeky and rebellious towards her parents. An early developer, she could easily have passed for sixteen when she was only twelve, and there was no lack of male interest, however unwanted.

Furthermore, at this crucial time in her life, Annie's father was forced to leave Friesland to take up a new job in Noord Holland and the family had to take in lodgers to supplement their income.

Jan was much older than Annie, a tall, well-built man in his thirties. At first he seemed pleasant enough, spoiling her with special treats. He soon discovered that she loved cheese and would creep into her bedroom and feed her pieces of Gouda, and there was an endless supply of her favourite fruit, dried dates.

Jan had a motorbike and would often take Annie on rides into the country. It seemed harmless enough. Yet it wasn't. His late-night visits to her room became all too regular, and shamefully they continued for over two years.

"He just wouldn't leave me alone, and there was nothing I could do to stop it. He was living in our home and I didn't know how to deal with the situation. It only ended once we moved to Noord Holland," Annie shares candidly, hoping her honesty will help others who have encountered similar molestation. "I didn't see my father that often and there was no way I could tell my mother; I knew it would break their hearts."

Annie's parents remained clueless as Jan sneaked into her room time after time. Never mind the dirty boat people – she felt even dirtier. She knew that what was happening was wrong, and it made her feel guilty and worthless, but at least somebody seemed to care about her.

"This is what's so deceptive about sexual abuse," says Annie. "It makes you feel bad, knowing that it isn't right, that you are being violated, and yet there are times when you find pleasure in it. Then you feel you are the one to blame, that somehow you are the one in the wrong, when in fact you are the innocent party.

"That is what bothered me for a long time, because I had come to find a kind of pleasure in it but I couldn't understand why when I knew I was being abused.

"It is such a confusing situation to be in. That's why my heart goes out to people who have gone through the same thing. I know how devastating abuse can be and the detrimental effect it can have on your whole life.

"You feel that a part of you is broken and only God can fix that brokenness. Thankfully, today I have been able to let go of my anger and resentment and forgive these men for what they did to me. That really helped me walk free of these ugly situations."

Annie has now come to terms with the abuse that occurred, but there is no doubt that her ordeal precipitated the need for some of the therapy she would have to go through in later years. The abuse made her feel worthless. Her self-esteem was shredded and she had little self-confidence.

Not surprisingly, she became an impossible teenager who wouldn't submit to anything her parents asked her to do. As a result, her mother seemed even more distant and cold, and although her father was affectionate, Annie resented the fact that he had not been there to protect her, and his heavy-handed discipline only made things worse.

"I can remember my dad beating me on two occasions, but my siblings say it happened often. He was remorseful on his deathbed, and cried out, 'I am so sorry for hitting you!' Of course, I had long forgiven him, as I loved him so much.

"And I had long forgotten the physical abuse I endured; perhaps I just put it out of my mind, like the sexual abuse," Annie says, thinking back to the 1950s. "But of course your siblings are always there to remind you of your childhood woes!"

One incident Annie does remember is the time her parents bought her new shoes and she refused to wear them because they didn't fit and hurt her badly. Her dad was so angry at her apparent ingratitude that he lashed out at her without thinking.

Another concerned a teenage crush she had on a certain bus driver, while the family were still living in Friesland. It happened around the time when Jan was sneaking into her room. Perhaps it was Annie's way of regaining some control over what was happening to her.

She was thirteen and the bus driver was twenty-seven; he was married but obviously enjoyed the young girl's attention. He never knew how young she really was, nor did he take advantage of her. Annie would simply get on the bus and wait for him to finish his shift, and then they would talk for hours.

Nothing ever happened between them, but this was one relationship her parents did find out about and they tried all they could to stop it.

"Annie, you can't go out with a married man. You have to stop seeing him!" her mother screamed.

"Who is he?" her father demanded over the telephone from Noord Holland.

Annie refused to listen to her mother or tell her father whom she was seeing. All they knew was that he was an older, married man who was a bus driver. Her parents eventually called the police and asked them to investigate, but somehow

Annie managed to dodge the situation and they never found out who the man was.

One day when her father was home for the weekend she was sitting with her parents in the front room of their home when she saw the bus go by. Her friend was driving, and she couldn't wait to meet him.

"I'll see you later," she announced, running out of the front door.

Her father, seeing the bus and putting two and two together, ran after her and grabbed her. "You're not going to see that man!" he shouted. "He has a wife; you have no business wrecking a marriage."

"You can't stop me seeing him," Annie retorted defiantly.

He pulled her back into the house where he took his hand to her backside, leaving the teenager in a flood of tears.

"You can't do this to me; I can't wait to get out of here!" she screamed. This only enraged her father more and he hit her again.

"You'll never amount to anything if you carry on like this," was all her mother would say – her usual judgment when Annie did something wrong.

"I can imagine how frustrated my father was with me. I told him that it was unacceptable for him to beat me, but he just didn't know what to do. He and my mother were under enormous stress knowing their daughter was seeing this older man and the fact that he was married made my dad so angry, yet he should never have beaten me like that."

Despite all that was going on in these turbulent years, Annie continued to reach out to the outcasts of society. Immigrants from Indonesia and Suriname became her closest friends and she would still clean houses whenever she had the opportunity.

Maybe it became a comfort to her. Perhaps cleaning for

others made her feel less dirty in herself. Whatever Annie's motivation, things seemed rather dark in her young eyes and it did not look as if there were any light at the end of the tunnel.

But deep down Annie knew that "God is light and in Him there are no shadows", and that "Jesus is the light of the world", and He was about to reveal Himself to her. She was about to receive a clear call from God.

When Annie was fourteen her mother packed up the family home to go and join her husband. Maaike and the five children moved to Noord Holland, where the Terpstra family were finally reunited. They settled in the city of Zaandam and for Annie it meant a new lease of life. It was like emigrating to a new world!

Yes, she would have to go to a new school and learn to speak Dutch properly, but it was so exciting to be in a city and at last she was able to put Jan behind her. Her heart longed for her immigrant friends and the boat people she had come to love, but Zaandam had no shortage of new people in need.

One night, while Annie was asleep in her tiny new bedroom in her parents' flat, she was woken by a reassuring voice in her ears. It was loud but also gentle, and it seemed to bring a sense of joy and peace, which flooded her whole room.

"Annie, *Annie!*" she heard God calling in an audible voice.

She knew the story of Samuel in the Bible, as her parents had read her the Scriptures, but somehow she had never expected them to come alive in this way.

"Yes, Lord?" she replied softly, as the young prophet had done. She knew instinctively that it was God speaking to her.

"I am calling you to serve Me," He said. That was all, but it spoke volumes to the fifteen-year-old.

"I will serve You all my life," she promised.

Despite her parents' shortcomings, unkind words, and limited understanding of the gospel, they had instilled a yearning for God in Annie from childhood. Now He was becoming a reality to her and she developed a great desire to serve Him.

From that moment when God spoke to her so clearly, Annie knew she was destined to live a life dedicated to Him. She didn't know if she would ever amount to anything... or what it really meant to be a servant of God. The clues were already there, but she would only really find out much later.

4

No freedom as a psychiatric nurse

"I'M FREE, I THOUGHT, BUT OF COURSE I WASN'T"

After Annie had suffered years of abuse, God had looked down and in His mercy revealed Himself to her. He had called her at the age of fifteen, giving her words of hope to cling to, but the enemy wasn't about to give up trying to destroy her young life.

The devil had tried to lead her off track through rejection, and physical and sexual abuse, and now that she felt called by God he was about to try to cause all hell to break loose in her life. Annie was fast realizing that life was an obstacle race and that she would have to learn to trust God to help her overcome each barrier in her way.

Following the move to Zaandam, Annie grew to love the hustle and bustle of city life. It was so different from the tranquillity of the Friesian countryside with its same old townsfolk. Here there were new people to meet every day and much more to do.

The family's new home was in a block of flats near a busy hospital. This immediately inspired the would-be nursing sister. She remembered the games she had played in the attic with her friends and, as she looked out of her bedroom window at the hospital every day, it seemed to be drawing her to its busy wards.

God had called Annie, but she didn't understand what He

wanted her to do. Her teenage mind assumed she would have to become a nun. That's the only way she thought she could serve God, and the fact that the nearby hospital was a Catholic institution meant that she would have to change denomination!

Her parents wanted her to attend confirmation classes in the Dutch Reformed Church but she didn't want to go, because she had come to accept the fact that she would have to become a Catholic.

She knew God's calling was on her life and she wasn't going to let anything stop her, neither confirmation classes nor financial difficulties. St John's Hospital became her spiritual haven and Annie set her mind on joining a convent.

"At my parents' insistence, I finally went to confirmation classes, but I couldn't go through with it. I told the minister the only way I could really serve God was as a nun. I didn't realize then that I could also serve Him in other ways."

Everything seemed to be going well for Annie in her new neighbourhood; she felt fulfilled helping to care for patients after school and at weekends, and she had started to see the hospital chaplain about fulfilling her vocation.

Just when the ordeal with Jan was behind her, it happened again. And this time with a person she really admired and trusted. Her protector and friend. The hospital chaplain became her next abuser, tipping Annie into a deep depression.

"I have to get out of here!" Her tongue was silent but she was shouting the words in her mind. Her brain was screaming as if about to explode. Once again she felt worthless, dirty, unloved, and unprotected, and her behaviour became impossible.

She even refused to go to school. "Annie, you've missed so many of your lessons... what about your education? You have to think of your future," her mother pleaded.

"You have to go back to school," her father interjected, the threat of another hiding in his stern voice.

"Never!" she replied defiantly. "You can beat me all you like; it's not going to change anything. I can't stand living here!" she shouted as she ran to her room and slammed the door behind her.

"And we thought she had settled in so well," her mother said. "Leave her, Harm; if you beat her, it will only make things worse. It breaks my heart; that girl will never amount to anything..."

"I just don't know what to do any more," her father said for the umpteenth time.

Lying on her bed, Annie sobbed and sobbed. "I just want to be free. I just want to be free," she kept saying to herself.

Freedom seemed to come printed within the pages of a local newspaper. Maaike had been peering at the endless lines of fine print in the classified section when she saw an advertisement that caught her attention.

"I've seen an advert," she announced. "It's for a hospital! They're looking for applicants from age fifteen, and you are going to apply."

By this time Maaike was at the end of her tether over Annie's behaviour; she couldn't cope with it any more and neither could her husband, so it wasn't long before the fifteen-year-old moved to Amersfoort, about a hundred miles from where her parents lived.

The hospital turned out to be a mental institution, but that didn't deter Annie. She was only too happy to have left home. "I remember sitting in my tiny room turning up the hem of my new nurse's uniform and thinking, 'Ah, I'm free!'," she says, "but of course I wasn't."

Training as a psychiatric nurse at the Sun and Shield Psychiatric Clinic in Amersfoort was a dream come true for Annie, who had by now turned sixteen. As there were four nurses named "Anne" she was allocated the name "Anita".

Caring for patients seemed to give her life new meaning, and of course she always focused on the worst cases.

She also loved spending time with her colleagues, again befriending those who were excluded and making them feel accepted and loved. It was fun to be with other girls her age, but gradually Annie began to realize they were being exposed to far more misery than they could deal with at such a young age.

She found herself surrounded by anguish, grief, and heartache, day in and day out, and it began to seriously affect her. She became increasingly depressed and her self-esteem continued on a downward spiral.

Patients who were clearly not in their right mind had no idea what they were saying, and she was sometimes subjected to horrific verbal abuse.

"You dirty little prostitute!" a patient once shouted at her. She knew the woman didn't know what she was talking about, but it was still a shock to the system, and the shocks seemed to keep on coming, one after the other.

Days later Annie overheard a patient talking about her in the hospital ward: "Wow, she's got sex appeal, hasn't she?" he remarked to a friend as Annie passed by. This was the worst thing anybody could have said to her – it brought back all the horrors of what the farmer, the lodger, and the hospital chaplain had done to her.

Annie wondered how much more she could take. Many of her patients were suffering from severe psychosis, and, although she loved caring for them, psychiatric nursing was beginning to affect her emotionally.

Despite her inner turmoil she managed to continue with the training. Her love of caring for people seemed to make things bearable, but her biggest problem remained that she felt so bad about herself. Her mother's words – "No good will ever come of you" – seemed to haunt her and she couldn't come to terms with the way she'd been violated by men.

At seventeen Annie was transferred to another part of the hospital and she remembers how her self-esteem was so low that she would listen at the doorway of the head nurses' office to find out if they were gossiping about her. Of course they weren't, but she was convinced they were.

"The doctors had a meeting every Tuesday and I had to take them tea. I would weep the night before because I was so scared that I would overhear them saying nasty things about me.

"There wasn't any reason to think this: I had a good working relationship with my colleagues, but I was paranoid that they might be criticizing me behind my back."

Even though she felt she was under close scrutiny, Annie would still open her heart to anyone who was being ostracized; she knew how they would be feeling. The nurses who had been sent over from Suriname to train in the Netherlands came from a different culture and were often looked down on by the other nurses. Annie became their protector. She took the time to talk to them and make them feel welcome, and stuck up for them at every opportunity.

Dedicating her life to others was rewarding for Annie despite everything she was dealing with, and for a while things seemed to be going better for Nurse Anita Terpstra, until something awful happened that caused everything to deteriorate...

It was just another day at the hospital in Amersfoort, where Annie had by now spent about three years. She would soon have a day off and be able to relax with friends. Things seemed to be looking up for the young nurse but, unbeknown to her, tragedy was about to strike.

Annie was supervising the patients in the lounge when one of them, a lady in her late forties, got up and headed for the door. "I'm going to bed," she mouthed, giving Annie a wry smile.

"I'll check on you in a few minutes," Annie replied kindly.

The cord was still around her neck when Annie found her hanging in the bathroom, her lifeless body dangling below her broken neck. She had used the belt of her dressing gown, tied to the high cistern of an old-fashioned toilet. Somehow it had been sufficient to hold her weight.

It was a horrific sight for Annie to witness and she cried out in shock and despair. She couldn't believe what had happened: just moments before, this patient had been sitting with her and everything had seemed normal. Now she was no longer breathing, and Annie felt responsible as she was on duty.

She acted as quickly as she could. Screaming for help, she grabbed a pair of scissors and cut the cord. The woman fell into her arms and Annie was able to ease her down to the floor. She tried everything she could to resuscitate her. Doctors came running but it was too late; there was nothing they could do.

"What happened?" a doctor demanded.

"She was with me just a few minutes ago; she did this in just ten minutes; just ten minutes ago she was alive, and now she's dead," Annie sobbed.

A terrible fear of death came over the young nurse. From that moment she became increasingly perturbed by the prospect of other patients trying to kill themselves, and overly cautious. She felt guilty for not preventing the incident and kept blaming herself. What she didn't realize was that through this devastating experience a spirit of suicide had transferred itself to her.

Some days later another unfortunate situation occurred, when one of Annie's patients managed to break out of the institution while she was on duty, and again she felt entirely responsible. All she could imagine was him hanging from a tree and her having another death on her hands. The thought was unbearable.

Annie couldn't sleep at all during the night the police spent looking for the runaway patient, using sniffer dogs to try to track his scent. Fortunately he came back at five o' clock in the morning when his hallucinations eased. Unfortunately for Annie, the anguish she experienced that night would soon take its toll...

5

God does have a plan

"YOU SHOULD HAVE DIED; IT'S A MIRACLE YOU'RE ALIVE!"

Annie was at her wits' end. She started to hate the psychiatric hospital and it was an effort just to get out of bed each day. She had become increasingly anxious, and feelings of worthlessness haunted her. She could not forget how her patient had killed herself and was overwhelmed by the fear she felt that other patients would end up in the same position.

It was all too much for her and the nurse became the patient. Annie suffered a nervous breakdown and needed treatment. Ironically, much as she feared for her patients' lives, she gave no consideration to her own. She started to focus on how she could end her life. It was a desperate cry for help but nobody seemed to be listening.

"I cut myself here, there, and everywhere," Annie recalls (she still bears the scars). "I broke a thermometer and swallowed the mercury, which is supposed to kill you, and I overdosed on sleeping pills more than once, but nothing seemed to work."

As a nurse Annie knew how much to take for a lethal overdose but somehow death eluded her. In hindsight it was God's grace that kept her alive, time after time, especially when she became so determined to end her life that she swallowed a whole bottle of Luminol sleeping tablets.

"I was unconscious for five days, and when I woke up I was unable to see; I was blind for several days," Annie remembers, shuddering to think how close she came to ending her life and wasting the God-given opportunities she has been given over the past nearly seventy years.

The Luminol disaster was a huge blow to Annie at the time: she knew she had taken enough to make sure she never woke up again, yet she had once again survived.

"God has a plan for your life, Annie!" the doctor tried to reassure her. "You should have died; it's a miracle you're alive!"

"No, doctor, God couldn't have a plan for me," she argued. "None whatsoever!" God might have spoken to her at fifteen, but that was a mere hazy memory when, aged almost twenty, all hope seemed lost.

Annie continued to see suicide as the only way out and was in and out of the hospital. She took more overdoses, and cut her wrists again. On one occasion she was put in a straitjacket to stop her from self-harming and she received electric shock treatment, which in fact added to her torment. While many painful memories were obliterated by the shocks, the treatment did nothing to fix the cause of her unhappiness.

Eventually Annie was sent home to her parents, the very last place she wanted to be. Freedom had now completely eluded her and she hated the fact that she had lost her independence. Worse still, her parents had to lock her up like a prisoner while she awaited admission to a psychiatric hospital.

"My will to die was so strong that I needed to be admitted to a mental hospital. So I was locked in a back room in my parents' home, where I couldn't get away and couldn't harm myself."

It was during this time that Annie's cousin, Ansje, asked her parents if they would allow her to take Annie to a gospel meeting in Utrecht. Although the Terpstras were reluctant to let her out of their sight, Ansje was also a psychiatric nursing sister and they knew their daughter would be in safe hands.

They were guilt-ridden for having let Annie leave home to train in a psychiatric hospital at such a young age, and felt responsible for allowing her to be exposed to the traumas of people in such mental anguish, a decision that had proved disastrous. What could they do to help turn this situation around? Perhaps the gospel meeting would have a positive influence, they reasoned.

It was Easter Monday 1963 and the speaker was a Dutch missionary by the name of Andrew van der Bijl, who became world-famous as Brother Andrew, the founder of the widely acclaimed ministry Open Doors.

Brother Andrew's exploits in Communist countries were already legendary, as he had risked his life to take the Bible into places where the word of God was strictly forbidden and would later publish the best-selling book *God's Smuggler*.

Annie was inspired by the stories he told of serving God. Hearing about his missions to foreign countries and how he often put his life at risk showed her that there were many ways to serve God besides becoming a nun. This kind of Christianity was really exciting, certainly not dull; however, she cannot remember anything about the service except what happened towards the end, because it completely changed her life.

Brother Andrew was standing to the left of the stage as he invited people to accept Jesus Christ as their saviour. The words struck a chord in Annie's heart and, as she looked over to the right of the stage, she saw a vision of Jesus coming towards her with His arms outstretched, reaching for her.

Annie jumped out of her chair in excitement and ran to the front. It was the most amazing experience of her life. She felt embraced by God's love and was instantly set free from any impulses towards suicide. All thoughts of self-harming also disappeared and her mind was completely at rest.

"When Brother Andrew appealed to us to give our lives to Jesus I clearly saw the Lord with His arms wide open to me and I ran to Him and found healing in His loving arms," Annie says, her face lighting up with a joy she has known ever since.

The transformation in her life was clear to all: Annie became a fervent evangelist. She developed a close relationship with God and her free hours were spent on street corners reaching out to others with her newfound faith.

Ansje knew how important it was for her cousin to be surrounded by believers who were committed to God's work. She took Annie to her youth group in the Dutch capital, Amsterdam, where she knew many Christians who would be instrumental in discipling Annie.

Their primary aim in life was to preach the gospel and they spent time each day reading the Bible and in prayer. On Wednesday evenings they would meet for Bible study and on Fridays they gathered for a prayer meeting. Then on Saturdays they would go into the streets of Amsterdam, sharing the gospel along the canals and even in the city's infamous red light district.

"On Saturday afternoons we would meet for sandwiches and then go out into the darkened city and have a street meeting," Annie recalls. "We would sing and play the guitar and testify, and people would give their lives to Christ as we shared the word of God and prayed for them. It was amazing!

"This was the most wonderful introduction to true Christianity," she goes on. "Our focus was purely to see God move in the lives of others, and there was no such thing as 'You are a new believer and you don't know what you're doing'. If you got saved on a Friday, then the next day you were out on the streets evangelizing like everybody else!

"It was a wonderful group of believers. Where I had been in the depths of depression, my life was now filled with joy. All of a sudden all I talked about was Jesus and what He was doing in my life. That's all we wanted. We didn't want anything else, just to do the Father's will."

Serving Jesus was exciting, but it wasn't without resistance. There were times when the young evangelists had rubbish thrown at them as they went from door to door, and at times the police in the centre of Amsterdam would ask them to stop what they were doing.

"But we could not be stopped," says Annie. "The excitement of seeing people saved was the greatest thing. We didn't go to our youth meetings to play ping-pong; we went to see people's lives transformed by the power of God. Even our holidays were dedicated to outreach.

"Do you think our idea of a vacation was to go to Hawaii? No! We would put a tent up in a village somewhere, where people were very religious, and we would go from house to house to invite people to our meetings. Sometimes we would have an egg or a tomato thrown at us, but it didn't matter. God was so real and serving Him was so exhilarating."

Looking back at her time as a new believer, Annie cautions Christians never to forget their first love, their enthusiasm for Christ, and the passion He inspires for winning souls. She is grateful to Ansje for taking her to Brother Andrew and for the role she played in her discipleship. Ansje later served as a missionary in Thailand for thirty-five years, an inspiration to Annie in her mission to Malawi.

Annie is also thankful to Brother Andrew and his far-reaching ministry, which has affected her life so deeply. Despite the many dangers he has faced over the years, including narrow escapes from death, he has been blessed with a long life and he's now back in Holland. Annie became a supporter of his work and he gave her a Bible, which she still treasures. She also met up with him during her time in South Africa, but more about that later.

"God does have a plan for my life," Annie finally realized, "and I know how I will serve Him. I will go to the ends of the earth for my beloved Lord and I will reach the unreached, those whom nobody loves and nobody cares about."

> **"For I know the plans I have for you," declares the Lord, "plans to prosper you and not to harm you, plans to give you a hope and a future."**
>
> (Jeremiah 29:11, NIV)

6

Go into all the world

"MY WHOLE FOCUS CHANGED WHEN I MET JESUS"

Annie was a different person once she had come to know Jesus. Every day she was discovering the significance of 2 Corinthians 5:17:

> Therefore, if anyone is in Christ, he is a new creation; old things have passed away; behold, all things have become new.

She had come a long way from the time when she was locked up in her parents' home, awaiting a place in a mental health institution; however, she was advised not to return to psychiatric nursing. She was told it would be like "going back into a den of ravening wolves", so she took a nursing position in a tuberculosis sanatorium in Zeesse, a town not far from Zaandam.

Annie had barely arrived when she found a new youth group to join, where she could continue being discipled and have fellowship with Christian friends. Her childhood concern for people from the Dutch colonies persisted and she was immediately drawn to a girl from Suriname named Ingard, or "Inge", as everyone called her.

Inge became a great friend to Annie, especially as she shared her passion for street evangelism. She also had a beautiful voice and played the guitar, and the two of them would regularly go out on the streets to share the gospel. Inge would attract passers-by with her singing and Annie would tell everyone how Jesus had transformed her life.

"I tried to commit suicide; I can't remember how often. But when God saved me, at the age of nineteen, I was set free. If there was hope for me, there is hope for you too," Annie challenged people as she shared her testimony.

"Inge and I just clicked and we would go all over the place to minister. We sang and preached at the railway station, even in bars," Annie recalls. "We just loved the Lord so much, and would lead people to Jesus. We were having a ball and each time somebody got saved we were overjoyed. That was a very special time!"

Annie was very excited about what God was doing in her life and was careful to guard her relationship with Him, as He was the one who mattered most in all she did. She was always ready to tell people about God and to share His love with others.

Just as when she was a child, when she had used her school breaks to help others, she saw holidays as being not just for fun but for being productive for the kingdom. Even as a new Christian she understood the importance of the great commission with which God charges every believer, to go into all the world and preach the good news to all creation (Mark 16:15).

Inspired by Brother Andrew's tales of exciting missions to foreign lands, Annie was eager to discover the world that lay beyond the Netherlands. She might have been just a young believer but God had given her a pioneering missionary spirit and a hunger for His word.

She realized that she couldn't go abroad straight away, but that her time would come. In the meantime she gave every spare guilder she could find to Brother Andrew's ministry, Open Doors.

"Why are you wearing such old clothes?" her mother would ask critically. "You can't afford to give *all* your money to Brother Andrew; what good is that going to do? You'd be better off getting yourself a new dress."

What Maaike Terpstra did not realize was that even at this young age Annie was sowing a firm foundation for her future ministry, and embracing a lifestyle of giving that would underpin everything she did and bring about many different harvests of blessing to others.

In addition to being impressed by the ministry of Brother Andrew, Annie had been introduced to the teachings of Rees Howells, a renowned Welsh revivalist who preached on faith and intercession. Rees and his wife had spent years as missionaries in Southern Africa and Annie felt God was leading her to attend his Bible school.

So she set her heart on studying at the Bible College of Wales in Swansea, but there was a problem – her father was not happy to let his eldest child go overseas. He wanted her to stay close to home.

Annie had to wait until her twenty-first birthday, when she would be able to make her own decisions. As soon as that day came, she jumped onto her bicycle and went to apply for a passport! A month later she was in the United Kingdom.

There was nothing stopping this determined young woman and so began a journey that would take her from the Netherlands to the UK, then on to South Africa, and ultimately to Malawi.

The UK was a whole new world for Annie and it meant mastering a new language. She had learned English at high school but realized she needed practice at speaking it. So before going to Bible school in Wales Annie decided to take up a job in

England as an au pair with a Christian family in Tewkesbury in Gloucestershire.

Having professed Christ as her saviour at a Pentecostal crusade, Annie thought everybody who was a Christian was on fire for God, but she was about to learn that this was not so. Although the family she stayed with were believers, they were more concerned about what she wore to church than with sharing their faith.

"It was the most difficult experience for me," Annie recalls. "Coming from the group of believers in Amsterdam, where all we talked about was what God was doing in our lives, I now found myself in a denomination where all they were interested in was that I get myself a hat!"

Annie was passionately in love with Jesus and although being an au pair was a full-time job she took every opportunity to escape into her bedroom during her breaks just to be with Him. She would cover her head with a blanket and pour her heart out to God. "I could never wait very long to tell Him how much I loved Him, and how precious He was to me," she says.

Annie's relationship with God grew stronger day by day, but she longed for genuine fellowship with other believers and couldn't find anybody to share with. Then she heard that an evangelist would be visiting the church, and she couldn't wait for him to come.

The day of the crusade finally arrived. The evangelist had a powerful voice, and Annie was moved as he sang one of her favourite hymns, "Down from His glory", written by William Booth-Clibborn in 1921. As he sang it was like a taste of heaven on earth.

> *Down from His glory,*
> *Ever living story,*
> *My God and Saviour came,*

And Jesus was His Name.
Born in a manger,
To His own a stranger,
A Man of sorrows, tears and agony.

O how I love Him! How I adore Him!
My breath, my sunshine, my all in all.
The great Creator became my Saviour,
And all God's fullness dwelleth in Him.

Annie had experienced God's salvation, and her heart was bursting to share her Lord and saviour. She tried to talk to the evangelist after the meeting but all he did was joke about her poor English and strange accent. She felt alone, a foreigner in a new country and a believer without fellowship.

"This is why it is so important for Christians to be planted in a strong local church," says Annie. "You need the ongoing support of the body of Christ to nurture you and encourage you to become all that God has called you to be."

Annie may have felt isolated but God was with her, and it was only a matter of months before she made contact with a church in Cheltenham that was more open to the work of the Spirit, and she was soon back out on the streets sharing the gospel.

She quickly realized that she could no longer stay with the family for whom she was an au pair. She felt stifled by their denominational traditions and of course, in their eyes, it was forbidden for a woman to preach.

This was a challenge Annie would have to overcome time and time again, yet she knew that God had called her "for such a time as this", like Esther in the Bible, and also like her fellow countrywoman Corrie ten Boom, who had survived the Holocaust to share the gospel worldwide.

From her study of the Scriptures it was clear to Annie that God was no respecter of persons (Acts 10:34); that all believers were one in Christ and gender was no barrier (Galatians 3:28); and that the great commission to go into the whole world and preach the gospel was given to *all* believers.

Furthermore, she knew that God had promised to pour out His Spirit in the Last Days on both men and women:

> **And it shall come to pass afterward that I will pour out My Spirit on all flesh; your sons and your daughters shall prophesy...**
>
> (Joel 2:28)

To prophesy is to speak under divine inspiration, and there was no stopping Annie. Her life had been turned around by the power of God: she had gone from deep depression and suicide attempts to joy, peace, and salvation. Jesus had done too much for her to allow her to remain silent.

Annie's preaching may not have been welcomed by the family in Tewkesbury, but her new friends in Cheltenham encouraged her to share her testimony of what God had done in her life, in order to help others struggling with depression and suicidal feelings.

"My whole life changed when I accepted Jesus Christ as saviour," she would tell any passer-by who would listen, and often God gave her opportunities to speak from her personal experience with people who had lost hope and were about to give up on life.

"Jesus can set you free from that spirit of suicide," Annie would tell them. "Don't even consider taking your own life; you may be out of it, but consider the mess you would leave behind.

"God delivered me from depression. My whole focus changed when I met Jesus. I realized how precious I was to

Him. He helped me to rebuild my self-esteem as I found out what the word of God said about me.

"I learned to see myself as God sees me. I realized that, as I am part of His workmanship, He places great value on me. Who are we to say to God that He didn't create us right? That we are inferior? God created us, so we couldn't possibly be inferior!"

Annie was not going to compromise her ministry by being held back by religious tradition; she knew she needed to find a new au pair job and place to stay, and started to pray that God would intervene in her situation.

The answer came swiftly. She got in touch with a couple from Oxford who were known to her through the youth group in Amsterdam, and they offered to employ her to look after their children. For a season everything was going well for Annie, and then, she says with a grin, "That's when I made my big mistake... I got married!"

7

Oh no, not Annie again!

"IF ONLY I HAD LISTENED TO MY DAD!"

Initially he seemed charming. His name was David, and he swept Annie off her feet.

She first saw him at the youth group in Amsterdam and remembers looking out of the window as he arrived from England. "What a handsome man; I like the look of him!" she thought to herself, but immediately dismissed the idea as he was ten years older than she was and lived in another country, and she thought he was probably married.

Several months later, Annie was in England herself and living in Standlake in Oxfordshire at the home of the couple who had taken David to Holland. "By the way, David is coming to visit us," they told her one day. "He'll be here for the weekend."

David and Annie met on 1 October 1965, started courting on 17 November, and were married three months later. So Annie never did get to Bible school in Wales, instead she had enrolled in "the University of Hard Knocks"!

David was a director of General Motors Finance Corporation in London and Annie was impressed by his job title. Maaike Terpstra had drummed into her girls that they must never marry a poor man, as she had done, and this was one piece of advice Annie considered worthwhile. She thought her mother would be proud of her at last.

Besides, David was convinced that Annie was the woman for him. Unbeknown to Annie, he believed that the woman

God wanted him to marry would be confirmed by the Scripture "God is love". Annie had inscribed this verse from 1 John 4:8 on the edge of her Bible. "This is it!" David had hastily decided.

In addition to this apparent sign of divine approval, David was fascinating to talk to and appeared to be very concerned for people's well-being. Annie had been introduced to him by trusted Christian friends, and although he had been married before, she wasn't going to let that bother her. "It was only for a year," she reasoned.

With the benefit of hindsight, Annie realizes that marrying David was not God's best for her; his father had been married several times, as had his grandfather, so he hadn't grown up with an appropriate example of how a husband should treat his wife. At the time Annie didn't have any inkling of this; to her it was very simple: she and David were in love, they were both believers, and it seemed that they had a bright future together.

Annie phoned her parents to tell them she had met her future husband and that she was bringing him home so they could meet him. The couple celebrated their engagement in Holland with Annie's family and shortly after that Annie moved from Standlake to London to make the arrangements for the wedding.

She arrived at the Chinese Mission House in Chelsea, where David had arranged for her to stay as he was a friend of the leader of the Mission. It was just six weeks before the wedding and Annie had many things to prepare for the big day, yet she still found time to reach out to people on the street.

"I always seem to find the 'down and outs', and while I was staying at the mission I met a young woman whom I started to talk to about the Lord. She was a prostitute, but desperate to leave that lifestyle behind her," Annie remembers.

"David wasn't happy about this and became intolerant of me reaching out to her. One evening this young woman came to visit me at the Mission House, which was not allowed, and David heard about it and became angry. We had a huge fight about it.

"The young woman was interested in God and I felt that, if I pursued her, she would be saved. David didn't have the same heart for people, even though he gave everybody that impression.

"I was already beginning to see signs of what would follow. I should have realized then how he would ultimately try to control my ministry, but I was young and in love and full of hopes and dreams...

"And everything for the wedding was organized... Although the thought crossed my mind, I felt I couldn't back out. Worst of all, I knew what my mother would say: 'Oh, no, not Annie again!' I could hear her tell my father. 'She will never amount to anything.' And I didn't want to hear that again."

The day of the wedding, 5 March 1966, came all too soon. Harm and Maaike Terpstra and Annie's sister Saakje came over from Holland to witness the marriage ceremony, which was conducted by the well-known Armenian evangelist Samuel Doctorian, founder of Bible Land Mission.

"Annie, you look so pale – are you OK?" Maaike Terpstra asked her daughter on her wedding day.

"Yes, *mem*, I'll be fine," Annie sighed.

Not easily rebuffed, Maaike had another question, which would really upset her daughter: "Are you sure you aren't pregnant?" she asked in a whisper.

"No, *mem*," Annie answered impatiently, ending the conversation. She couldn't tell her mother that the problem was that she wasn't sure what she was letting herself in for.

"It wasn't the best day of my life; I felt that I was making a mistake," Annie observes today. "I just didn't know how to back out of the situation. I was in a different country, I was still rather naïve, and I just didn't see a way out. I felt I was being swept into something I would regret, but it was too late to stop it."

Annie loved living in the UK, but it was to be only a stepping stone. Barely a year after she had arrived there she would be heading for the southern tip of Africa. In fact, just eleven days after the wedding David was transferred to Johannesburg, and he and Annie spent their honeymoon on the ship to South Africa.

Right from the start it was clear that David's work came first, at the expense of his marriage. He spent their honeymoon studying towards bettering his qualifications, and although Annie was keen for him to get ahead, it *was* their honeymoon, after all, and she felt neglected.

"He spent the whole twelve-day cruise studying and it was as if I didn't even exist! I tried to talk to him, but that only made him angry," Annie says.

Things got worse when the couple arrived in Johannesburg. They started off staying with friends of David in Honeydew, a suburb on the outskirts of the city. It was hard for Annie, living in a house with people she hardly knew and with her husband nowhere to be seen.

The move to South Africa meant another new country for Annie to adjust to. She was now a married woman, yet she still had much to learn about how to function in the world. For instance, she didn't know she could use an estate agent to find a flat to rent or that she could look for properties to let in the classified advertisements in the newspaper. So she went from door to door in Johannesburg's most densely populated suburb, Hillbrow, looking for suitable accommodation.

She eventually found a place in Smith Street in Joubert Park, where she and David lived for two years. Despite the couple's strained relationship their first child was born in

1967, a boy named Samuel. In 1969 David was transferred to Port Elizabeth and the family moved to the east coast of South Africa. A daughter, Rebekah, was born that same year.

Annie loved living by the sea and taking the children to the beach, but it wasn't long before David was transferred back to Johannesburg, where they lived in Germiston before moving to the affluent suburb of Bryanston. A second son, Paul, was born in 1971 and a second daughter, Esther, in 1977.

Though there were times when the couple seemed happy, it grew harder for Annie as her husband became ever more controlling and less tolerant of her spending time with God or ministering to others. She had to toe the line or risk major confrontation.

But she had children to care for, and they became the focus of her attention. That made it easier for Annie to cope with her husband's working around the clock. "He was a complete workaholic who would hardly consider his family, as he was scarcely ever home," Annie says. "He wasn't even having an affair at that time – his work was his mistress!"

When Annie was five months pregnant with Paul, Brother Andrew came out to South Africa to establish Open Doors in Johannesburg, and Annie and David went to meet him. Annie remembered that providential night in 1963 when she had given her life to God at his meeting in Utrecht, and the Bible he had given to her, which she has kept all these years.

Once again she was enthralled by his stories of how he would take Bibles into Communist countries, defying this godless ideology and making the Scriptures available to the underground church. "He had secret compartments in his combi where he would hide hundreds of Bibles," Annie recalls, "and he would lay hands on these and pray that God would give him safe passage, blinding the eyes of the guards at the border posts."

For once, David was inspired by something other than his work and expressed a desire to accompany Brother Andrew behind the Iron Curtain, but his heart wasn't really in it and, besides, Open Doors did not encourage people with children to travel into Communist countries as the dangers were so great.

At one time Annie had also considered travelling with Brother Andrew to Russia, but this was not to be. Thankfully, the Iron Curtain has since fallen, and in her own way Annie too has had to tear down many personal barriers and obstacles that have stood in her way.

On the one hand her marriage started to fall apart, yet on the other her ministry in South Africa began to take off. She wondered how long she could endure her marriage, yet she knew how much God hated divorce and that it was not an option for Christians.

Harm Terpstra had wanted to keep his daughter close to home but Annie had had other ideas. "Had I only listened to my dad, I believe life would have taken a different turn and I would not have endured all those years of difficulty," she says.

This may be so, but one cannot regret a union that produced four children, and God does cause all things to work together for good (Romans 8:28). God used this unhappy marriage to establish Annie in Africa, where she would reach out to the oppressed people of South Africa at the height of the apartheid era.

8

Watch out, devil, Jesus is coming!

"THEY WILL LAY HANDS ON THE SICK
AND THEY WILL RECOVER"

Weighed down by her marital problems, Annie felt she was running out of options. David had been asked to leave the church where they were worshipping in Bryanston and she didn't know what to do, but God's plan for her life was continuing to unfold.

Annie heard about a young couple who had just started a new ministry in Randburg, Ray and Lyndie McCauley. The year was 1979, the ministry was Rhema Bible Church, and it was going to have a great impact on South Africa. It would soon grow to more than twenty thousand members and Ray McCauley would become an international Christian leader and nation-builder.

The services at the Constantia Theatre in Rosebank were lively, filled with faith and the hope of a better future for South Africa. A Bible-believing church, it also broke all the apartheid rules. This was a groundbreaking ministry in which people of all races were not only welcomed but celebrated – something Annie supported wholeheartedly. Despite her husband's disapproval she had always believed in equal rights.

She lamented the fact that David would not allow her to invite her old friend Inge from Suriname to visit her in South Africa because he thought it might be a problem for her to be seen in their "European-only" neighbourhood. Every time Annie raised the matter, David would lose his temper – but that did not stop Annie from befriending the black African people.

She remembered the so-called "dirty children" she had played with while growing up in the Netherlands. Society had been quick to reject them and contact was forbidden, just as it was unheard of for white people to venture into South Africa's volatile townships, but Annie was about to challenge all that. With an apostolic zeal for breaking new ground, she would once against find herself going against the flow.

From the time Annie arrived in South Africa, she had longed to get back to the street ministry she'd been involved with in Holland, but had felt held back by David. "All I wanted to do was go out onto the streets of Hillbrow to reach out to the homeless, the prostitutes, and the drug addicts, but I had a husband who did not understand this woman who was on fire for God and wanting to help others."

Annie was moved to tears whenever she was exposed to the poverty of the African people and she wanted to do something, *anything*, to help them. In the early 1980s, when her children were older, she felt the time had come, but it would require money, so she got a job. Driving to work each day in the industrial suburb of Wynberg, Annie would pass Alexandra Township and weep as she saw the squalor its people were living in.

"Alexandra, or Alex, as we called it, was a devastating place," Annie says. "One square mile with about three hundred thousand people crammed together, most of them living in makeshift shacks. It was a poverty-stricken mess, filthy, foul-smelling, and full of crime. Even today it is considered one of the most dangerous places in the world... and I would cry out to God as I went past and say: 'Father, what can I do?'"

Annie didn't know how to start meeting the needs of the people of Alexandra. She thought of making a pot of maize porridge, known as "mealie meal", and sharing the gospel as she endeavoured to feed the hungry. Although she had experience of street evangelism overseas, this was a different continent, and she was unsure how to proceed. She felt out of touch with ministry because she had spent the previous decade focusing on bringing up her children.

Then the call of God came, and with it empowerment. Annie was attending Rhema's first "Faith Convention" in 1980 when one of the ushers came up to her with an African woman and asked a pointed question. "This lady wants to know why Rhema is not doing anything in Alexandra Township, especially when the needs are so great."

Nobody knew what was in Annie's heart and of her desire to reach the poor, but she knew in that moment that God was calling her to Alexandra... "I'm coming!" she responded immediately, with no regard for the dangers that lay ahead or the friction it would cause with the South African Police Service.

True to her word, Annie met the woman the following week and they decided to start holding meetings in the lady's home – even though it would be difficult for Annie to travel into the township, they would do it anyway. Unlike her shack-dwelling neighbours, this lady at least had a roof over her head, and though the house had only one room, it was a start.

"We had our first meeting that Saturday, and of course I was full of faith, full of power, and full of glory," Annie recalls. "Nobody stopped me from driving into Alex and although there were only nine people I wasn't perturbed because I knew we were just getting started. I had to be both song leader and preacher. My pulpit was a bread tin on top of a table and of course I preached my heart out!"

Annie talked passionately about the power of God to transform people's lives, just as Ray McCauley had taught her. By attending Rhema, she had come to know the importance of responding to the great commission:

> Go into all the world and preach the gospel to every creature. He who believes and is baptized will be saved; but he who does not believe will be condemned. And these signs will follow those who believe: In My name they will cast out demons; they will speak with new tongues; they will take up serpents; and if they drink anything deadly, it will by no means hurt them; they will lay hands on the sick, and they will recover... And they went out and preached everywhere, the Lord working with them and confirming the word through the accompanying signs."
>
> (Mark 16:15–17, 18, 20)

Annie knew the power of God's promise that "they will lay hands on the sick, and they will recover". Pastor Ray had often challenged his congregation to do this: "It's so easy to pray for the sick," he would say. "You just need to find a head and lay your hands on it!" And so Annie boldly asked if anyone would like prayer.

"It is amazing what God did in that first meeting," Annie recalls. "The lady had a son named Peter, who was an alcoholic. He said he wasn't 'on the bottle, he was *in* the bottle, with the cork on top!' That's how deeply he was into alcohol. I laid hands on him and prayed for him to be delivered in the name of Jesus, and God set him free. I know because he continued to come to the meetings and he never touched alcohol again.

"The first meeting was a miracle meeting! God always shows up where the needs are greatest. There was a man with asthma and the Lord healed the asthma; there was an old granny who was nearly blind and she left the meeting able to see much better than before. There was a lady who had a large tumour on her chest, like a third breast, but it had disappeared by the time she got home. This was God at work!"

After these miracles, Annie thought the service would be packed out the following week and that the room would be too small to contain the crowd, but when she arrived the following Saturday there were only six! This was a disappointment, but Annie decided she wasn't going to let this upset her and continued in faith. As she often says, "I'm not moved by what I see or by what I hear; I am moved only by the word of God."

God had called Annie to Alex, and she knew that He would prosper the work there. She was also convinced that He would give her complete protection. After all, she always had Psalm 91 tucked under her arm, in the Bible she carried, as her heavenly insurance package! Though her life would be threatened by gangsters and she would be arrested by the police, she would not be deterred.

The South African Army and Police Force were a constant presence in the township as they endeavoured to keep law and order and root out the African National Congress (ANC), which was banned because of its resistance to the Nationalist government. Its leader, Oliver Tambo, was in exile, and the world's most famous prisoner, Nelson Mandela, was still behind bars on Robben Island.

Annie was of course suspected of being an ANC member, but she never was; she just wanted to help the people and it didn't matter what political party they belonged to. She soon became known among the people as "Sister Annie", and they would flock towards her as she came to distribute food and clothing.

The fellowship began to grow steadily, and from the one-room house they moved to a school hall and then into the larger hall of a men's hostel. Before long the mayor of Alexandra heard about Annie and offered her an office in the municipal buildings, fully kitted out with everything she needed, at no charge. A Dutch Reformed minister, the mayor was also a member of the ANC, but his secret was safe with Annie. All she wanted to do was to follow the example set by her saviour:

> **"For I was hungry and you gave Me food; I was thirsty and you gave Me drink; I was a stranger and you took Me in; I was naked and you clothed Me; I was sick and you visited Me; I was in prison and you came to Me... Assuredly, I say to you, inasmuch as you did it to one of the least of these My brethren, you did it to Me."**
>
> (Matthew 5:35–37, 40)

Annie had negotiated with one of South Africa's major grocery stores, Woolworth, to be allowed to collect surplus food that was about to pass its sell-by date. There wasn't anything wrong with the food, but by law the shops had to withdraw it from their shelves, and for the people of Alexandra this was a lifeline.

"Clothing also came in by the bagful," Annie says, looking back on all God accomplished in Alexandra through people's simple obedience to the Scriptures. "What a blessing it was, to help clothe people who were desperately poor. I would pick up babies from their begging mothers, take them to my office, and give them a bath and a meal. I can still remember the joy on those mothers' faces. That would inspire me to go back the next day and do more.

"Of course, there was also a negative side... I was threatened because of the young people who were accepting Christ as Lord and forsaking ancestral worship. There were also many times when they tried to steal my car, but Jesus protected me."

Annie was getting into her car one day when five men armed with screwdrivers approached her. "What do you want?" she asked bravely.

"We want your car, madam..." one answered somewhat respectfully, which Annie thought was strange because she knew many people who had been carjacked, and some had been left for dead.

"You're not getting my car!"

"We want your car; otherwise we're going to stab you."

"You're not getting my car. This car belongs to Jesus; now go!"

The men left and, surprisingly, they waved at Annie as she drove past them! "I will never forget that; it was amazing," Annie says.

In another incident, two shack-dwellers tried to steal Annie's briefcase. One distracted her by asking the time and the other took off with her case.

"In Jesus' name, put it back *now!*" she shouted, and the man dropped the case immediately.

And so with great faith in the word of God and the boldness to go where others would not, Rhema Alexandra was born – a ministry that would quickly grow to accommodate a network of home cell groups across the township and which is still touching lives today.

God was showing Himself to be more powerful than all the witch doctors combined. Often as she would drive into Alex Annie would shout at the top of her voice: "Watch out, devil, Jesus is coming!"

9

A tormented wife and mother

"I PRESSED INTO GOD, INSTEAD OF TURNING AWAY FROM HIM"

Although Annie's first two years of ministry in Alexandra were fulfilling, things at home were very difficult. Her marriage was breaking down and her family continued to experience trauma.

Annie is no stranger to the plight of the many women who have been verbally or physically abused by a man. She reluctantly shares some insights into her first marriage not to expose her former husband, as she has forgiven him, but to help other women who have been mistreated, battered, or abandoned.

David and Annie had been married for only a few weeks when he first hit her. It happened shortly after they arrived in Johannesburg, while they were still staying with his friends in Honeydew. David would leave early in the morning for work and return late at night, practically ignoring his young bride. He was thirty-one and focused on business, while she was just twenty-one, far away from her family and in need of love, reassurance, and affection.

Annie felt lonely and neglected, and as they were so far from the city centre it was as if she had been abandoned in the Bushveld. "David, you're like a stranger to me," she cried, trying to make him understand. "How can you leave me here alone all day and all night? This isn't what marriage is about; this is *not* what I expect of a husband."

66

David was not a man to be questioned, and he lost his temper. "How dare you speak to me like that? I'm tired of your whining," he shouted as he slapped her, pushing her out of his way. "I don't want to hear another sound from you."

Annie was shocked by the way she had been manhandled, and burst into tears. She felt worthless, devastated that her new husband could be so insensitive to her needs. She had experienced this same feeling of hopelessness before, when she'd been violated as a child, but this was a new kind of abuse and it hurt just as badly.

"David, *please...*" she appealed, thinking this would be a one-off incident.

"Not another word," he interjected as he slapped her across the face. Annie had been silenced and, even if she had been able to find the words, this was not something she could talk about.

She definitely couldn't speak to David's friends, and was embarrassed to show her face as they had almost certainly heard the commotion. Annie cried herself to sleep... this was the start of seventeen years of abuse that would cause her pain and heartache, which she would not have survived had it not been for her strong faith.

The enemy knows our weaknesses and he keeps trying to use them to derail us. He would use David to bring back all those feelings of worthlessness Annie had experienced as a child, and unfortunately this would force her to revisit the dark pit of despair that she had experienced as a trainee nurse.

"I had God's word hidden in my heart, so it was impossible to break my spirit," says Annie, "although there were times when it came close. Ultimately my first marriage was a time of spiritual growth, despite my ex-husband's jealousy of my relationship with Jesus and the abuse I endured."

From the start, David was a very private person and would shut Annie out of his life in many ways. Nobody was allowed in his study and he would lock its door even if just going to the toilet. He was obsessed with keys and locking things away. For example, photographs and videos of the children were always under lock and key and Annie was not allowed to see them.

"I couldn't understand this strange behaviour," she confides. "I realized I was in trouble because my husband was trying to make me feel that I had no value. I was not going to accept this, of course; I knew the truth, but at the same time I felt constantly suppressed.

"Worse still, when the children came along, he suppressed them too and for years I felt I had to protect them from him. This placed a huge strain on me."

Annie found a reason for the behaviour of her workaholic, stay-away husband when she discovered in 1972 that he was having an affair with his secretary. They had been married for just six years and she was devastated, but somehow things started to make sense. Nevertheless, this revelation compounded her sense of rejection and she felt betrayed and unwanted.

Annie knew how hard it would be to confront David and that she would have to wait for the right time. This would prove difficult, as she was booked to travel to the Netherlands to visit her parents and introduce them to their new grandson, Paul, who was eight months old. She thought of postponing her flight to deal with the situation, but that wasn't possible and so she went to Holland.

Shortly after Annie arrived, she had another shock when she discovered she was pregnant again. She wrote to tell David the news and he was furious. "I don't think you should have this baby," he wrote back, "and if you do, you'd better just stay in Holland."

Annie was distraught at his reaction and felt obliged to take the blame for their tempestuous relationship as letters flew back and forth. She poured her heart out to him and he replied, justifying his actions. David eventually confessed to the affair and told Annie he wanted a divorce so he could marry "the love of his life".

Annie was four months pregnant when she returned to an empty house. David had moved out, but it wasn't long before he came back to taunt her with his wedding plans. This was distressing for Annie, and, emotional and overwrought, she started throwing things at him. David was enraged; he grabbed her, dragged her into the toilet in the hallway of their home, and locked her inside.

It seemed hours that Annie was left alone in the dark, the light switch being on the other side of the door. She felt claustrophobic, boxed in like an animal in a cage, for a matter of hours, yet in reality she had been a prisoner in her marriage for years.

Annie was traumatized to the point that after this incident she could never use that toilet again, or even her neighbour's when she visited him, as he had a similar house and it was too painful to relive the nightmare.

Eventually David opened the door to a flurry of footsteps. An ambulance crew had arrived to take Annie to a private psychiatric clinic. David was having her committed. He never told anyone where Annie was and she felt helpless, without any support from family and friends, and unable to make any decisions for herself.

"My wife is in no condition to have another baby so soon," he told Annie's doctors. "I think it's best that her pregnancy be terminated." What he didn't tell them was that he was divorcing his wife to marry his girlfriend and he didn't want another baby messing up his plans.

It took years for Annie to forgive herself for what happened, as you will read later, and it was harder still for her to come to terms with the loss of her baby once she was discharged from the clinic.

For some reason David decided to go home with Annie – it seemed that he was unable to make up his mind whether he wanted to keep his family together or pursue a new life with his secretary.

For months he would come and go, disappearing for days on end. The affair finally fizzled out and he told Annie that he had come home for good. The couple did their best to make things work.

Four years later, Annie found herself pregnant again. It was quite unexpected, but this time there was no way she was going to let anything happen to the baby. Their youngest daughter, Esther, was born in 1977 and whereas David had been a harsh disciplinarian with Samuel, Rebekah, and Paul, his baby girl could do no wrong.

As the years passed Annie continued to busy herself with her children's lives; this was ministry of a different kind, but just as rewarding. General Motors continued to swallow up David's time and the same old problems gnawed at the marriage. Annie had learned to toe the line and keep the abuse at bay, but it was becoming impossible for her to cope with the way she and her children were being controlled.

"In 1979 my feelings for David became so bad that I would go to bed and not be able to sleep because I was thinking about how I could get this man out of my life, especially when he upset the children," Annie confides.

For a brief moment, it seemed there was hope for Annie and David's marriage when they started attending Rhema Bible Church. Annie realized she needed help before she did something stupid. She had prayed unceasingly about the situation and was led to Rhema.

"I will never forget what Pastor Ray said at the first service

I attended," Annie remembers. "'There are people here with depression and marital problems and I want you to come forward and I'll pray for you.'"

Annie had never seen people physically struck by the power of God and she was quite sceptical about it. Nevertheless, she went forward. She was first in the prayer line, but the pastor prayed for the others before her. Then he came back to Annie... "You foul spirit, leave her now!" he commanded, in Jesus' name.

"I fell to the floor like a sack of potatoes," Annie recalls. "I crumbled onto the floor and when I got back on my feet I was totally free. I ran around the whole day telling everybody how free I was. It was a wonderful feeling."

Annie believes she had been oppressed by a demonic spirit and God had delivered her instantly. The depression lifted and she knew the Lord was calling her back to active ministry to help others be set free. Some months later, during that providential camp meeting, she responded to the call to go to Alexandra.

When Ray McCauley saw what Annie was achieving in the township, he invited her to attend Rhema Bible Training Centre, to broaden her knowledge of the Scriptures. However, Annie knew her husband would never allow her to go unless he accompanied her. By now Ray had come to know the challenges Annie was dealing with and he didn't think it was a good idea for David to attend.

"If you don't accept his application I can forget about coming, because it will cause such misery in our lives, especially for the children, and I can't do that," Annie told the pastor. So David was accepted by Rhema Bible Training Centre for the class of 1982 along with Annie, and the couple spent the year attending classes each evening from Monday to Friday.

Ray was right to be concerned, because six weeks before their graduation a situation developed over which David was nearly asked to leave. He had also become increasingly unsupportive of Annie's ministry. He had left the high-powered world of finance and started his own business, a recruitment company, but it was floundering. As his efforts began to fail, he became very jealous of Annie's success.

"Harassment from the police in Alex and the dangers of people who wanted to harm me were not my biggest problems," says Annie. "My biggest challenge was my husband. He would do all he could to prevent me from going to Alexandra, and on the few occasions when I brought somebody home from the township he chased them out of the house, which was very upsetting."

The marriage had deteriorated beyond repair and Annie knew she had to get out. She had been slapped and kicked and had her ribs broken, but even worse were David's verbal abuse and the control he sought over her life. She had to endure mental agony as well as physical pain, but what caused her the greatest distress was the way her children were also being abused.

"What would I say to a woman in that situation?" Annie reflects. "Counsellors will tell you that, if your life is in danger, you need to get out. But that is easier said than done. I pressed into God, instead of turning away from Him, and I trusted the Lord to get me to a place where I was financially secure enough to make the tough decisions I had to make to protect myself and my children."

10

Rescued from the jaws of hell

"ALEXANDRA IS FOR JESUS!"

Despite her marital woes, Annie had such an intimate relationship with God that it overflowed into the streets of Alexandra, enabling many others to come to know Jesus as well.

"I used to stand on beer crates, anywhere in Alex, and I would preach the gospel," Annie recalls. "I'd tell the people that God wanted to save them, heal them, and set them free. I'd reach out to the 'down and outs' and tell them Jesus loved them!"

It was a simple message, backed up by loving practical action, and it would bear much fruit. Rhema Alexandra continued to grow and with it came persecution. It was one thing to feed the hungry and clothe the poor, but another to preach salvation in Jesus Christ alone, and especially freedom from fear.

There was one group who thrived on keeping the people mired in superstition and fear and who saw themselves as all-powerful: the witch doctors, or "sangomas", as they are called in South Africa. Of course, a certain Dutch lady was not going to be intimidated. She would tackle them head-on.

Annie's first real confrontation with the sangomas of Alex Township began when she intervened to protect a young woman in her church who had suddenly stopped coming to meetings.

"What's happened to your daughter?" Annie asked the girl's mother.

"She doesn't want to come to your church any more," the woman replied.

Annie found this hard to believe, as she knew the girl had experienced a genuine encounter with God and there was no way she would turn her back on Him. She had come to Rhema Alexandra after abandoning her baby and had been ridden with guilt. She'd given her life to Christ and had been deeply repentant. Annie had prayed with her and reassured her that she'd been forgiven.

"Tell her we love her and are praying for her," Annie told the girl's mother, knowing intuitively that the message wouldn't be passed on.

Annie later discovered that the young woman was being trained to be a witch doctor. Her parents were frightened when she started having nightmares about her brother being involved in a car accident. They had concluded that this was because the ancestors were angry, and the only way to protect her brother was for her to become a witch doctor.

"Witchcraft is still prevalent all over Africa," Annie discloses. "It's part of keeping people in bondage to fear, but I'm not afraid of witch doctors, because I know that 'He who is within me is greater than he who is in the world'. When I heard that this girl had been taken to become a witch doctor, I started searching for her immediately. I knew it wouldn't take long, because I knew every corner of the township."

When Annie found the girl, she knew she had to proceed cautiously. She asked if they could meet some afternoons and started to study the Bible with her to build up her faith. Annie knew the girl's faith had to be strong enough to allow her to leave without being paralysed by fear. "Let me know when you're ready and I'll help you get out," Annie promised. "I'll take you somewhere safe."

The day came when the girl was brave enough to leave. "Sister Annie, let's get out of here!" she cried. Annie told her to bring whatever she could, including everything associated with becoming a witch doctor. "The two of us made a fire and we burnt the lot!" says Annie.

This was the way evangelist Reinhard Bonnke dealt with the charms, amulets, bones, and *muti* (traditional medicinal items) collected on his crusades, and Annie knew the importance of destroying these as an act of repentance.

Annie provided refuge for the young woman with a friend in Rivonia. She had been rescued from the jaws of hell itself. But such a victory did not come without a price; there would be repercussions. First, it didn't take too long before the witch doctor worked out what had happened and Annie was summoned to the mayor's office.

The witch doctor and the girl's mother were both there, and although Annie had previously enjoyed a good relationship with the mayor, it was clear he was very angry. An ordained minister, he had given her much support, yet it was obvious whose side he was taking now.

"How could you have kidnapped this child?" he demanded to know.

"I never took her against her will, and she's not a child. She is twenty-three years old. How can you, as a minister of the church, allow a young woman to become a witch doctor?" she asked politely, but the question remained unanswered.

"You know more than anybody that our children have to submit to their parents," he replied.

"But she's no longer a child," Annie argued. "How can you as a 'dominee' (preacher) be against me in this?"

"I am also the mayor, and I have to be fair to everyone. After what you've done, you had better pack up your things," he asserted. "As of today, you no longer have an office here."

"You shouldn't have done this," warned the witch doctor. "You're making the ancestors very angry and they will come for you. Your life is in danger."

"Be very careful," added the girl's mother. "If my daughter doesn't come home very soon, you're going to die."

Though the loss of her office was a blow to Annie and her ministry to the poor, the death threats were like water off a duck's back. She knew God was greater, and that the power of His protection was much stronger. Psalm 91 was too much of a reality in her life for her to be intimidated by any death threat:

> **He who dwells in the secret place of the Most High**
> **shall abide under the shadow of the Almighty.**
> **I will say of the Lord, "He is my refuge and my fortress;**
> **my God, in Him I will trust."**
>
> (Psalm 91:1–2)

Annie refused to stop protecting the girl and her friend's home continued to provide sanctuary. They carried on attending Rhema Bible Church together in Randburg and the girl became a firm believer and never returned to the township. Salvation was a price Annie was always willing to pay for, even with her life.

A short time after the altercation at the mayor's office, Annie was leaving the township when a car pulled up in front of her, forcing her to stop. Annie saw a gun pointing towards her as she looked across at the driver. "Jesus!" she mouthed at once, repeating the Lord's name over and over.

This was a moment she had known could come at any time and she felt fear trying to take hold of her, but she also knew the promise of Romans 10:13, that "whoever calls on the name of the Lord shall be saved". Annie had been cornered. She couldn't drive on; all she could do was pray.

Her aggressor glared at her, waving the gun from side to side; it seemed to be happening in slow motion. It was just a few moments, but it seemed like an eternity. Annie had come close to death before, but then she had wanted to die. Now she had everything to live for! But there was a gun in her face.

"If you touch me, you will find out what will happen," Annie shouted at the top of her voice. "If you touch me, you touch my heavenly Father, and He will deal with you. And if you want God to deal with you, then you are in trouble..."

Without a word, the driver lowered the gun and drove away. Nobody can say for certain whether he had wanted to shoot Annie or just scare her, but Annie believes God shielded her from death that day.

As the church continued to grow Annie realized she needed help. She was experiencing difficulties at home, with a husband who didn't support the ministry and would sometimes hide her car keys so she couldn't drive into Alex. Besides, she still had four children to care for. Annie felt led to bring in an African pastor with whom she'd been at Bible school, Pastor Moses, and his wife, Mimi, who could help run the church.

One day Annie was giving Mimi a lift home to Alexandra when they came upon a group of witch doctors gathering in a field close to the road. A righteous anger rose up in Annie and she knew she had to stop and confront the powers of darkness. She got out of her car, stood in front of the witch doctors, and started shouting the name of Jesus...

"Jesus, JESUS, J-E-S-U-S!" Annie shouted out, louder and louder. The gun incident had given her proof that the name of Jesus is stronger than any other name. Then she began to challenge the witch doctors by questioning their ability to heal. "You call yourselves traditional healers, but Jesus is the only true healer," she declared boldly. "He alone is the real miracle-worker!"

Within a matter of minutes the witch doctors had moved away. "Mimi, Alexandra is for Jesus!" Annie exclaimed, as they drove off in triumph. "These witch doctors are not going to have Alex. The township belongs to Jesus!"

Annie sensed that God was using this to show Mimi and the believers in Alexandra that they had to learn to take a stand for God in their community and be courageous in the face of witchcraft and intimidation. Annie not only believed this, she lived it. She wasn't afraid of being robbed or even of dying.

Alexandra was a violent township filled with all kinds of crime and the police felt it was their duty to protect Annie, but she didn't want to have too much to do with them because they were seen to be the enemies of the people. The police had often come to her office (when she still had one) and asked questions about certain individuals they suspected of being ANC members.

Annie knew that the more she accommodated the police, the less she would be able to minister to the people. She often tried to dodge the police as they tried to tail her car, a situation that was bound to come to a head, and of course she would sometimes end up on the wrong side of the law.

One of these times was late one night when she had driven into the township to give some young people a lift home from youth club. "It was nearly midnight and of course a white woman in Alexandra at midnight was unheard of, according to the police, so they took me into custody!" Annie remembers with a grin.

She couldn't believe she had been apprehended by two officers and escorted to the police station. All she could see was the funny side. She had done nothing wrong, and here she was being treated like a criminal. She thought the situation was hilarious and burst out laughing. When she heard what the officer said over the police radio she laughed even more.

"Ons het hierdie mal wit vrou in hegtenis geneem. Dit is middernag en sy is in Alexandra en sy lag en lag. Ons dink sy is dronk!" ("We have arrested this crazy white woman. It is midnight and she is in Alexandra and she keeps laughing. We think she is drunk!")

Being from the Netherlands, Annie could easily understand their Afrikaans, which is similar to Dutch, and she laughed even more loudly. However, when she got to the station she soon realized this was no laughing matter and quickly "sobered up".

"You shouldn't be here. You know there are separate areas for blacks and whites in this country," the station commander warned, in accordance with government policy.

"But this is my ministry; this is where God has called me..." Annie tried to explain.

"Do you know what these hooligans are going to do to you?" the commander interjected. "They mean to kill you."

"No, they are not going to kill me."

"What makes you so sure?"

Annie opened her Bible up to her favourite piece of Scripture, Psalm 91, and started reading. The commander soon realized she was not drunk and told her to get out of his office and go home immediately. Thankfully she was allowed to go without being prosecuted.

Ministering in Alex was not without some laughs, but the dangers were real. Undoubtedly, Annie was rescued many times from "the jaws of hell", as she put it. She felt that the devil was doing all he could to destroy her, especially through her marriage. Sometimes she felt like running away from her problems as she drove towards the township, but, as she was learning, life is an obstacle race and you can't run away; you have to face the barriers head-on.

11

My fight for my children

"IT'S OVER, DAVID; I CAN'T TAKE ANY MORE"

Death threats, attempted carjackings, and robbery were not the biggest barriers in Annie's way – her greatest problem at the time was her husband. She felt blocked by him in so many ways as he sought to control her life and thwart her ministry. But worse than this was seeing her children being mistreated in a similar way.

The boys were given a hiding if they did anything wrong, and though he never beat the girls they received their fair share of punishment. The children would try hard to please their dad but David was a perfectionist, and nothing was good enough for him. Instead of getting the affirmation they needed, Samuel, Rebekah, Paul, and Esther would often end up feeling rejected.

Mealtimes were particularly stressful for the whole family. The children would start getting nervous as supper drew near because they knew their dad would soon be home and they would be rapped over the knuckles if their table manners weren't perfect.

"You could never have a dinner without David complaining about something," Annie recalls. "We would be shaking as we waited for him to come home, because we never knew how he was going to react.

"He would punish the children in ridiculous ways. We had bought a plot of land and he would make them weed it for hours. This made no sense at all. And, if he came home late and found dog mess on the pathway, he would wake up one of kids and get them out of bed to clean it up, even in the freezing cold of winter."

David was a very strict father and Annie couldn't bear it when the boys were beaten or when he criticized the girls. She felt controlled and now she could see him exercising the same sort of control over the children. He was continuously making up new rules that had to be obeyed or there would be angry outbursts.

"I don't want any of you in my study," he would remind the family at dinner. "It's my private space and nobody is allowed in there."

He would often take photographs of the children but they were his private trophies and were kept locked away in his study, with nobody allowed to see them.

"I never saw any pictures of my children while they were growing up," Annie admits, sadly. "They were out of bounds, in his study, and I wasn't allowed in. To this day I can't explain this behaviour."

Many years later David sent a disk containing photos to the children, but Annie felt uneasy as she started to look at them. It brought back all the anguish of a time she felt had been stolen from her. "Do you realize that these photos have been hidden from me all these years?" she said. "I can't look at them now; I wanted them *then*." She could never understand why David was obsessed with locking things away. "Perhaps it was just another way of controlling us," she muses.

Annie constantly felt as if she had to walk on eggshells to ensure she didn't upset David; likewise, the children always had to be on their best behaviour to avoid being punished, yet whatever they did to please him, it never seemed to be enough.

David would also use the children as pawns to manipulate Annie. When he had had her committed to the mental health clinic he had taunted her that he was going to send them to a children's home if she didn't do exactly what he instructed.

"I'll tell the Methodist Home in Benoni they'll have to take the children because their mother is insane and unable to care for them," he threatened.

Annie had tried to fight for their unborn child's life at the time, but she had realized she was also in a struggle to protect their other three children.

It was unbearable for her to think of Sam, Rebekah, and Paul being taken away from her, and she was convinced David would actually carry out his threat. She knew she was being manipulated, but she had to do as she was told. Besides, she was outnumbered by David and the doctors he had persuaded to force her to have an abortion.

Years later, once Esther was born, David became determined to turn their four children against Annie. This was after he had become jealous of her outreach into the township, and he went behind Annie's back and tried to poison their minds against their mother. "Your mother loves Alexandra much more than you," he would tell them.

One day Annie came home and David was sitting with the children in the lounge waiting for her. "We've decided we're all going to leave you unless you stop going to Alexandra," her husband announced. "You must choose between us and Alex." It was an ultimatum.

Annie could see the insecurity in her children's faces and her heart ached. "You know I love you more than anything," she reassured them. "I'll never abandon you; I'll always be here for you."

She decided to submit to her husband's wishes and take time out from ministry. She didn't have a problem with submission; she just couldn't bear the way he wanted to control her every move. She knew she could never forsake her calling, but she had to be sensitive to what was happening at home.

The truth was that Annie loved her children passionately, a love which today has overflowed to hundreds of abandoned children in Malawi. She would have done anything to protect and nurture her four children. What she didn't realize was that she would end up having to protect them from their own father.

She had learned to handle David's abuse, whether verbal or physical, but there came a time when she could not allow her children to be subjected to it for one more day. The last straw came when her eleven-year-old son Paul had a friend to sleep over.

"Mom, can we use the pull-out settee in my room?" he asked excitedly.

"Sure, my boy," Annie answered, thinking nothing of it – that was what it was there for.

"Why is the settee opened out in Paul's room?" David demanded when he came home.

"The boys want to sleep on it..."

"Well, they're not sleeping there. They can just sleep on his bed; I don't want that used," David insisted, interfering as he had so many times before in simple household decisions a mother would usually be responsible for.

Annie was upset because that was what their son wanted, but she knew it was not worth having a major argument about it. But, when the two eleven-year-olds had a shower and spilt water all over the bathroom floor, all hell broke loose.

"How can you boys make such a mess?" David shouted at them. "Now you're going to see who's boss in this house!"

Annie heard the commotion and hurried into Paul's bedroom to see what was going on. David had pinned Paul against the wall and was punching him over as his friend watched in fear.

This was the end for Annie. She had finally reached breaking point. She knew she couldn't allow this marriage to go on a moment longer, for her children's sake.

"Stop it, *stop it*, David!" she screamed. "Leave the child alone!" she cried, forcing her way between her husband and her son.

Taken aback, David let go of Paul and it looked as if he were about to punch her as well.

"It's *over!*" Annie screamed at him. "I don't want you any more," she cried repeatedly. "I can't live with you any more."

Embarrassed, David walked away, beckoning to Annie to come to their bedroom where they could discuss the matter privately.

Annie stormed into the room and started packing his clothes. "Get your stuff out of here!" she insisted. "You can go into the guest room for now, but we're finished."

Samuel was fifteen when Annie and David split up; Rebekah thirteen, Paul eleven, and Esther five. There were tears of course, as well as relief as the children sat down to meals without fault-finding or upsets. Eating together was no longer an ordeal, yet it would be hard for the four children to grow up without a dad at home.

David continued to see them over the next year and ensured that Annie received monthly child support, but then he suddenly disappeared and the support stopped. Annie would not hear from him for three years.

She realized the fight to protect her children was not over; it had merely taken a new direction. She now had to look for the best possible job to support herself and four children on a single income. Her ex-husband may have forsaken the family, but God had not.

He began to bless Annie's working career. She was promoted to group credit manager in a public company and eventually opened her own credit control business. Not only did she manage to keep the children on track, she was also able to build a house for the family.

When David finally re-established contact with Annie in 1987 he told her he had moved back to England and was missing the children after three years with no communication. Yet he refused to provide an address for them to get in touch with him.

"I'm not going to sue you for child support," Annie assured him. "I don't need your money, so there's no problem in giving me your address." She had decided that she wasn't going to get involved in an ugly legal wrangle that would only cause more pain and distress.

"I can cope very well on my own; I don't need your money, David, but I do want the children to honour their father," she told him. "Because that is what the Scriptures command; otherwise their lives are going to be negatively affected."

He finally gave Annie an address and she arranged for the children to write to him. She had always taught them to respect their father and told them that, no matter what he had done, God still placed a high value on his life and they should too.

David had returned to the UK at the age of fifty and had been unable to get a job; he had remarried, and he and his wife had been forced to live on income support. He could not afford to see the children, so Annie sent them one by one to England so they could re-establish their relationship.

Today, the children are all happily married, which is a testimony to God's goodness and to answered prayer. They all still live in South Africa.

"From the moment my children were born, I broke every curse that had come down through the generations over their lives," Annie says. "I also broke the curse of divorce. I thank God today for what He has done in their lives; the boys are such great husbands and the girls are a delight as wives."

Sam and his wife have four children and live in Johannesburg, where he is a leader in a large church. In tribute to his mother, Sam quotes Luke 9:23 where Jesus makes a sobering statement: "If anyone desires to come after Me, let him deny himself, and take up his cross daily, and follow Me."

"In a single sentence, Jesus tells us what it means to follow Him," writes Sam. "It takes an uncompromising, radical, all-or-nothing commitment each day to surrender all that we are and everything that we have to Him. And, when I think of people like this, my mum is the first that comes to mind.

"I have been enormously blessed by having a mother who demonstrates through her life what it looks like to be a genuine Christ-follower. Her devotion to God inspires me to live beyond myself and to trust God completely. If more Christians showed just half the commitment to following Jesus that my mum has, the world would be far better off."

Rebekah and her husband also live in Johannesburg. "The biggest lesson in life that my mother taught me was: 'Wherever you go, you take yourself with you.' It has always made me think twice about my motives in any situation I find myself in."

Paul works for an investment bank and he and his wife and three children live in St Francis Bay. "Mom, you are my inspiration," he says. "When I think of all you've achieved, I'm inspired to achieve more. You're my hero!"

Esther and her husband live in Margate with their three children. "The greatest gift my mom gave me was teaching me to have faith and to know that God is always in control," she says.

The children jointly bought an air ticket to bring their father out to South Africa in 2008 so that he could see his grandchildren, and of course Annie ended up contributing towards the trip. She was always pleased to see the children show respect to their father.

"I have always encouraged my kids to keep up their relationship with their father, because the Bible says, 'Honour your father and your mother that you may have long life.'

"The fight for my children has been immensely rewarding; there have been twists and turns, but God has been faithful and I'm blessed by each one of them and by my ten wonderful grandchildren," Annie says.

"I love them dearly, and I'm so grateful to God for what he has accomplished in my family in spite of all we've been through."

12

God hates divorce

Going back to 1983, David was furious with Annie for intervening to protect their son after he and his friend had made a mess in the bathroom. He insisted he was right to discipline the boy and that it was wrong of Annie to interfere. He was further enraged when she started ranting about their marriage being over.

"Who punches an eleven-year-old boy?" Annie asked him some time later. "You're fortunate I didn't call the police and press charges." She hadn't considered reporting David for the physical abuse *she* had sustained, but this was different. This was *her child*...

David was a highly successful businessman who had provided the best he could for his family, and yet he had never learned how to truly love his wife and children. He had not grown up with a godly example of family life; instead, there was many a night when he had to help his father home from the local pub, and he had had a succession of stepmothers.

David's father had had little understanding of how to nurture a family and, although a Christian, David hadn't understood the concept of loving his wife as Christ loved the church; neither had he realized the need for a father not to exasperate his children.

Despite his abusive behaviour, David did not want to

88

see his family torn apart. He reluctantly gave in to Annie's wishes, packed his personal belongings, and moved into the guest room, hoping the situation could be resolved. He was certainly not going to leave – Annie would have to divorce him first!

Pastor Ray had advised Annie that, if there was going to be a divorce, she should not be the one to instigate it; David would have to divorce her.

The stalemate continued for weeks. David kept on asking Annie when he was going to be served the divorce papers, but she wasn't prepared to initiate proceedings. In the meantime, the lawyer David had engaged was a fellow believer, who was trying to keep them together.

A handsome man with endless charm, David seemed very much the eligible bachelor – and it wasn't long before he had found a girlfriend and everything changed. He now wanted to move on with his life, and filed for divorce against Annie.

Though she was expecting them, Annie was still very upset when she received the papers. Far from celebrating her newfound freedom, she felt guilty and confused. "Because I'd initiated the separation I realized I was the originator of the divorce, and the guilt began to set in and I started to have second thoughts," she admits.

"This was mainly because I was concerned that I would lose my fellowship with God and I knew that, if I lost that, I would have nothing left. I thought that because I'd started it, I had sinned, and that if I didn't repent of my sin, I would lose my relationship with God, and that was much more important to me than having a bad marriage."

Annie pleaded with David to hold back on the divorce, but he said it was too late. In an echo from the past, he told her he was going through with it because he wanted to marry another woman. Annie came to the conclusion that, even though she felt guilty about starting the break-up, there was now no turning back.

One of the most hurtful things for Annie as the divorce settlement was discussed was David's claim for the forty thousand rand he insisted was due to him to cover all the money she had given away to the people of Alexandra. He alleged that this had come out of her housekeeping money.

Although Annie had been working at the time, her salary was considered part of David's as they were married in community of property meaning that everything acquired during the marriage was owned jointly, and he gave her no say concerning the money she had earned.

This claim hit Annie hard, and, even though David never received the money, she couldn't believe that he could be so spiteful. But there was worse to come.

Though the couple had previously lived in a large upmarket home, which they had owned, David had sold it several months before the break-up and they had moved into rented accommodation. He had done this to finance his new personnel consultancy business, which wasn't doing very well, and this meant that after the divorce Annie was left with nothing but her car.

The divorce came through in October 1983 and David got remarried in June 1984 to his third wife. At the time of writing, he has recently divorced his fifth wife.

"If you asked David about our seventeen years of marriage you would get a totally different story from the one I have shared," Annie says, "because he never considered himself to be abusive in any way. The children have tried to get him to acknowledge the way he mistreated us, but he has never done so."

Annie accepts her part in the breakdown of her first marriage and has been able to repent of it and find forgiveness.

"God is always ready to bring healing and restoration to a marriage in trouble, because He is the God of restoration," she shares. "But marriage involves the will of two people, and God will not go against a person's free will. He hates divorce, yet He does recognize it.

"God spoke to me clearly and I had to see things from His point of view, despite the fact that my marriage had become so unbearable. At first I was overjoyed to be set free from seventeen years of agony, in which I had had to protect my children, but then I had to reach the point where I would allow God to talk to me about what had happened.

"If you want to speak to God, then you have to talk about everything. The Lord had been talking to me about this sin and I needed to realize it *was* a sin and that I had to repent of my part in it and ask for forgiveness, which I did. I also had to learn to forgive myself for getting divorced."

Annie was reassured by the promise of 1 John 1:9: "If we confess our sins, He is faithful and just to forgive us our sins, and to cleanse us from all unrighteousness." She accepted that divorce meant falling short of God's ideal; this was no hasty prayer of confession but the reflection of a heart submitted to God in deep repentance.

Annie also had to learn to forgive David. She began to understand that she could not expect God to forgive her unless she did so. This was the central message of Christianity, that Jesus had died on the cross to forgive the sins of all mankind – but that forgiveness could not be received unless or until we forgave others.

Annie remembered the words of Jesus in Matthew 6:13–16: "For if you forgive men their trespasses, your heavenly Father will also forgive you. But if you do not forgive men their trespasses, neither will your Father forgive your trespasses."

"Lack of forgiveness towards a particular person is like taking poison and expecting the other person to die," somebody had once told her. And so Annie let go of all the hurt, the pain, the abuse, the anger, and the resentment. "Yes,

I had been through a traumatic period of time with David, but God had set my mind free of all the painful memories."

Annie also knew that if she wallowed in self-pity and harboured ill feeling against David she would embitter the children's minds against their father and their lives would be filled with anguish. She had to make sure she had released all the bitterness that threatened to linger in her heart and stifle the life out of her future.

> **Pursue peace with all people, and holiness, without which no one will see the Lord: looking carefully lest anyone fall short of the grace of God; lest any root of bitterness springing up cause trouble, and by this many become defiled...**
>
> (Hebrews 12:14–15)

Having been taught the principles of faith by Kenneth Hagin at Rhema Bible Training Centre, Annie knew how to trust that God would remove from her path the obstacles she now faced – the loneliness, financial challenges, and uncertain future. She had heard Mark 11:23 preached on so many times, but she knew that it was also dependent on Mark 11:25:

> **For assuredly, I say to you, whoever says to this mountain, "Be removed and be cast into the sea," and does not doubt in his heart, but believes that those things he says will be done, he will have whatever he says. Therefore I say to you, whatever things you ask when you pray, believe that you receive them, and you will have them. And whenever you stand praying, if you have anything against anyone, forgive him, that your Father in heaven may also forgive you your trespasses. But if you do not forgive, neither will your Father in heaven forgive your trespasses.**
>
> (Mark 11:23–25)

"Mountain of poverty and joblessness, be cast into the sea," Annie had boldly declared. "God is going to give me a job that will take care all of our needs and still be a blessing to the people of Alexandra."

She thought back to how God had provided a job for her years before. "If He did it for me then, He can do it for me again. He is that same, yesterday, today, and for ever!"

She and David had been going for marriage counselling at the time and a psychologist had recommended that she go back to work, to take her mind off her unhappy marriage. Annie had thought of returning to nursing, but it would have meant retraining.

Instead, she did what she had done to find accommodation when she and David had first arrived in South Africa – she went from office block to office block to find work. And, when all the doors seemed shut, she sat in the foyer of a company one day and began to sob.

"Why are you crying?" a man enquired kindly.

"I need a job, and nobody wants to employ me... "

"Do you think you would be any good at credit control?" the man asked.

"I could try."

"Well, then I'll give you a try!"

That was the start of Annie's career in credit management, and she quickly began to climb the corporate ladder. While working at Plessey, she had been introduced to a gentleman by the name of Blackie Swart, the chief executive officer of Terexco who had been keen for her to come and work for him.

Years later, the month before David disappeared and stopped paying maintenance, she got a call from Mr Swart, asking if she would come and see him because he wanted to offer her a job.

It was like the story of Joseph in the Bible, when he had been left forgotten in prison but the butler finally remembered him and recommended him to Pharaoh. Blackie Swart had mentioned in a board meeting that he needed a new group credit manager and his secretary had remembered Annie.

"Do you recall that lady?" she asked her boss, reminding him of Annie.

"Yes, she would be perfect; see if you can find her!"

It didn't take the secretary long to locate Annie – they were both members of the same church, Rhema!

"You're the best credit manager I know, and I want you to work for me," Blackie Swart told a very grateful Annie. "Just tell me how much I need to pay you!"

It wasn't long before Annie became Director of Credit at Terexco, giving her the resources she needed to minister in Alex and to pay for her children to attend schools in Bryanston, so that they were not disadvantaged by the hardship so often brought to a family by divorce.

Having been through divorce and yet having been able to rebuild her life by faith, Annie's aim is to offer hope to the people she comes into contact with, including those who have been divorced or widowed and women who have been beaten or abandoned. She also has a particular concern for single mothers struggling to bring up children on their own without child support.

She knows the anguish of the many young girls who have been molested or found themselves pregnant and unsure of what to do, and she knows from first-hand experience the pain of women who have had to give up their babies.

Annie is constantly ministering to women and believes that what God has done for her, in overcoming divorce and rebuilding her life, He can and will do for others. He can turn things around for any woman facing abuse or at a crossroads in her life. She believes God will make a way where there seems to be no way, and that ultimately He will "restore the years the locust has eaten" (Joel 2:25).

"God hates divorce, but He loves people. He is compassionate and forgiving and He can make all things new. Though you think your life may be over, He can give you a new start. As the saying goes, 'We can't go back to the beginning and start over, but we can start again from now and have a brand new end.'"

13

A beautiful spiritual daughter

"WE HAD NOTHING, BUT WE HAD
EVERYTHING!"

In January 1984 Rhema Bible Church held a land dedication service for its new building in Randpark Ridge. It was a historic day for Annie and many others as Reinhard Bonnke delivered a far-reaching prophetic word that would affect her future and that of many of her friends.

"This is the nesting place of the divine eagle," he prophesied. "And many, many eagles will be sent out from this nest; they shall go all over the world, taking the word of God to the nations."

One of those "eagles" was, of course, Annie Chikhwaza, who would leave South Africa to become a mother to the nation of Malawi; others included international evangelist Rodney Howard-Browne and a multitude of people who would find themselves all over the globe, touching lives in different countries.

One of the best-known of these is Wendy Alec, the co-founder of the global broadcast network GOD TV, which reaches over six hundred million people with revolutionary Christian programming.

Wendy and her husband, Rory, have become well known in evangelical circles since they started GOD TV in 1995, but back in 1983 it was barely a dream. Wendy hadn't even met

Rory at the time, but that was all about to change, with a little help from a friend named Annie!

Annie first met Wendy Koefman at David's office before they separated. Wendy was at Rhema Bible Training Centre at the time and working part-time for David's recruitment company. The two women quickly struck up a friendship when they discovered they went to the same church.

Following a spate of personal confrontations at General Motors, David had received a telex from the company's headquarters telling him he needed to work on his people skills. When he was put on probation for three months, he decided to leave his highly paid job in corporate finance and venture into his own business.

He started the personnel consultancy using the capital he received from the sale of the house where he and Annie had lived and he employed Wendy, whom he had met through Rhema. Annie felt sorry for Wendy because she knew how difficult David could be.

As in his home environment, everything in David's new business had to be locked away and he was the only one with the keys. It was hard for his staff to work like this and Wendy became just as perturbed as Annie was by David's obsession with keys.

Furthermore, the relationship problems David had been having at General Motors had not gone away, and working in the recruitment company became increasingly challenging for Wendy. Annie would often end up consoling her.

Annie became very fond of her younger friend, whose mother was overseas, and Wendy began to see Annie as a 'spiritual mother'. They would go to the hairdresser's together and go shopping for clothes, Annie taking an interest in helping to groom Wendy along with her daughters, Rebekah and Esther.

When Annie's marriage came to an end, she moved into a house of her own with the children. It was a large property and when Wendy needed new accommodation she went to stay there. They would pray together, go to church, and share the joy of knowing Jesus. Although she was remorseful that her marriage had ended, this was a season of healing in Annie's life and she and Wendy shared many happy times.

"Neither of us had a proper income at the time," Annie recalls. "I'd been angry with David for investing all we had in his new business so I'd stopped working and, now that we were separating, I couldn't find a job. All I was receiving was five hundred rand per month child support from David and he wasn't paying Wendy very much at the personnel agency."

Wendy wasn't happy working with David and soon found another position working half days in a pharmacy so she could continue with her Bible school studies. Ultimately, her future did not lie in business recruitment; she was more focused on recruitment of another kind – winning souls through creative evangelism!

"We were in the worst situation we could ever have been in financially," Annie recalls. However, for a whole year God provided miraculously for us: people would stick envelopes of money under the front door and we were able to get vouchers at church for groceries.

"Friends would often come over and I remember a particular day when we had a houseful of visitors and the table was laden with food. Wendy and I looked at each other and laughed and laughed. The Lord had provided for us so bountifully. We hardly had a penny to rub together, but joy was overflowing all the time. We had nothing, but we had everything!"

Having worked for Annie's ex-husband, Wendy knew a little of what her friend had experienced over seventeen years of marriage and would become a great support to Annie as she faced the future as a single mother.

"Wendy is like my child," Annie says. "She lived with me for eighteen months and God really knitted our hearts together. We were so excited about the word of God and the promises given to us as believers that we could step out in faith and believe Him for the impossible, because all things are possible with God. Wendy always had enormous vision and it was inspiring to dream such big dreams!"

For Wendy, this was a season in which her Christian life was growing in leaps and bounds. She was able to devote considerable time to following up new converts at church and counselling those in need. She would also spend many hours in prayer and could often be found interceding at the back of the church building. This was a time in her life that she describes as her "wonder years".

"Wendy enriched my life in so many ways. I also felt blessed that I could help her, and that did something for me. I watched her grow in the Lord and develop in spiritual confidence as we spoke the word of God to each other and prayed together," Annie says. "It seems God uses me with young women in this way, as I've been privileged to disciple many girls who have come to Kondanani as missionaries."

Wendy sometimes sang at Rhema and Annie would encourage her to go further in her ministry. "You're an excellent psalmist; more people need to hear you sing!" Unfortunately Annie was having a break from the ministry in Alex following her divorce so she wasn't able to take Wendy to minister in Alex, but she did take her on a ministry trip to Rustenburg, which would turn out to be a date with destiny.

"Wendy and I would sometimes talk about our romantic attractions," Annie says. "I eventually had a gentleman friend named Les; we were on the same spiritual wavelength, but neither of us was attracted to the other and we knew it would never amount to anything...

"In any case, I wasn't going to date just anybody and bring one man home to meet the children after another. I would never have done that to my children. I'd decided I wouldn't enter into a romantic relationship unless I knew it was likely to lead to marriage, and God would have to do a miracle for me ever to get married again!

"I was quite happy being single. Wendy, on the other hand, was young and ready for a relationship. We had watched *The Thorn Birds* on television and she fancied Richard Chamberlain, but I knew God had better in store. Besides, I knew she preferred men with longer hair!"

Annie knew a pastor in Rustenburg who had once worked for David, and when she needed to find a boarding school for Rebekah she considered the town the ideal location as she knew he would be on hand if her daughter needed support.

"My friend Wendy can sing beautifully," Annie had told the pastor, while making arrangements for Rebekah. "Would you like her to come and sing in your church?"

"That would be great," he replied. "Would you arrange for her to come this Sunday?"

So Annie and Wendy arrived that Sunday morning, Wendy oblivious to the fact that she would meet her future husband that day. Rory was more alert because he had chatted to the pastor the day before and said, "I believe the Lord has told me that I'm going to meet my wife tomorrow!"

"I can still remember Rory sitting there, going bright red when he saw Wendy," Annie recalls. "He was on leave from the army and had very short hair. I could see Wendy wasn't interested initially, not one little bit. But he pursued her, and she became more interested as his hair grew longer!"

The trip to Rustenburg was a divine appointment and Wendy writes about it in her book *Against All Odds: The Story of GOD TV's Visionary Pioneers*:

> **Sometimes, I have to confess, in the hectic, pressurized lifestyle of the GOD Channel, I look back longingly on those wonder years! The angels were no doubt working hard, for one weekend in God's blueprint – I was invited to minister at a church in the small mining town of Rustenburg.**
>
> **"I don't want to go to Rustenburg!" I stated to my long-standing friend, Annie Chikhwaza, who now runs "Kondanani" looking after HIV/AIDS orphans in Malawi. She looked at me with the glint of God in her eye. "You need to go."**
>
> **I arrived at the morning service and there, leading the praise and worship, was a vibrant young man who played the keyboards in a manner that immediately got my attention. Music was still my passion. This talented young man was Rory Alec.**

"What a privilege it was for me to play even a small part in bringing this extraordinary couple together," says Annie. "Little did I know then how much they would accomplish together and what a far-reaching ministry they would have. GOD TV is an amazing global outreach that has transformed many lives, and it's been a huge part of all we've accomplished in Malawi."

Rory and Wendy were married in 1987 and Annie watched with delight as she saw these two gifted musicians pool their talents, from writing rock operas to other gospel music projects, including an award-winning music video. "They tried their hand at quite a few things, but their greatest desire was to be used in Christian media," Annie says.

"Wendy is extremely creative and I remember her sitting in her room writing day after day! It's amazing for me to think that the forerunner to *The Chronicles of Brothers* was written in my home. I would encourage her by saying that it would one day be a movie. Chronicles is now a series of bestselling books, they're brilliant, and I believe we will soon see them in the cinema."

Annie was happy to see Wendy starting to live the dreams they had talked so much about, and Rory and Annie became good friends, a friendship which has crossed the years and the continents.

When Rory and Wendy's television-commercial production company, Alec Gene Productions, was established, Annie celebrated her friends' success as she watched their commercials on television. And, of course, being in credit management she was always ready to caution Rory lovingly, especially if she saw him in a new car!

They lived in the same suburb, and Annie would visit the couple in their large thatched house and join in taking their two Ridgeback dogs for a walk. It was a joy for her to see them doing so well, but she was also there to encourage her spiritual daughter and her husband, when recession hit South Africa and advertising budgets were cut.

Rory and Wendy were devastated when they started to lose important clients owing to the economic downturn. Key staff were poached and the production of new commercials was postponed. Adding insult to injury, their car was stolen. It was a hard time for them as they came to terms with losing everything. Then Wendy discovered she was pregnant, and of course Annie was there to support her through the pregnancy.

Rory and Wendy were forced to move back to Rory's hometown, where they would need to stay with his parents while they awaited the birth of their eldest child, Samantha. "I remember so clearly the day she was born," Annie says, "when I went to Rustenburg to see her for the first time.

"Samantha was a pretty little baby with dark hair, but I was concerned for Wendy as she did not seem to be too well. I insisted that she see a doctor immediately, who diagnosed septicaemia, and fortunately she recovered quickly after that."

Annie knew that the loss of Alec Gene Productions and of their home was not the end for Rory and Wendy, that God was only getting started with them. She saw the valuable lessons the Lord was teaching them and prayed for them daily. She felt that God was about to do something new in their lives.

Annie had learned from personal experience how to cope with shattered dreams. God had helped her to rebuild her life and she would call Wendy regularly to strengthen her faith and tell her not to give up.

"If you put yourselves in a position where God can use you, nobody can stop you," she would tell Wendy. "If you do that, His plan for your life's calling will be fulfilled!"

14

A vision for Africa

"GOD CAN TURN THINGS AROUND!"

When Annie got divorced in 1983 she was asked by the leadership of Rhema Bible Church to take a two-year sabbatical from ministry to rebuild her life and focus on her children. In 1986 she returned to the township and by 1991, as an area leader for the church, she had established fifteen home cell groups, covering an area that extended from Alexandra on the outskirts of Johannesburg to Allandale, a suburb of Midrand, halfway to Pretoria.

In addition to the weekly meetings on Saturdays, which had grown exponentially from that first meeting in the one-room house, she had also started Sunday afternoon services. God's work was being done as Annie and her team preached the gospel and prayed for the sick as they distributed food and clothing.

Annie now had two colleagues assisting her, Pastor Moses and Pastor Thomas, one of her spiritual children. It was still considered objectionable by the authorities for a white woman to go into the townships and Annie was grateful to her friend Pam Duffield, who was also prepared to break the rules. Pam would accompany Annie into the township once a week to lead a cell group, which she considered a great blessing.

The police were constantly pestering Annie. The banned ANC movement continued to work undercover against the National Party government and she witnessed social injustice on both sides of the political divide. "There was so much violence and so many people were beaten up for no reason at all," Annie recollects.

"Madam, my wife has been arrested!" came the frantic cry early one morning as Annie was woken by her phone. "The police have taken her and I don't know what to do," lamented the man, who was a member of her church. Annie got dressed and drove to Alex as quickly as she could.

A neighbour had falsely accused the woman of breaking into their house, but when Annie went to check out what had happened she could see this wasn't the case. The window had been broken from the inside, not the outside. It was clearly a fabrication. She didn't know whether this was politically motivated or just tribal infighting; it didn't matter. She had to protect the innocent.

Annie was horrified to find out that the woman had been arrested at three o'clock that morning and that she had been beaten even though she was pregnant. Annie immediately went to the police station and refused to leave until the woman was released.

She told the station commander that she had been to the alleged scene of the crime and that the police had insufficient evidence to hold the woman. He became angry when Annie threatened legal action if they didn't let her out, but owing to her persistence they finally let the woman go. "I held a 'sit-in' at the police station!" Annie recalls.

Annie was immensely relieved; she had been praying under her breath the whole time, trusting that God would help them, and now she was able to ensure that the woman received treatment for her wounds and was reunited with her husband.

She didn't realize it at the time, but God had sent her to Alex as an agent of His peace. She didn't take sides; she simply sought to care for the people and bring God's peace into a troubled situation.

**Blessed are the peacemakers, for they shall be called
sons of God. Blessed are those who are persecuted for
righteousness' sake, for theirs is the kingdom of heaven.
Blessed are you when they revile and persecute you,
and say all kinds of evil against you falsely for My sake.
Rejoice and be exceedingly glad, for great is your reward
in heaven.**

(Matthew 5:9–12)

The more Annie reached out to Alexandra, the more she realized the need for the church of Jesus Christ to minister to people across the three dimensions of spirit, soul, and body. She wanted to start income-generating activities with the people but the church leadership insisted this was beyond her remit. They let it be known that she was working hard enough and that the focus of her ministry should be primarily spiritual; in other words, Annie was told to concentrate on evangelism.

She eventually resigned as an area leader at Rhema as it went against her conscience just to preach the gospel and not to attend to other areas in the lives of the needy. She then set up a not-for-profit organization named Tandanani, which means "Love one another" in Zulu (a forerunner of Kondanani), in order to help the people of Alex earn an income.

Annie remembered a much-quoted Chinese proverb: "Give a man a fish and he will eat for a day. Teach a man to fish and he will eat for a lifetime." This was a simple yet profound concept that she felt would multiply the church exponentially if believers just put it into practice.

Annie wanted to do things the Rhema leadership didn't consider a core part of their mission at the time; she was a forerunner, constantly breaking new ground, but she knew they would ultimately follow her example.

"What is the point of preaching the gospel and not developing the people?" Annie would ask. "I wanted to start income-generating activities with the people, but they didn't see that as the role of the church. My heart is not just to give a fish but to teach people to fish; otherwise you keep them reliant on charity, and that is not a long-term solution."

Rhema later embraced the concept of being both "evangelistically potent" and "socially relevant" and introduced an entire range of community development programmes that preached the gospel in tandem with feeding the people and helping them to feed themselves.

"We have to be part of the solution and not part of the problem," Pastor Ray had always preached, a phrase that had inspired Annie. Now he started to teach about the church reaching out as the hands and feet of Jesus in all areas of life. "We have to find a need and meet it, find a hurt and heal it," he would often say.

Meeting needs and healing hurts were an everyday part of the ministry of Rhema Alexandra, but Annie was just as focused on empowering her congregation to extend healing hands themselves and she constantly taught them the power of sowing and reaping, assuring them that, as they gave to others, they could trust God for a harvest.

This increasing community development dimension of Annie's ministry in Alexandra meant she had less time to spend at work. It was difficult being a company director and having to attend the board meetings of several companies while balancing her family life and her ministry. So she resigned from Terexco and started her own management consulting business.

Her time became her own, and God continued to show his favour to Annie as she built up credit control teams which she could send into companies when needed to combat bad debt.

The business became successful because God was using it to finance His work: provision for the vision!

"The children and I were so grateful to the Lord for His faithfulness. There was enough to maintain our home and still give to Alexandra; even so, I could never save, because the needs of the township were so great. I spent any money we had left over each month on food and clothing for the people there. So all my money was used up, but I'm not sorry, because I sowed many seeds, which I'm still reaping from today!"

Annie ministered in Alex for thirteen years, until she knew every corner of the township. "People used to complain about how it stank, because the smell was horrific, but – you know what? – I couldn't help but love the smell of Alex because God loved the people and I was glad to have the opportunity to minister to them and see the Lord move in great ways.

"I loved the place and I loved the people. But I didn't want them to stay in that squalor and in poverty. I was convinced that, as they responded to the word of God, they could trust that He would provide for them. So it was a joy for me to teach them the Scriptures – passages such as, 'The Lord is our Shepherd; I shall not want; He leads us into green pastures, He prepares a table before us'... 'I have never seen the righteous forsaken or their seed begging bread'... 'God supplies all our needs in accordance with His riches in glory'... These were some of the verses my congregation knew off by heart! They had the revelation that God wants His people to prosper and be in health as our souls prosper!"

After more than a decade of pouring her energies into the turbulent streets of Alexandra, God was ready to move Annie on to her next assignment. The ministry she had founded would live on, and Alexandra Bible Church remains the largest congregation in the township to this day.

Before she left Alexandra, Annie was given a piece of land right on the border of the township for a church to be built. She was delighted when a couple she knew signed the land over to her, and she was overjoyed to be able to give it to Rhema Alex as a lasting legacy of all that had been accomplished, despite the many obstacles that had stood in their way.

Annie had learned so much in Alex; it was an excellent preparation for what lay ahead. A vision for Africa had been growing in her heart for several years and she knew God was calling her to continue to help alleviate poverty. She also knew only too well the ravages of a new disease that was bringing Africa to its knees, the scourge of HIV/AIDS, and she felt God was opening her heart to serve the innocent victims of this pandemic.

Annie is not entirely impressed with the world's attitude to development in Africa. "The United Nations keep the people of Africa as subjects of charity, just throwing bags of maize or rice at them. Though commendable in the short term, this is not a long-term solution.

"It keeps the people down and out, and if you are the subject of charity, you can be told what to do, what to eat, what to wear, and where to go. My vision is to empower people through the gospel and through development so that they can make their own decisions, including having an opportunity to decide to receive Jesus Christ as their saviour.

"Africa is a continent rich in resources: it has gold, platinum, diamonds, oil, wildlife, unspoilt landscapes, and wonderful people, and yet so much money has been poured into aid to Africa because the mindset of the Western world does not understand what is really needed to develop Africa. More than aid, the people need to be empowered."

Africa faces many challenges, not the least of which are poverty, disease, political corruption, witchcraft, and tribal hatred, but Annie's vision is that the church can help overcome these scourges as every believer does their part to reach this vast continent. "Africa can be a great continent for God," she declares, "and even though there are desperate situations, God can turn things around!"

15

Where shall we marry?

"YOU'RE A WOMAN OF GOD, YOU'LL LISTEN"

About eight years after Annie began her new life as a single woman she received a telephone call from an old friend, a pastor by the name of Lewis Chikhwaza. It was a momentous conversation. Although he asked a simple question, it would be difficult for her to answer. And, when she finally did, it would change her life and ministry for ever!

Annie had first met Lewis in 1982 when they were students at Rhema Bible Training Centre. Originally from a Catholic background, Lewis had established Holy Cross Ministries in Bvumbwe, near Blantyre, but had come from Malawi to South Africa to study at the college after hearing how God was using Rhema to restore key truths to the body of Christ.

He particularly supported the revelation that healing had not passed away with the early church, as he had witnessed his wife, Elizabeth, being supernaturally healed. She had also been set free from demonic oppression, and Lewis wanted a more thorough understanding of the message of faith and the gifts of the Holy Spirit.

Lewis had experienced the power of God at work in healing and deliverance and he wanted to see this in his own ministry, so he went to South Africa. He started the Bible school year staying at the residence of the Malawian ambassador in Pretoria; however, it took him over an hour to get to Johannesburg each afternoon and an hour to get back late each evening. It was a tiring daily commute and he soon realized he needed to find accommodation closer to Rhema.

"Would anybody be able to assist a pastor from Malawi with accommodation?" the dean of the college, Graeme Cross, asked the students. Annie was surprised when David's hand went up! Despite his shortcomings, David seemed to want to help in this instance, and Lewis came to live with Annie and David and their family for the academic year. Fortunately they had a five-bedroomed house!

"That was in February 1982," Annie recalls. "What a privilege it was to be at Bible school together, to focus on God's word each day, and share our newfound knowledge of the Scriptures with one other. Lewis soon became part of the family; we adults became good friends and the children loved their 'Uncle Lewis'. Esther was still a little girl and he would sometimes take her to nursery school."

Lewis worked at Rhema during his year in South Africa and became friends with many of the pastors. He would also sometimes accompany Annie into Alexandra to minister to the people. They clearly felt the same concern for the downtrodden.

"He was a great house guest," Annie remembers. "He would eat anything I put in front of him, but he must have longed for some *nsima* (the thick maize porridge that is the staple food of Malawi).

"We missed him when he went back to Malawi, but of course we kept in touch. My ex-husband David and I and our four children visited the Chikhwaza family in Bvumbwe in December 1982, and Lewis came to South Africa and stayed with us twice after that. We often spoke of how we could help him extend his mission field in Malawi."

Annie would share with Lewis and Elizabeth the latest adventures in her outreach into Alexandra and how God had helped her overcome many obstacles. They were amazed at how her life had been supernaturally protected and laughed over her run-in with the police, when she had been arrested for being "drunk".

Lewis was inspired by the work in the township and was desperate to see God move in his own country. "Annie, I can't wait for you to come and minister in Malawi," he insisted.

On his return home from Bible school, Lewis found that he could no longer identify with the doctrine of Holy Cross Ministries and started a new work known as Bible Faith Ministries, which grew rapidly, and he became the overseer of several churches in Malawi and neighbouring Mozambique.

In July 1990 Lewis called Annie to invite her to speak at his Easter Conference in April the following year, and Annie readily agreed. She had long set her heart on a mission to Malawi, but then tragedy struck.

Annie was shocked to hear from Lewis just a few months later that Elizabeth had passed away. She was only fifty-two but was diabetic and suffered from high blood pressure. She had collapsed suddenly and died and to make things even worse, Lewis's son Stephan had also just passed away, just nine days after his dear mother.

Elizabeth and Lewis had ten children, and he was devastated to have lost not only his wife but also a son. It was a dark time for him, and Annie did her best to comfort her friend and encourage him to turn to God and forge on with his ministry. Following a time of mourning, Lewis decided to go ahead with the conference.

Once a prosperous businessman, he had fallen on hard times, and, with the death of his wife and son, things were deteriorating further. Lewis was the first black man in Malawi to own a bus company, and the first to open a driving school. His businesses had brought him prominence and he became a Member of Parliament.

Lewis's company was called Ulendo Transport and at one time his buses would transport the people of Malawi up and down the nation's long, narrow territory via roads running parallel to one of the world's largest freshwater lakes. For a season his business did well, and in 1971 Lewis bought a farm, where he and his family lived in a large colonial house.

However, in 1976 the bus company came under judicial management and Lewis lost everything except the land he owned. Fortunately he was able to keep the forty-three-acre property, but he never had the funds to finish the renovations he had started on the ten-bedroomed house or to maintain it over the years.

An unbeliever at the time of the collapse of the bus company, Lewis thought all hope was lost, especially since his wife had become very ill. This was many years before Elizabeth's untimely death and Lewis took her from witch doctor to witch doctor to try to find a cure, but of course they did not have the answer. He finally came into contact with a Christian preacher with a deliverance ministry, who came to the house and started casting out demons.

Elizabeth's health was completely restored at the time. Lewis was amazed, and he immediately committed his life to Christ. From that point on he had a new joy and his heart was filled with love and a desire to share it with others. He felt called to ministry and shortly after that he started Holy Cross Ministries.

A few years later, he felt led to spend a year at Rhema and managed to raise the funds to go to Johannesburg. He was immensely grateful for David and Annie's hospitality and, although he had witnessed first-hand the breakdown of their marriage, he was sorry to hear that they had divorced.

Now Annie was coming to Malawi and Lewis was eager to show her his country and share her ministry with his congregation. By the time she arrived for the Easter Conference he was nearing retirement age, but, as every believer knows, there is no such thing as retirement in God's kingdom!

God was about to give Lewis a complete new lease of life and it would come in the form of a godly woman with boundless energy and an unstoppable passion for brightening people's lives. There was only one problem: she had first to get her head around the idea!

Annie was used to the poverty of Alexandra, but this didn't prepare her adequately for the desperation she would find in Malawi, one of Africa's poorest countries. It seemed that everybody was poor, even her pastor friend.

"I was fetched from the airport in what I call a real 'township car'!" Annie recalls with a smile. "Its makeshift windscreen was made of plastic and we had to push it to get it started! But we had the most wonderful meetings and we sowed many seeds of revival, which would later bear much fruit."

Annie soon had an inkling of Lewis's growing affection for her, but was going to make it very clear she wasn't interested.

Once the conference had ended Lewis dropped a bombshell: "I want you to be my wife," he told Annie, assuring her how much he had come to love her. "Will you marry me?"

"Lewis!" Annie exclaimed, visibly shocked. While she thought he had a wonderful personality and she felt drawn to him, she knew it was foolish even to consider living in such poor circumstances.

After ministering at the conference she was sure God was calling her to Malawi, but she felt that had nothing to do with

Lewis Chikhwaza! She would somehow have to come up with a plan to get him out of the way.

"You're a great friend, Lewis..." Annie answered, "but I can't consider marriage right now."

It wasn't that she didn't find him attractive, but how could she accept such a proposal, she asked herself? She thought of her children, although they were mostly grown up (her youngest was in her last year of school). What arrangements could she make for Esther?

A hundred questions flooded her mind. She thought of her comfortable home – there was no comparison to Lewis's house. How could she give up her business, her car? It was unthinkable to give up everything to marry a man who was struggling to make ends meet. Besides, he was from a different cultural background.

"Where do you think will be the best place for us to get married?" Lewis would ask Annie each time he phoned.

"I can't marry you, Lewis," she told him repeatedly.

But he was undeterred. He kept on phoning and always ended up asking the same question: "Johannesburg or Blantyre?"

"Lewis, we're not going to get married!" Annie would protest, trying to put him off.

"You're a woman of God; you'll listen," he said knowingly.

Although God continued to speak to Annie about Malawi, she didn't want to hear anything about Lewis.

"I lived in one of the most affluent suburbs of Johannesburg. I had my own company. An Audi SE 500 was in my driveway, the top of the range," she recalls, "and now I had this pastor who didn't have a penny to his name wanting to marry me! It sounded ridiculous. But he wouldn't stop phoning!

"I knew God was calling me to Malawi, but I felt I had to get rid of this man first," she says. "I didn't want to risk going to a new country and finding myself in trouble because I had a jealous man on my hands."

In October 1992 Annie flew to Blantyre to tell Lewis that she was going to come and live in Malawi, but that he wasn't the reason for her move. However, during the flight she prayed, "Lord, if Lewis is your best for me, then that is the best. I just want your best. Make it clear to me.

"He's a man of impeccable character and vast wisdom," Annie acknowledged to the Father. "And he's a very loving man, but do You have any idea how hard up he is?"

From the airport Annie and Lewis took a taxi to the nearby Shire Highlands Hotel, where they sat under a jacaranda tree, a myriad of purple florets shading them from the hot African sun. It may have been a romantic setting, but Lewis was quick to get down to business.

"When are we going to get married?" he asked.

Annie's plan was to make him see that he couldn't afford her. And if this hadn't been obvious on her first trip, she was going to make it abundantly clear on the second. Lewis now didn't even have a car to fetch her from the airport. Things had gone from bad to worse.

"Please, Lewis, I know God is calling me to Malawi, but marriage is another thing altogether. Besides, you lived in my home for a whole year and you know my lifestyle," Annie answered, labouring the point about her standard of living.

Lewis just smiled, knowingly. "What does God want you to do?" he enquired patiently.

"OK, if you'll fix up your big house I'll marry you," Annie exclaimed as part of her strategy to put him off, thinking he would never be able to accomplish such an impossible task.

"No problem!" he said. "I'll fix it."

"But how are you going to do that?

"Ah, well, I have a spare plot and I'll sell it," he replied with a twinkle in his eye.

"We'll see!" she said, not realizing that the land he spoke of was inhabited by squatters and would prove impossible to sell.

But somehow in that moment Annie just knew that marriage to Lewis was God's plan. "This is the man I want you to marry," she felt the Holy Spirit say deep in her spirit.

Annie had reached the point at which she was prepared to do what God wanted more than what she wanted. Doing God's will was far more important to her than the guarantee of a comfortable life.

"Father, if Lewis is your best for me, then I will submit to what You want," she whispered.

"This is it, Annie!" she thought to herself.

She had gone to Malawi determined to tell Lewis that she was moving to the country because God had called her, not because of him. But God had other plans, and, when she returned to South Africa ten days later, she was engaged to be married.

She had resolved to do things God's way, but she felt she needed to gain the acceptance of her children and church family. The children all knew Lewis well and they had no objection, nor did any of her friends. The pastors at Rhema were also pleased to confirm their approval.

The momentous telephone call came in mid-1993, two years after Lewis had made his first proposal. "Now, Annie, where shall we marry?" Lewis asked for the umpteenth time.

Annie finally gave him the answer he had been looking for. "It has to be Blantyre!" she said.

16

The derelict house

"ANNIE, YOU'LL NEVER BE POOR,
NEVER!"

Set in forty-three acres of farmland, the large, ten-bedroomed structure seemed out of place in comparison with the neighbouring villages and their brick huts with untidy grass roofs. A remnant of a past era, it was no longer the colonial farmhouse of former days. It was now little more than a partitioned barn, filled with bags of maize and infested with rats.

It was certainly spacious enough, along with its many outbuildings, but it was dilapidated and exposed. Only one of the rooms had functioning window panes; the glass in the other windows had been either removed or smashed, leaving the rooms open to the elements: wind, rain, spiders, crickets, snakes, bats, and any other unmentionable intruder.

The floors were dusty, the walls dirty. There were leaks here, there, and everywhere, puddles of water, mould, and damp. Several internal doors were missing or broken and built-in cupboards had been gutted. There was no running water, no fitted kitchen to speak of, and a bathroom that doubled as a storage room. The kitchen was an iron shack at the back of the house.

The locks on the exterior doors were broken and nothing was secure. The house seemed uninhabitable – yet people were living there. This was Lewis's home. This was where a new bride would spend her honeymoon!

Annie thought back to her days growing up in Holland and how she would show her love for people by cleaning their houses; this was just a new challenge. Nevertheless, the thought of living in such a dilapidated house frightened her as she contemplated her move from South Africa to Malawi.

"Poverty, poverty, poverty!" The word seemed to haunt Annie as she came to terms with her decision.

Lewis had given all he had to his ministry work; he had reached the normal retirement age of sixty-five and had no income-generating prospects. Annie asked God how she was expected to survive and experienced many a sleepless night as she woke from nightmares about her future and her concerns about Lewis's ability to provide.

"This wasn't faith in action. I knew God was my provider, yet I was riddled with doubt and fear and the Lord really had to deal with me," Annie confides.

A mutual friend of Annie and Lewis, prominent South African evangelist Elisha Mashingwane, offered Annie some encouragement: "If Lewis is God's best for you, Annie, then he's God's best!"

"One thing I'm sure of, Annie, you'll never be poor, never!" the evangelist told her. "So don't worry!"

Despite Elisha's prophetic words, Annie knew the road ahead would be challenging, but she could not forsake the calling. Overcoming a fear of poverty was just one more barricade to be surmounted in her obstacle race. Another was letting go of her comfortable suburban lifestyle.

"I was struggling to give up the slightest thing," Annie admits. "I realized that, although it had been so easy in the past to sing the song 'I surrender all', I now found myself in a situation where I couldn't even surrender a single piece of furniture. It was mine, and I couldn't let go!"

Though Annie appointed an estate agent to sell her house,

it seemed an impossible task. It was 1993, the year before South Africa's first democratic elections, and the country faced an uncertain future. There was a glut of properties for sale owing to a spate of last-minute emigration, and very few properties were being sold as hardly anybody wanted to buy, particularly with a mortgage rate of close on twenty-two per cent.

It would take a miracle for Annie's house to be sold, to settle her mortgage and release the funds she needed to send a container of her household contents to Malawi.

"One evening, as I walked through my house, I confessed my sin to the Lord," Annie confides. "I asked Him to change my heart, for I seemed to be so attached to my worldly belongings. I had to get to the place where if I didn't sell the house, I didn't sell it. If I couldn't take my furniture, then I couldn't take my furniture. I had to come to a point where I was prepared to surrender all.

"The Lord worked on my heart as I allowed Him to and it wasn't long before I gave everything away in my mind, without feeling stressed about it. It was just after this that my house sold and the Lord allowed me to take my furniture with me."

By now, all Annie's children had left home except Esther, and Annie arranged for her to board with a close family friend. She got quotes for the relocation of the things she had decided to take to Malawi and began to pack up. Though she stood to lose everything, she knew the promise of Mark 10:29–30:

> So Jesus answered and said, "Assuredly, I say to you, there is no one who has left house or brothers or sisters or father or mother or wife or children or lands, for My sake and the gospel's, who shall not receive a hundredfold now in this time – houses and brothers and sisters and mothers and children and lands, with persecutions – and in the age to come, eternal life."

Annie attended her final service at Rhema Church, where she had done so much for the ministry in Alexandra. She was called to the front at the end of the service and Pastor Ray laid his hands on her and prayed for her future work in Malawi.

The wedding day was set for 7 August 1993 and Annie arrived just a week before. As it was a second marriage she had requested that the ceremony be as simple as possible. Though she had been single for ten years, she still felt awkward about the fact that she had been divorced, and didn't want too much fuss. However, she now found herself in a different culture. Annie ended up with five bridesmaids and two page boys, including some of Lewis's grandchildren, and there were five hundred guests at the reception!

"One thing I was sure about was that this was a new beginning and I was determined to wear white," Annie shares. "So I dressed in a beautiful white blouse, with a long flowing white skirt and an elegant white hat, and of course I had a bridal bouquet of pink roses!"

In accordance with Malawian culture, both Annie and Lewis had to have an "advocate" as part of the wedding procedure. Lewis's relative the Chief Justice of Malawi was appointed as Annie's advocate and she stayed at his home the night before the marriage ceremony.

The morning of the wedding Annie was fetched in a large gold Mercedes, owned by one of Lewis' former partners from the bus company. Although the bride was on time, the driver was late, which upset the pastor leading the service. He agreed to continue with the ceremony, but he refused to preach!

"I've yet to hear of anyone in Malawi being exactly on time, so I wasn't at all pleased with him!" says Annie.

In true African tradition the bridal procession took several minutes to make its way up the aisle as Annie was brought in by her advocate, walking three paces forward and two back while the crowd sang joyously. "It took ages to get to the front," Annie recalls, "but it was fun!"

Annie had insisted that her children should not travel to Malawi for the wedding because of the costs involved, and she thought it was going to be a small private affair, but it was anything but. The reception was held at a school hall and attended by the entire community.

It was a major celebration with a large wedding cake, pieces of which Lewis and Annie had to feed to each other in keeping with the culture. Annie also had to kneel in front of all thirty-five of the special guests sitting on the stage and offer them slices of cake.

Many people contributed to making the wedding a memorable day. The only thing Annie found strange was the Malawian custom of throwing money at the bride and groom. It seems that the main purpose of a wedding in Malawi is to shower the bridal couple with as much cash as possible.

One by one different groups of people were called upon to give money to Annie and Lewis. "Now it's the turn of the pastor's wives to give," the master of ceremonies said. "Now it's the turn of the government ministers; now it's the turn of the villagers... " and so it went on.

Despite all the kwacha notes that were literally thrown at them, the value of the local currency wasn't strong and there was insufficient money to go away on honeymoon, but at least there was enough for the newlyweds to spend their first night together in a hotel.

Annie was in for a rough surprise the following morning, as her new husband's family came to the hotel at six o'clock to say goodbye. This was another African tradition, and she would have to get used to it.

Annie wondered why the family came to say goodbye, as many of them would be her neighbours. The honeymoon destination was, after all, a certain "derelict house".

At least she got to live in the one room that had windows. She had decided to look on the bright side and was only too happy to be doing what she believed God wanted, with the man she loved. She knew Lewis adored her and that was all that mattered.

Annie tried to make their bedroom as comfortable as possible. "Yes, it was difficult to get to sleep with the rats running riot in the ceiling, but I got used to it! I never went to sleep without socks on in case they bit my toes in the night."

Her new husband needed to be fed, so Annie quickly had to get to grips with her African "kitchen". "This was the iron shack outside," she laughs, "with a fully portable stove – three large stones in a triangle! I'd have to make a fire in the middle to cook our food! It worked very well, nothing I couldn't handle."

Bathing was another adventure for her, as there was no running water. Water had to be drawn from the well in buckets and poured into a large drum on the outside fire until it was hot. Then the bath inside the house had to be filled, bucket by bucket, but fortunately for Annie there was a servant to help with this.

"I lay there in that old bathtub, surrounded by broken milk cans, old tyres, bags of cement, and all sorts of rubbish, and I laughed and laughed and laughed! And I asked the Lord, 'Father, how did you ever get me out of my tiled bathroom in Bryanston into this?' But I was happy!"

Though there was no running water, there was at least electricity, so Annie did not have to use gas lamps and candles, like most of her neighbours. "Fortunately I could use a heater in winter, and when I wanted a slice of toast, I'd simply put a piece of bread over the bars!" she says, making the best of her new surroundings.

"It was quite an experience living in my 'new home', but I was happy, and when you are doing God's will it really doesn't matter where you are! Yes, it was a massive change, but I was thinking of the ministry opportunities ahead and, at last, I had a loving, caring husband by my side."

As the couple had very little money, Annie thought she had better start doing something productive. She had brought her sewing machine and some Laura Ashley™ and Biggie Best™ material with her, so she started to make a range of bathroom sets and pillowcases. She began selling them and sold one after another. By November she had so much work she needed to employ a tailor to help her.

"Never ever just sit and think, 'What am I going to do now?'" Annie advises. "Whatever circumstances you find yourself in, do something pro-active. Move into what God has for you. Nothing is impossible for those who believe!

"I had made up my mind that I was going to make it. Why? Because I firmly believed the Scripture verse that says: 'The people who know their God shall be strong, and carry out great exploits' (Daniel 11:32). Get to know God, get to know who He is, and find out what adventures He has for your life."

Annie could see how poor the people in her new community were. She realized she needed to include them in her entrepreneurial ventures, and would start many different projects to help the people living in the little thatched shacks in the surrounding village.

Annie had finally passed her test of obedience. Six weeks after she and Lewis were married, they were able to move into a rented house on a seven-acre property next door to Lewis's farm. It would be ideal for their needs and it would come just in time to accommodate Annie's container of furniture!

17

My fight for Lewis's children

"I'M GOING TO WALK IN LOVE"

On her marriage to Lewis, Annie became stepmother to his nine remaining children: Dorothy, Ellen, Angela, Jeremiah, Victor, Agatha, Agnes, Madalo, and Doreen. Lewis was sixteen years older than Annie and his children were grown up, though some of them hadn't left home. He also had thirty-five grandchildren at the time.

During those first six weeks of marriage Annie found herself living in one room in a close community of several family members, with much to learn about African culture. Misunderstandings and family tensions were inevitable as the new woman of the house took her place and it was to prove hard for her to overcome the obstacle of being considered an outsider. "I was overjoyed to be married to Lewis, but my joy would be sorely tested," Annie recalls.

Living in the farmhouse with Annie and Lewis were his son Jeremiah and his wife, Cecilia, and their three children; Lewis's youngest son, Madalo, aged twenty; his youngest daughter, Doreen, aged eighteen; and three of his teenage grandchildren, Jo, Andy, and Roger. His daughter Agnes was also living on the property, in a five-roomed cottage adjacent to the house, with her husband, Nicolas, and their five children.

Malawian culture seemed to underpin everything and Annie would gradually discover more about it. For example she needed to be seated lower than her husband and younger people and servants would kneel to talk to her. Lewis had been married for thirty-two years and had never sat at the same table as his wife. He and his sons would sit at one table and Elizabeth and the girls at another. This is the way many families in Malawi eat their meals to this day.

"The way Lewis and I lived together, it was as if there were no cultural differences or unfamiliar customs in our relationship at all," Annie points out. "I think he was glad to leave that behind him. His children, however, looked at me with their Malawian eyes, expecting me to be like their mother, and I was of course very different. They knew nothing of where I'd come from or the lifestyle I was used to."

The Chikhwaza children were not well off and they assumed that, because Annie had come from South Africa, she was wealthy. They welcomed her at first because they thought they would benefit financially, and then became resentful when they didn't. Immediately after the wedding they started to look to Annie as their provider, and when she made it clear that she couldn't possibly be that, they were not happy.

They were also upset because they felt their father had set aside some of their cultural traditions. "She's turning our father into a white man," Annie overheard them complaining. In spite of this they still addressed her as "Mommy" or *Mai* (the Chichewa word for mother), as a mark of respect to Lewis.

It was hard for Annie to face being ostracized by the children, but she had always had a heart for the poor and the oppressed and she was determined to go out of her way to be kind to them.

When they came asking for bread or sugar she would gladly give them what they needed. However, she knew she had to challenge their mindset. If she was to help the people of Malawi she had to start with her new family. She had to teach them that God did not want them to rely on charity and that He would bless the work of their hands.

"The Bible says, 'If anyone will not work, neither shall he eat'," Annie quoted 2 Thessalonians 3:10 as she tried to reason with the three teenage grandsons living in the house.

She wasn't being mean; she just wanted to encourage them to do more with their lives than sit around at home. The young men were not happy being told off by a woman and started muttering about Annie to the village people. Seeds of ill feeling began to take root.

By now, Annie's sewing endeavours were bringing in sufficient income to provide for Lewis and herself. The bathroom sets and pillowcases were popular, and as each set sold Annie was able to purchase new material to make more.

There were now sufficient funds to rent a house, and when the property next door to the farm became vacant, Annie jumped at the opportunity. It was perfectly situated, enabling her and Lewis to have their own space, while still being close enough to the farmhouse – the hub of the income-generating projects Annie was planning to alleviate poverty in the community.

Annie saw their new rented home as God's provision for Lewis to build their marriage without the stresses of living in such close proximity to others, in a community where boundaries were easily blurred. It would also mean that she could take delivery of the long-awaited container filled with her furniture!

When Annie and Lewis moved, they continued to use their room at the farmhouse for storage; however, this proved unworkable, as things started to disappear. She found it hard to believe their property was being stolen, especially since the perpetrators had to be from the local community, which included her new family. But the thefts continued, one after another, and Annie realized she and Lewis would have to do something about it before they had nothing left.

"I planted a vegetable garden and it was there one evening and gone the next morning!" Annie remembers. "I went to pick some carrots and found that they had disappeared. The next day I went for a cabbage and they were all gone. I would gladly have shared the vegetables with the neighbouring villagers if they'd just asked, but they didn't, and I began to feel they had no respect for me at all. The more I planted, the more the vegetables would disappear. It was very frustrating."

Annie knew God had called her to minister to the needs of the community, but how could she do this while she was at loggerheads with her own family members and with the villagers who were stealing? It became a struggle for her to confront the culprits, and, with regard to her stepchildren, she made a decision: "I'm going to fight for these kids and show them the love of God."

Deep down, she knew that her battle was not against flesh and blood, but against spiritual forces working against her. And the more the devil tried to cause division and strife, the more Annie clung to God.

"I'm going to walk in love," she resolved as she set about assisting the family in whatever way she could. The biggest need was for the grandchildren to be educated, and Annie would do her best to teach them and she and Lewis would help finance their schooling. Lewis was supportive of his new wife and upset by the way she was being treated, and did his best to try to keep the peace.

As a pastor, Lewis shared Annie's desire to win the people of the surrounding villages to Christ and he encouraged her to reach out to them through entrepreneurial projects similar to the ones she had been so successful with in Alexandra.

To start with, Annie found the money to buy twelve hundred chickens for one of the grandsons, Roger, to manage so he could earn an income from selling eggs. But it was not long before the chickens disappeared.

She was disappointed but undeterred. She knew she couldn't give up. She had to keep her eyes on Jesus and stay focused on her calling.

Annie wanted to empower families in the village economically and she began to include the womenfolk in her needlework initiative. She invited them to come to the farmhouse, where a large crowd of ladies could often be seen sitting on the lawn learning candlewicking, a kind of embroidery, and quilting. Each Tuesday Annie would receive the embroidered squares the women had made, pay them for their work, and give them material for the week ahead.

While reaching out to the community, Annie remained committed to winning Lewis's children over, but not all of them shared his faith in Christ and love for their neighbours. They were mostly still steeped in cultural traditions, superstition, and fear of witchcraft. When anything went wrong in their lives, they were convinced somebody had put a curse on them or wanted to poison them.

Lewis and Annie had been married for only eight months when tragedy struck his family again. His daughter Doreen came to visit them at the rented house on the seven-acre property and she did not look well. Everybody thought it was just the flu, but, having been a nurse, Annie was concerned it was something worse.

Annie insisted that Doreen come and stay with her and her father so she could care for her properly. When she started to lose weight rapidly, Annie realized she was very ill. Doreen had no money to pay for medical treatment and Annie gladly paid her hospital bills.

"We did everything we could for Doreen," Annie recalls. "Lewis and I were fighting for her life and I nursed her for days. When she developed meningitis we took her to a private hospital, but they said there was nothing they could do for her."

Doreen lasted only a few days at the hospital before she passed away. It was heartbreaking for Annie, as she had become close to her stepdaughter. Lewis of course was devastated to lose another child, and it was a good thing Annie was there to comfort him and the rest of the family.

As the funeral approached Annie thought back to a strange request Lewis had made before Doreen died. "Ask her if she had anything to do with her mother's death," he had instructed his wife, thinking that if anybody would be able to find out it would be Annie. Weak but still conscious, the girl insisted that she hadn't.

Although Lewis never truly believed that Doreen had been involved in Elizabeth's death, he wanted to put to rest the rumours he had heard. Annie then discovered that many villagers in Africa never attribute death to natural causes. They believe it is because of either poison or witchcraft.

Annie was still trying to understand the ways of the Malawian people, and the funeral was to be a traumatic ordeal for her. Doreen's body was taken from the hospital to the farmhouse, where she was laid out on a bed ready for the mourning to begin. Annie had to lead the women mourners: a cloth was placed around her head and she had to stay next to the body for twenty-four hours.

The wailing went on through the night as the people of the community came to pay their respects. The mourning was primarily in Chichewa, but every now and then they would break into English.

"Mommy, mommy, *Mai, Mai*, why didn't you close the gates of death?" they wailed. "Why did Doreen have to die?"

Annie did not realize that they were addressing her. She had never experienced anything like this in her life and she couldn't understand what they were saying. Later when the whole family gathered to discuss the burial she began to understand...

When Elizabeth's brothers started to make all the arrangements, Annie could not understand why Lewis was not consulted, as he was Doreen's father. But in Malawi, in the absence of a child's mother, it is the uncles that have the final say. They are known as *amalume*, which means "the keepers of the children of their sister".

"The uncles sat with Lewis and me and I felt as if I were being investigated," Annie recalls. They asked me all kinds of questions, almost implying that I had something to do with her death. 'Why did she die? How did she die? Why was this not done? Why was that not done?' I was taken aback and I asked Lewis what was going on."

Lewis couldn't answer Annie then, but he later explained the cultural connections concerning death and witchcraft, and she was horrified that they could even consider she had anything to do with Doreen's passing when all she had done was love and care for her. After Doreen's death, however, she could see that Lewis's children were beginning to distance themselves from their stepmother.

"I could have handled some things better," Annie acknowledges. "But I didn't know how to treat them at the time, especially in respect of their way of thinking. I didn't understand how they saw things. But I did love them, and tried to do my best to support them."

Annie's fight for Lewis's children would become an ongoing mission to empower them, care for them, and walk in love and forgiveness towards them. Unfortunately for Annie it would almost become a fight to the death.

18

Marriage suits you well

"YOU HAVE JUST BLOSSOMED!"

A short time after Annie and Lewis were married, they went to South Africa to visit her children. She was overjoyed to see Sam, Rebekah, Paul, and Esther and for them all to celebrate with her and Lewis.

By now Annie had come to call Lewis "daddy" and he affectionately addressed her as "mommy".

On a visit to Rhema, the couple met one of the church's senior leaders, Joe Peter, whom they both knew well. "I can hardly recognize you," Pastor Joe teased Lewis. "Marriage to Annie seems to have suited you very well. You have just blossomed!"

Their marriage was indeed flourishing, but then Annie discovered they had been married only under "customary law", the way most couples in Malawi are wed – something she found alarming.

She knew she and Lewis were husband and wife in God's eyes as they had exchanged vows in church, but she wanted to ensure their marriage was recognized by the courts. So, in October 1994, fourteen months after their first wedding, Annie and Lewis married before a registrar. "I had to be sure!" she says with a grin.

Annie also needed assurance about something else. "Daddy, What about your promise to fix the ten-roomed house?" she reminded him.

"Mommy darling, we must sell that spare plot," Lewis answered. "There are squatters, but they must go."

The Chikhwazas eventually drove over to Lewis's second piece of land, where people were living illegally. (By now they had purchased a vehicle and, although it was far from new, it was a giant leap from the makeshift "township car" Annie had found so amusing.)

Lewis knew it would take a good deal of negotiation to get his land back, and they had come prepared to placate the people. Annie had made a large pot of soup and was ready to exercise her considerable charm.

"*Muli bwanji*?" Lewis greeted the group of people who had quickly gathered to see what they wanted. He was saying, "How are you?" in Chichewa, an everyday Malawian greeting.

"What do you want?" a man asked suspiciously.

"We want to give you some soup," Annie replied kindly. But, hungry as they were, nobody came forward to get any. "We also have biscuits," she offered.

What Annie didn't know was that in Malawi people don't eat soup! To the Malawians, soup is the gravy they eat with their maize porridge, so Annie had made a bit of a cultural blunder.

"This is Reverend Chikhwaza," one of the squatters shouted, identifying Lewis. "He is the one who wants to take back the land."

"We don't want your soup," they shouted. "Go away. We're living here now."

"You're illegal. I am the owner, and I want you to leave," Lewis retorted.

A woman grabbed a packet of biscuits, tore it open, and started throwing them at Annie and Lewis. "*Iwe choka! Choka!*" she yelled. This was the way Chichewa speakers would tell an animal to scram. It was very rude to use this term to a person, and Lewis got the message loud and clear that they had better leave.

A large crowd had formed as others came to see what the commotion was about. Lewis and Annie were outnumbered. "We'd better go," he whispered to Annie, guiding her towards the car.

"The squatters began to chase us and I had to run with that big pot!" Annie recalls. "We never did get them off that land. God would have to find another way to provide for us and for that derelict house to be renovated."

Like Lewis, Annie was blossoming in her marriage, despite the challenges she faced and the delays in fixing the house. In the meantime she was very pleased to be in their rented home. This was a three-bedroomed house, with a lounge-cum-dining room, two bathrooms, and a small veranda.

Of course, after the container had been unpacked, she felt much more settled in Malawi. She was glad to be surrounded by familiar things and to have a place where her children could visit.

"It was not what I'd been used to, by any means, and the kitchen was small and ugly," says Annie, "but I made a home of it and I was happy.

"If we're prepared to humble ourselves before God, He will elevate us. If we are prepared to do what He tells us, He will reward our obedience," she reflects. "I could have said, 'I'm not going to live in this mess' and never married Lewis, but then I would have missed out on a really great husband and I would never have had what I have now.

"I wouldn't have the life (and life in abundance) that Jesus promised. Because it is only when we are doing God's will that we can find true fulfilment."

Annie's second marriage was quite unlike her first. She now had a man who loved her and wanted to spend time with her. He never felt threatened by her and would encourage her to stretch herself and do more for God. In turn, she would affirm and honour him. "It was so different being married to a man who was focused on loving me as Christ loves the church," Annie reveals.

God was clearly blessing Lewis and Annie, their marriage, and their work. Annie was grateful to be able to make an income from sewing, and wanted to teach others to do the same. She began to teach more and more of the village women the arts of candlewicking and quilting.

It was a challenge, as the women were illiterate, but they eventually got the hang of drawing the patterns onto calico. Next they had to learn how to candlewick by hand and finally they were taught to use the sewing machines that had been donated to the project. Before long, beautiful candlewicked quilts were being made to fulfil orders from Annie's contacts in Malawi, South Africa, and Holland. Many of these quilts would be sent across the globe.

Being married to a pastor, Annie knew the importance of empowering fellow pastors' wives of different denominations, and she started a network for them named "Helpmates in Ministry". She applied for entrepreneurial funding from the Dutch government, and was awarded enough to train twenty-seven women in income-generating projects, from baking to sewing, leather work, sisal-bag-making, quilting, and other crafts.

Annie then promoted these ladies to be trainers so they could empower another twenty-three women, which meant a total of fifty who were able to generate a new income by setting up their own small businesses.

Annie loved apples, and she thought she could benefit the whole community, including the Chikhwaza family, by planting an orchard of apple trees. So she and Lewis found the money to plant fifteen thousand apple seedlings as a long-term investment. "We were brimming over with ideas for new income-generating projects all the time," Annie says, "and many, many of the little business start-ups we initiated were beginning to flourish."

A brick-making project was also set up to provide for building and renovation, which employed a large number of village folk. God was starting to transform lives in the local community and He was about to do a miracle for the Chikhwazas.

One day as they were talking on the veranda, or *khonde*, as it is termed in Malawi, Lewis started reminiscing about his days as owner of the bus company. "You know the government took Ulendo Transport from me in 1980, when we couldn't make a loan repayment to the bank. They put us under judicial management, but the company was supposed to be returned to me after the debts were paid," he confided in Annie.

"Did they ever pay you your share?" she asked.

"No, Mommy, they were supposed to, but they never did, even though I put in a claim."

That had been fourteen years ago and the whole matter was long forgotten, but Annie sensed that she should pursue it. For Annie there was nothing like a challenge, especially when she believed she had heard from God, and she would not take no for an answer.

The company was taken into receivership in 1980 and never went into liquidation; neither was it returned to Lewis. In 1990 he and his partner had gone to the lawyers, but they were getting nowhere. Lewis asked Annie to look into the matter.

In 1993, after investigation, it became clear to her that the government had been wrong, and she opened a claim.

Annie discussed the matter with the Vice-President, who referred her to the Minister of Trade and Industry. Lewis knew both men from his time in government and, after several meetings, much persistence, and some high-level negotiation with the senior state attorney, the government finally authorized Lewis's claim.

"After three months we received a cheque – without even going to court!" Annie says. "It was a miracle! And it wasn't even a huge battle, though it was the start of one."

God had rewarded Annie's tenacity with a miracle of provision. The windfall would make a huge difference. They could go ahead with an overseas trip they had been planning for years and they could start renovating the ten-roomed house, at long last!

Annie and Lewis were excited to be able to join a group from Rhema Johannesburg who travelled to the USA to attend a Rodney Howard-Browne conference in Lakeland, Florida. On the way back they visited Europe to see family and friends.

This was the first opportunity for Lewis to meet Annie's family in the Netherlands, and he received a warm welcome. "They just loved him," says Annie, "and they spoiled him rotten. My mother even joked that I now had competition, as she thought he was such a nice man!"

Annie and Lewis posed for photos in front of Annie's childhood home in Friesland, the church where they had worshipped as a family, and Annie's primary school.

Lewis in turn loved Holland: coming from Africa, he couldn't believe he could hold snow in his hands and "walk on water", as he put it. It was actually an iced-up canal!

The couple also visited the UK to see their friends Rory and Wendy Alec and find out more about the new Christian broadcasting venture they had heard so much about. Annie longed to spend time with her spiritual daughter, and to share with Rory and Wendy what had already been accomplished in Malawi, despite the obstacles in their way.

Rory and Wendy were growing into a formidable couple able to make a worldwide impact through media, and Annie knew it was not for nothing that their paths had crossed a decade earlier. Lewis and Annie too were becoming a spiritually formidable couple, who would in turn have a great impact on Malawi.

They may not have had children of their own, but their love for each other and for God would overflow and give them many spiritual children and many more babies and toddlers to care for.

Annie has always had a special concern for children, and it broke her heart to see how many toddlers in Malawi were malnourished and in need of nurture. God gave her the idea of starting a nursery school and she set about converting a large shed in the grounds of the ten-bedroomed house into a sanctuary for the poorest village children. The building was large enough to accommodate forty energetic three-year-olds, who came daily to play together and receive food, clothing, and medicine.

"I was overjoyed to see these little lives respond to our love and care," Annie says. They were no longer lethargic and miserable and, most of all, I knew we were sowing good seeds of the word of God in their lives. The school was also a great way to show the love of God to the community."

When the time came to name the school, Annie knew it had to focus on Jesus' greatest commandment, to love one another. And so it became known as "Kondanani" Nursery School, using the Chichewa word for "Love one another". It was officially opened by the then President of Malawi, Bakili Muluzi, and would be the forerunner of a much greater vision for Africa's children.

19

Get off "our" land or we'll kill you

"IF YOU'D MARRIED ONE OF US,
YOU WOULDN'T HAVE THIS PROBLEM!"

When Lewis started to renovate the farmhouse, his children became very upset. They knew this is what he had promised Annie, and they were concerned that it was being done just for her. Their father was nearing seventy and they were worried about what would happen if he suddenly passed away. They were concerned about losing their inheritance, thinking that he would leave everything to his new wife.

From the start of his second marriage Lewis had made it clear to both Annie and his children that their inheritance remained unchanged, that on his death they would still receive the forty-three acres of land, excluding two acres that would go to Annie. There was a clear understanding that Annie would not inherit the estate, but they started to question this.

"When Lewis and I got married, we discussed the land and it was agreed that, if anything happened to him, I'd be given two acres of land only, which I was happy with. Two acres was more than generous and would have been sufficient for a person on their own."

Annie and Lewis had several family meetings to set their minds at rest, but the children were convinced that Annie would gain everything if Lewis died, leaving them with nothing. They believed she had clouded their father's mind, and exercised an evil influence on him. They also felt they had a right to dictate to their father how he should spend the money he had received from the government payout.

Immediately after the cheque arrived, Lewis received a letter from one of his sons telling him that the family had decided how the funds should be spent. Lewis ignored the letter, and Annie found it by accident two months later. When she read it, she was dismayed that the children felt they could interfere in their father's affairs, but she thought it would be wise to find out whether this kind of behaviour was part of their tradition.

"Although I didn't like it, I felt I had to make some allowances," Annie remembers. "I went to see two prominent Malawian leaders, the Hon. Justice Unyolo and Revd Pieter Mbeve, and they confirmed that the children had acted inappropriately.

"I approached the particular son and told him that his letter was not acceptable and that we would not allow our lives to be controlled by the children. In spite of this, they were all given some of the money.

"What the children don't know is that, if I'd had my way, they would have received double what Lewis decided to give them, but he was very angry with them for interfering."

Even though they had benefited financially from the windfall, the children were furious that their father would not accede to their wishes and were convinced they would be left with nothing after his death. Growing resentment now turned to anger and open hostility.

It was no secret to Lewis and Annie that the children were plotting against their stepmother, and had she been a lesser woman she would probably have given up the fight and gone back to South Africa. But she believed God had called her to Malawi and so there was no going back. She would stick it out, no matter what.

Annie was trusting God to resolve the family tensions, but she did wonder what they were saying about her. She thought of Joseph's brothers plotting to throw him into a pit and how the conversation must have gone. She sensed that a similar discussion must have taken place among her stepchildren, and she wondered how it might have played out...

"This cunning white woman is going to steal our land," she imagined Dorothy telling her siblings. "She has to go!"

"We have to get rid of her," she could hear another of the children saying angrily. "Perhaps she will have a car accident..."

"Maybe we can get her deported..." She pictured one of the sons trying to come up with a lesser evil, to placate his brothers and sisters; after all, he *was* a church minister.

Annie thought of each of the children in turn and what they might be plotting. "If she lives, our land will be gone," she imagined one of the girls saying. "We will have to get the villagers to sort her out..."

"Yes. Let's kill her!" was the outcome of her imagined scenario, given the events that followed. But had any of the children dared defend her for the good she was doing? Even one? And what would Doreen have said, had she been alive? Would she have put in a good word for her stepmother?

But these were just thoughts whirling round in her head. In reality, of course, Annie did not know who had said what, but the children did attempt to get her deported through the efforts of a relative who was a prominent legal figure, she was involved in a suspicious car accident, and ultimately the time did come when they would try to take her life by causing the villagers to gang up against her.

By now one of Lewis's grandsons was training as a motor mechanic and Annie and Lewis would regularly support him by paying him to service their car. It was after one such service that Annie was involved in a bad accident.

"We were on our way to church in Chiwembwe, one of the townships, when all of a sudden Lewis lost control of the vehicle," Annie recalls. "He wasn't speeding, nor was the weather bad, but the car ended up in a ditch. It wasn't Lewis's driving, and when we saw that all the damage was on the passenger side of the car, where I'd been sitting, I thought it was suspicious."

Annie was rushed to hospital in Blantyre, where it was discovered she had broken her back. She had to lie still for seven weeks and it was only with the help of two Bible school students from Rhema that she was able to keep her outreach projects and the nursery school going. They had come for six months' practical experience and were able to oversee things for her.

It seemed like a flashback to Alexandra Township, where her ministry had been going so well but her home life was so challenging. The Lord was blessing the entrepreneurial projects but her stepchildren were starting to make her life impossible.

When threats of deportation and a suspicious accident did not seem to scare Annie, the children became even more determined to get her to leave. But they didn't know the courageous resilience of the Annie who had braved gangs of knife-wielding thugs and angry witch doctors in Alex!

"The children tried to make my life a misery in so many ways," Annie shares. "But I wasn't afraid. I had the Lord as 'my strength and shield' and, besides, I was not going to run away, because God had given me a vision for Malawi. He had told me where I was to be and I couldn't abandon that calling just because things were getting difficult, but it was going to get worse, a lot worse."

The tactics of those who work against God are not new; if they can't intimidate you with fear, they will try spreading lies, and it was not long before some serious allegations about Annie were circulating in the surrounding villages as the children tried to enlist the sympathy of the people to support them in their "inheritance dilemma".

The most serious of these lies and the one that hurt Annie the most was the rumour that she had been involved in Lewis's first wife's death. Despite the fact that everyone knew that Elizabeth Chikhwaza had died from a diabetic condition exacerbated by high blood pressure, it was now said that Annie had killed her so she could marry Lewis and get all his money.

The story was ludicrous: Annie hadn't even been living in Malawi at the time, but, even so, many people in the villages started to believe it.

But the lies were about to come even closer to home. When another of Lewis's children passed away suddenly, the other children were convinced she had to be responsible for his death. They could now vilify Annie in the eyes of the villagers by telling them she had poisoned their brother.

Lewis's youngest son, Madalo, was a tall, well-built, good-looking young man whom Annie had tried to support in every way.

"When I first came into the home I did everything to help him complete his education. We enrolled him in a private school, bought what he needed, and gave him money for the extras he still had to buy, but he disappeared with the money, we didn't see him for several days, and he never went to school."

Madalo became a heavy drinker and began to have epileptic fits. Annie and Lewis took him to see a medical consultant in Blantyre about his epilepsy and the professor told them it would stop if he curbed his drinking, but that was easier said than done.

Tragically, on 5 September 1996, at the age of twenty-three Madalo was found dead. He had suffered an epileptic fit, fallen with his lips pressed against his nostrils, and suffocated, an awful way to die.

When Annie got the telephone call at the farmhouse she was heartbroken, especially since she now had to tell her husband that another of his children had passed away. "It was dreadful news for Lewis and the whole family," she remembers. "We were both distraught and all I could think about was how I could comfort my husband."

As Lewis sat trying to come to terms with the situation he suddenly looked up at Annie and said, "Mommy, you know they could hold this against you..."

"Against *me*?" Annie answered in shock. "What's this got to do with me? I have nothing to do with it."

"Even so, I'd better take you home right now. Let me deal with this; I don't want you involved."

When Lewis saw his children, his fears were confirmed. They were quick to accuse Annie of poisoning their brother. Although they knew he had epilepsy nobody else knew about his condition. As far as the villagers were concerned, he was alive and well one day and dead the next. It was very easy for them to believe he had been poisoned, and who was close enough to him to do it other than his stepmother?

One of Lewis's pastors went to warn Annie: "*Amayi*, get away, because they are coming. They think you killed Madalo, and now they're coming to kill you."

A crowd of angry villagers came to the house, but Annie wasn't there; she had already taken refuge at a friend's home nearby. "They of course forgot about the saving power of God, and I managed to get away, sensing angels encamped around me," Annie says.

Although she wanted to be at the funeral, Annie was relieved that she couldn't attend for her own safety, especially as she hadn't forgotten the ordeal of having to lead the mourners after Doreen's death.

"These new allegations were beyond my imagination," Annie says. "Death is never natural to the majority of Malawians; its cause is either poison or witchcraft. It was therefore not difficult for the children to make the villagers believe that their 'white stepmother' had poisoned a young man who had looked so strong and healthy the day before. Revenge is very much part of African culture, and I was condemned to death."

At a post-burial meeting, Lewis was given his own death sentence: "You and your wife must never come onto this farm again," instructed one of his sons. "If you do, you'll be killed. We won't do it ourselves; the villagers will do it."

"Get off our land now," Dorothy threatened, "or the villagers will kill you..."

Lewis was distraught as he was chased off his own land and a band of his rogue grandchildren took over the farm. But it wasn't just a farm; it was also a community development centre where hundreds of people came to earn a wage each day and a nursery school where Annie was caring for forty children.

"I was back there two days later, trusting God for my protection," Annie says. "I had a lot of responsibilities on that property and there was also the nursery school. But I was never to see my little ones again. Every person working for Lewis and me was warned that, if they continued in our employ, 'Something bad would happen to them' – and for a Malawian that is enough to make them stay away."

Annie and Lewis went to the police to ask them to intervene in the situation, but they were reluctant to get involved in a family matter. "If you'd married one of us, you wouldn't have this problem!" the station commander told Lewis.

20

Today you'll see your shame

"IT WAS ALL MALICIOUS PROPAGANDA"

Lewis Chikhwaza was heartbroken, still grieving the loss of Madalo, and now it seemed he was losing his farm as well. A godly and peace-loving man, he was now faced with all-out war.

It pained him to think of how he had brought his children up to serve God and to see how they had instead become consumed with hatred. They knew the biblical commandment to honour their parents, they knew how to show respect to their father in accordance with their culture, and yet they sought to bring dishonour to him and to the Chikhwaza name.

It hurt to come to terms with the fact that his children would resort to death threats and that some of his thirty-five grandchildren were petty thieves. He also knew he had to make a stand for what was right. God had called him to be a pastor and to uphold the standard of His word, including the Ten Commandments, which his family seemed to have rejected.

He wondered how they could sink so low as to think it was acceptable to dishonour their father, steal, bear false witness against their neighbour, and covet their neighbour's house. Most of all he was grieved that they had forsaken the greatest commandment of all those that Jesus had given His disciples, to love one another.

Kondanani ("Love one another") was the name of the nursery school on the farm property yet it was demolished with a furious hatred that gave no thought for the children so desperate for its loving care. Lewis's children and grandchildren ruthlessly closed everything down to ensure there was no need for Annie or Lewis ever to return to the property.

"They smashed the nursery school to pieces," Annie laments. "Everything I'd tried so hard to build to help the people was gone. It was all destroyed."

By 26 September 1996, eight Chikhwaza grandchildren were firmly in control of the farm and the police were doing nothing about the situation. Lewis and Annie could see what was happening from their house nearby. The teenagers would regularly patrol the grounds of the farmhouse to show off their power, and each morning and afternoon it seemed as if they were doing military exercises aimed at intimidating them.

Then there were the death threats... but these were nothing new; they had been going on for months. Annie remembers one of the worst: "I opened the letter in horror. It was addressed to me, but unsigned. There was no need; I knew who it was from. 'You don't belong here, you don't belong among us. We have an AK47 ready for you' was all it said, but it spoke volumes."

Lewis immediately wanted to install shutters to cover their bedroom window, but Annie didn't take the threats as seriously as he did. "We can't live with our bedroom window all covered with wood," she told her husband.

Lewis had been concerned that they would be shot through the window while they were sleeping. He understood the culture and the danger they were in. "We'll have to hire some watchmen, then," he replied. The next day he arranged for a security guard to be stationed on their property day and night.

Lewis's fears were justified. Some weeks later he and Annie were woken late one night by a commotion outside their room. Several men had broken into the house but they couldn't get through the locked bedroom door. Fortunately the guard had disturbed them, and they had fled.

While some of Lewis and Annie's belongings had been stolen, they were clearly the targets, as a panga knife was found lying in the passageway the next morning. The couple had had a narrow escape.

"We can't go on like this. We need proper security, more watchmen, and a rifle," Lewis resolved. That morning he arranged for five security guards to be stationed at their house. One of them had a licensed firearm.

While Lewis felt he and Annie needed protection, he had no intention of attacking anyone. But now that his grandsons had taken over the farm it was a volatile situation, and he wondered how he could best end the conflict.

He still hoped the family feud could be resolved through negotiation and he called his brother to come from Lilongwe to try to reason with the family. He also tried time and time again to get the local police at Bvumbwe to come to the property to remove his grandsons but they wouldn't come, even though they had previously arrested them for theft.

He appealed to the local Member of Parliament for the area and to the traditional chief at Bvumbwe, but nobody wanted to get involved. He also tried other police stations, telling them that he and his wife were in danger of losing their lives, but they reiterated their policy that they could not intervene in family matters.

Lewis had previously reported his grandsons to the police for stealing and of course it had caused friction between him and his children as they came to their own children's defence.

"I have over thirty grandchildren and a number of these are criminals," Lewis wrote in a statement to the police. "My wife and I have lost over one hundred thousand kwacha worth of goods: clothing, iron sheets, shoes, blankets, tyres, batteries, radios, motor spares, eggs, chickens, bags of maize, and many other items.

"In the past three years I have taken these kids to Bvumbwe Police Station about six times, and the reason for doing that is to get the police to help us recover the stolen items from the people around us who have bought them. This is what has angered my children.

"These boys have now robbed me of my house. I can't believe they think that they can chase away the owner of a home and make him homeless. According to the law, they have no right. And, in our custom, children should look after their parents, not rob them."

Annie and Lewis resolved that if the police would not come to the farm to question the grandsons, then they would have to take them to the police station themselves.

"These boys are known criminals; perhaps we should send the guards over there to apprehend them and I will take them to the police station myself," Lewis suggested to Annie.

"We'll have to disguise the guards" Annie replied, "otherwise the grandsons will recognize them and run away, I'll find some stockings to put over their heads."

A headline in the *The Star* would later read: "PASTOR HIRED MASKED MEN." Dated Monday 11 November 1996, and written by Frank Vinkhumbo, it was filled with inaccuracies:

> Macabre details about an alleged plot by a Bvumbwe
> pastor and his white wife to eliminate his "troublesome"
> children who are gunning for a share of his estate are
> emerging... It is believed that a gang of about thirty,
> including Safe Guard security personnel, donned
> women's pantyhose to massacre Pastor Chikhwaza's
> children.

The family wrangle in the household of Pastor Lewis
Chikhwaza of Bible Faith Ministries reached a climax
on the night of 29 September when a group of about
twenty-five to thirty men, covering their faces with
masks and wielding knobkerries, pangas, machetes, and
axes, stormed the premises where Chikhwaza's son and
grandsons were sleeping.

It is alleged that the gang were under instruction
to kill one of Chikhwaza's sons, and one of his
grandchildren. One of his daughters claims that the
instructions to eliminate the two came from their
stepmother and father...

One grandson managed to slip away; however, the
gang got hold of two of Chikhwaza's grandchildren who
were fast asleep. It is alleged they were tied up and taken to
Chikhwaza's rented house where the pastor shouted at the
guards to kill them, while his wife Annie could be heard
laughing. They were afterwards taken to the garage and
beaten up before being shepherded to the police station.

In reality, neither Lewis nor Annie had ever given any instruction
for anyone to be "massacred", "killed", or "eliminated"; they
simply wanted to take the boys to the police station. They knew
that the son who was mentioned in the article wasn't even
there at the time, as he was at his home in Chiwembwe. So he
was never even a target. "It was all malicious propaganda," as
Lewis described it in his diary.

Furthermore, the boys weren't beaten and Annie certainly
wasn't laughing; these were all fabrications based on the
children's "eyewitness" accounts and their erroneous thinking.
The report also mentioned a maid named Lucy, who was said
to have been "tortured", which was preposterous.

The truth was that out of the seven grandsons who had

taken over the farm, five of them managed to escape and Lewis was able to take only two of them to the police station, where they were held for questioning. The other five came back later and took control of the farm. "So we were back to square one," Annie sighs.

Lewis could hardly sleep that night and at five o'clock on Monday 30 September he drove to his son's home to inform him what had happened the night before. His son was furious and the meeting did not last long.

However, at about midday, six of Lewis's children arrived at the farm. They were very angry with their father for taking the boys to the police station. They called him over and started to verbally abuse him.

"Today you will see your shame," one son warned his father.

"Today you will experience what you have never experienced in your life," another son kept repeating, implying that Lewis had better be prepared to "meet his maker".

Lewis was devastated. "My daughter Dorothy said words that cannot be written down on paper, really nasty words. My other daughters uttered words that cannot be mentioned. I was shocked."

He warned the six children that they were bringing a curse on themselves, and started to walk away...

The threats were mounting and the authorities didn't seem to care. Lewis's cousin was a senior judge in the High Court, who believed the lies the children had been spreading. Lewis and Annie wondered how far his cousin would go in siding with them and blocking their urgent need for protection.

Lewis had told him continually that the children were lying and that there was no truth to their claims. He tried to gain protection from the courts by means of a restraining order, but his cousin managed to block him every step of the way.

That Sunday night, while Lewis and the guards were dealing with the grandsons, Annie had managed to get in touch with the State President. He had opened the nursery school, and Annie told him how the school had been destroyed and asked for his help.

"They are threatening to kill my husband and me," Annie insisted.

"But they are only threats," he replied

"Yes, but they are *serious* threats!"

"What evidence can I give the Inspector General?" the President asked. "There is nothing I can do until something has actually happened."

The following morning, 26 September, while Lewis was meeting his children, Annie went to the Dutch Consulate in Blantyre to tell them she needed protection. "I wanted the Dutch government to know that my life was in danger and that I was not being afforded any protection by the Malawian government or the police. But they couldn't do anything, as they too said I had not yet been harmed.

"It was a very trying time; I knew I had God's protection, but I wanted to ensure that the authorities knew what was going on," Annie says. "If I hadn't had the word of God so firmly implanted in my spirit I wouldn't have been able to bear the pressure that was on Lewis and me at the time."

Isolated and alone, Annie and Lewis would have to rely purely on God. The police had baulked at the idea that "Reverend Chikhwaza and his wife Annie could be killed by their own children".

The Dutch authorities could offer no support; even the most powerful man in Malawi could do nothing... but God had not given up on the elderly pastor and his wife, whom he had called as a missionary to bring hope into the most hopeless of situations. The Bible states that perfect love casts out fear, and love would ultimately prevail.

21

Kill him! Kill her!

"SURELY HE SHALL DELIVER YOU
FROM THE SNARE OF THE FOWLER"

Monday 30 September – "It was scheduled to be the 'day of my execution'," Annie says, looking back on that fateful day. "The family also intended it to be 'The day of Lewis's shame'. Yes, it was one of the worst days of our lives, but God was with us and I still had my heavenly insurance policy, Psalm 91."

Lewis was upset when he returned from the early-morning altercation at his son's house in Chiwembwe. His son was angry to hear that two of his teenage boys were being held by the police and, worst of all, that it was their grandfather's doing.

They two men had argued, and Lewis was wondering what action his children would take next. When he got back, Annie tried to reassure him over breakfast that God would see them through the family crisis.

> You shall not be afraid of… the destruction that lays
> waste at noonday.
>
> (Psalm 91:5–6)

It was now midday and Lewis and his brother from Lilongwe were told that a mob was gathering on the farm. They went to investigate because they were led to believe that this mob was about to wreck his house.

What was in fact happening was that a crowd of village

folk were gathering to attack Lewis and Annie themselves, having been promised a piece of the land if they helped the Chikhwaza children do away with their father and stepmother.

Annie kept watch from the window of their sitting room, to see what was going on at the neighbouring farmhouse. She could see that a quarrel had erupted and within minutes people started descending on the house from all directions.

The angry crowd was growing in number and she knew her husband was in grave danger. All seven of his surviving children were now at the farmhouse; they were blatantly threatening to kill their father, and she felt she had to get to the police station to ask for help.

Annie drove to the station about one and a half miles away and begged the commanding officer to come to the farm to see what was happening. She finally managed to persuade two policemen to accompany her. She knew better than to get involved and went home. The policemen took Lewis and his children to the station, where they could discuss their grievances against one another.

While they were at the station, a group of villagers began to attack Annie and Lewis's watchmen and some of their staff. Lewis's nephew, who worked for him, was captured by one of his grandsons and stripped naked, and his clothes were thrown into the fire of the farmhouse's outdoor kitchen.

In the meantime, Dorothy had left the police station by taxi and come back to incite the crowd. "We will give you a piece of the land if you help us kill our father and stepmother," she told the villagers, echoing the promise the children had been making to them all week.

"You know she is a murderer!" Dorothy incited them. "Let us avenge the death of our brother, Madalo."

There were plenty of bricks at hand, thanks to the brick-making project Lewis and Annie had started to refurbish the farmhouse. It also provided work for the community, but nobody cared about their livelihood now; they were consumed by revenge and ready to throw their jobs away.

The crowd, led by Dorothy and the grandchildren, started attacking the watchmen, throwing bricks and stones at them and trying to grab the one rifle they shared between them.

The watchman with the rifle, Laison Bandula, started shooting into the air to scare the people and stop them advancing towards Lewis and Annie's home, but they kept attacking him with bricks. In the chaos a young pregnant woman, Eunice Maliko, was killed. She died instantly, an innocent victim caught in the line of fire, who did not deserve to lose her life in that way.

Four other people sustained bullet wounds. One of these was Lewis's own granddaughter, Louise Chikhwaza. Tragedy had struck Bvumbwe and it was all so unnecessary.

By now it was half past three in the afternoon and the mob quickly scattered before anybody else was hurt. The women carried Eunice's body into the farmhouse and started to care for the injured. The watchman fled to the police station to hand himself in and give up his weapon.

A thousand may fall at your side, and ten thousand at your right hand; but it [destruction] shall not come near you.

(Psalm 91:7)

Just after this tragic confrontation, Lewis arrived back from the police station. He was met with chaos – women wailing as they mourned, injured teenagers in need of medical assistance, and the ground strewn with bricks. He was shocked when he heard that a precious life had been lost, and worried about his granddaughter.

It was all very upsetting for him as he felt the violence was so uncalled for. It also raised new security concerns. Where was Annie; was she safe? He couldn't find the watchmen and Annie was nowhere to be seen.

He went over to their home but it was all locked up. He kept calling for Annie but heard nothing. He thought she must have escaped and decided to return to the station to update the police on what had happened. Lewis was thinking only of Annie, but his life was now equally at risk.

By now, incensed by the death of Eunice, the mob had regrouped and were making their way to Lewis and Annie's house to take revenge. They were told that Annie had ordered the watchman to start shooting at the crowd and that she was now responsible for the "cold-blooded murder" of Eunice as well as the "poisoning" of Madalo.

"As I was walking towards my car, I saw my daughter Dorothy coming towards me with a large mob of people, dancing and ululating and giving orders," Lewis later wrote. "A man wielding an axe was heading my way and my children were standing there waiting to see their father hacked to death..."

Lewis realized there was no time to get in the car and drive away – he would have to run for his life, so he headed towards the Bushveld.

"Chop him with the axe!" Dorothy commanded as the man chased after Lewis. "Kill him now!" In the meantime the crowd had surrounded Lewis's car, smashing the windscreen and slashing the tyres. "Leave the car alone," Dorothy instructed. "We can use it."

He shall give His angels charge over you... in their hands they shall bear you up.

(Psalm 91:11–12)

"I couldn't believe my children had hired a man to attack me with an axe, and I had to run for my life, but God saved me from this bloodthirsty man. Somehow the man tripped and I was able to get away and hide in the bush until after dark," Lewis later wrote.

"I believe an angel came and delivered Lewis," Annie says with a grateful smile. "That is the only explanation I can give, because, given the circumstances, if that man had caught up with him, he would most certainly have been killed." Mercifully, Lewis had survived, but now the crowd focused their attention on the woman they had come to hate so much.

It was now four o'clock in the afternoon and Dorothy told the mob to break into Annie and Lewis's home. Many, many cottage pane windows were shattered and the front door was kicked in by the sheer weight of the mob, enabling eight angry villagers to gain access.

All this time Annie was hiding under the bed, crying out to God and asking Him to intervene in the situation.

"Never has there been a time in my life when I was so totally in God's hands. I said to Him; 'Father, today I know, if You want me alive I will be alive; if You want me dead I will die'."

Annie couldn't believe what was happening: it was like a film being scrolled in slow motion. "I wonder what I should call this movie afterwards..." she remembers thinking to herself.

She heard Lewis calling for her, but decided not to answer, as she knew it would only put his life in more danger. She listened to the ominous sounds of his car being smashed, but all she could do was pray. She heard Dorothy shouting lethal instructions and she knew there was no stopping her.

"Kill her!" Annie heard her say repeatedly, along with a string of swear words. "Kill the white bitch."

> **He shall call upon Me, and I will answer him; I will be
> with him in trouble; I will deliver him.**
>
> (Psalm 91:15)

It was a terrifying situation for anyone one to face, especially
a woman on her own, defenceless against a large crowd. The
shouts grew louder and the destruction of her home reached
an eerie crescendo as she heard glass shattering and doors
being forced open.

All the while, the footsteps were coming closer, her
bedroom door was being bashed and bashed until it finally
gave way. All Annie could do was call on the name of the Lord:
"Jesus, Jesus, Jesus," she mouthed repeatedly.

"She's under here!" a man shouted to the others.

"Grab her by the hair and pull her out," another instructed.

"Let's get her outside and see justice done!"

"Kill her! Stab her with the panga," Dorothy Chikhwaza
directed the crowd.

She didn't touch Annie herself, but continued to give
instructions to the angry mob. Lewis's children had warned
the couple that they would be killed, but not by them. They
would get the villagers to do it, so that they couldn't be blamed.

Annie was kicked, stoned, and bashed. She was beaten
on the head and her leg was slashed with a panga. There was
blood everywhere, but all the while she somehow felt cocooned
in the love of God. She focused on her heavenly Father, and
the word of God that she had buried so deep within started to
surface as she remembered the promises of the Scriptures:

> **He shall cover you with His feathers, and under His wings
> you shall take refuge.**
>
> (Psalm 91:4)

"It was such a frightening situation, but I was completely

reliant on God," Annie says. "I was so aware of being under the shadow of the Almighty, cushioned from the horror of the attack. I remember clearly thinking that if they killed me it would be a short cut to heaven, and it held no fear for me; in fact, I had great peace."

Annie didn't feel the pain at the time, though her tendons were cut and her right leg was slashed. But her head had been badly beaten, she was drifting in and out of consciousness, and her lifeblood was ebbing away.

"Fortunately I didn't have any broken bones, but my head was swollen well beyond its normal size and I suffered nerve damage in parts of my body – I have no feeling in them to this day.

"As I lay there in a fetal position, with blood gushing from my leg, it must have looked as if my intestines were hanging out, and the mob left me for dead. One thing I'm sure of: if the police hadn't come when they did, I'd never have survived."

At the height of a crisis, it seems that God will often use the unlikeliest of rescuers. For Annie, it was those two policemen on their bicycles, coming to stop a crowd of two hundred people with sticks, stones, and pangas.

There was no police siren, although she later wondered if they had rung their bicycle bells! "It was quite comical, really, but I certainly wasn't laughing at the time," she says with a grin.

Surely He shall deliver you from the snare of the fowler.

(Psalm 91:3)

Annie's loyal tailor had witnessed the brutality of the attack and run to the police station to call them to come and intervene.

"Police, police!" one of the villagers started shouting at the crowd, giving the signal to disband. The mob thought their mission was accomplished: Annie was lying motionless on the ground, and they were convinced she was dead. It was time for them to disappear before they were arrested.

The mob quickly dispersed, leaving one lone villager to face the police. He was taken for questioning but nobody was ever arrested for the attempted murder of Annie or even for assault and grievous bodily harm. Thankfully, though, she was still alive, albeit only just.

By now the watchmen had returned and alerted a friend of Annie's to what had happened. Maria lived nearby and came immediately in her car and rushed her to the emergency room of the nearby Agricultural Research Centre. "It was there that I was sewn up like a Sunday roast chicken," Annie laughs.

Jokes aside, Annie's injuries were serious, and it would take several months for her to recover. From the Research Centre she was taken to hospital in Blantyre and finally to South Africa to receive further medical care.

"The pain was unbearable but I was just happy to be alive. This was not the first time the evil one had tried to kill me; I remembered how, in the depths of teenage depression, I had tried to take an overdose, and I recalled the doctor's wise words to me: 'Annie, God has a plan for your life!'

"God *did* have a plan for my life, and He also had a plan for Malawi. The devil had done his best to stop this plan from being accomplished, and he would certainly delay it for many, many months, but ultimately love would win out over hatred and God's purposes would prevail.

"I knew that God had preserved me," Annie concludes, "just as He will preserve any believer in a time of great trial if they put their trust in Him and confess the truth of the Scriptures."

> "Because he has set his love upon Me," says the Lord,
> "therefore I will deliver him.
> With long life I will satisfy him, and show him My
> salvation."

(Psalm 91:14, 16)

22

Annie must leave

"IT'S THE PEOPLE OF MALAWI WHO
ARE THE REAL VICTIMS"

In the days following the savage attack, the Malawian media went into overdrive:

"Villagers raid Reverend's house – Four injured."

"Enraged Dutch woman orders: SHOOT THEM!"

"Watchman kills woman, surrenders to police."

"Dutch woman in family feud."

These were just some of the headlines. The story had all the ingredients needed to sell newspapers, and it didn't seem as if the editors cared whether the reports were accurate or not. The Chikhwaza children and the villagers were quick to share their distorted version of events, stoking the ill feeling towards Annie and putting her life in further danger.

Annie was lying in agonizing pain in her hospital bed in Blantyre when a journalist walked into the ward and started commiserating with her about the assault. "Look at you; justice needs to be done!" he said, pretending to take her side. "Can we please have a photo?"

The result was an article on the front page of the *Daily Mail*, which carried a shocking photograph of Annie's swollen and bruised face. Though the article was filled with lies from her stepchildren's "eyewitness accounts", the photograph clearly revealed to the whole nation just how badly she had been beaten up.

Entitled "Villagers raid Reverend's house – Four injured", the *Daily Times* article of 4 October correctly reported that the young pregnant woman, Eunice, had been killed and that Annie and three others had been injured, but it also contained several misleading insinuations.

"The Reverend is on the run," it disclosed, implying that Lewis had something to hide, whereas in fact he had fled for his life.

"The nightmare started after Annie Chikhwaza's stepchildren, who are Reverend Chikhwaza's own, were beaten and tied to trees after being attacked by a group of men wearing masks," the article stated, incorrectly. In truth, none of Lewis's children had been tied up or beaten; it was only two grandchildren who had been apprehended and taken to the police.

"Mrs Annie Chikhwaza took over as housewife after the mysterious death of the Reverend's former wife five years ago" was the line that hurt Annie the most, as it gave the impression that she had in some way been linked to Elizabeth's death when she hadn't even been in the country at the time and the woman had clearly died of natural causes.

The article did at least acknowledge Annie's injuries, although it did not convey their severity. "The villagers allegedly 'sorted her out' with stones and other missiles until she collapsed and was driven to the hospital," it said. However, the accompanying photograph spoke volumes.

"I made the headlines for a few days with my terrible picture on the front page," Annie recalls. "As they say, 'a picture paints a thousand words', but so many of the news reports were inaccurate because the media were getting their information from the children."

In an article in *The Star* on 4 October 1996, headlined "Enraged Dutch woman orders: SHOOT THEM!", journalist Frank Vinkhumbo reported the children's concerns:

> **Pastor Chikhwaza has seven surviving children who feel their stepmother is misleading their father and is bent on grabbing property through marriage. The children, speaking through one of their elder sisters, also claim that Annie ill-treats them.**
>
> **They also suspect that Annie had a hand in the death, last month, of their brother Madalo, whom they allege was poisoned. Annie, they said, did not attend the funeral, thus enhancing their suspicions. She alleged that the stepmother wants to have total control over their father because of the forty-three acres of land and the house he owns...**

Annie of course had never "married Lewis for his money"; far from it – she had become the family breadwinner, assisting her retired husband. Nor had she mistreated Lewis's children or shown anything but kindness to his son.

The news report also alleged that Annie had shot at the crowd with "what looked like a pistol", which was another lie, as she and Lewis had never owned a firearm. Neither did she pass a gun through the window to her watchman, as a "so-called" eyewitness claimed.

A week later, in a follow-up article, boldly entitled "ANNIE MUST LEAVE – Villagers vow to kill her", Frank wrote a news story that was obviously meant as a warning to her to leave Malawi for good:

> **The South African woman Annie, married to Pastor Chikhwaza of Bvumbwe, would be lucky to step back into the village she lives in and walk out of it unscathed. The**

> people of the village have vowed never to see her there
> again as the mere sight of her will remind them of the
> macabre cold-blooded murder of Eunice Maliko, 26, who
> was shot on Monday, allegedly because Annie ordered a
> watchman to open fire on a group of villagers.
>
> Villagers have vowed that peace will not reign should
> Annie go back to the village after being discharged from
> hospital. Speaking at the burial of the late Eunice last
> Wednesday, one of Chikhwaza's children said they no
> longer welcomed the presence of Annie in their midst.
> "It's painful that there can be bloodshed just because of
> a woman," lamented one of Chikhwaza's daughters, who
> declared "We don't want Annie; we have had enough of
> her."

Reading Frank's reports, it was clear to Annie that, although
she had survived the assault, her life was still very much in
danger and she had no choice but to lie low for a while. A *Star*
reporter echoed this warning:

> The estranged wife of Pastor Lewis Chikhwaza of
> Bvumbwe has gone into hiding for fear of her life. This
> follows threats from irate villagers who have vowed for
> nothing short of her blood in return for the murder of an
> expectant mother, who was shot dead in cold blood last
> Monday.

Annie and Lewis were never estranged, although the ordeal
had been a great strain for them both. The truth was that they
had been reunited at the hospital and jointly came up with a
plan to get Annie safely out of the country.

Although Lewis had to remain in hiding for three months,
he visited Annie in hospital every day and they were able to
encourage each other and pray together.

"Thank You, Father, that you have brought us out of this terrible situation. In the normal way of things we should have been dead, but thanks to Your great mercy we're alive, and You still have a great plan for our lives," Annie prayed.

"Thank you, Father, that You have been faithful to protect us and bring us through this time of great trial. We give thanks to You for this!" said Lewis.

Annie kept her spirits up in hospital by testifying to everyone how God had helped her get through a terrible situation. Lewis kept repeating his favourite expression: "What a faithful God!"

Finally, in an article headlined "Dutch woman in family feud", Malawi News Online gave their perspective on what had happened:

> An irate Dutch woman married to a Malawian clergyman recently ordered her watchguard to shoot relatives of her husband who were involved in a family feud with her over property. In the shoot-out, an expectant woman was shot dead while three people sustained gunshot wounds.
>
> The Dutch woman, Annie Chikhwaza, married to Pastor Lewis Chikhwaza of the Bible Faith Ministries of Blantyre, sustained multiple injuries when a horde of angry villagers descended on her, executing instant justice.
>
> The feud is about a forty-three acre piece of land belonging to Chikhwaza in Bvumbwe, on the outskirts of Blantyre.
>
> Annie Chikhwaza was brutally stabbed and terribly beaten and left for dead. And Reverend Chikhwaza ran for his life as a hired man was running after him to hack him to death.

Annie had never ordered the watchman to shoot her husband's relatives; she and Lewis had simply hired an armed security guard to protect them after they had received death threats. But it was true that an angry horde had tried to execute what they saw as justice and that she had been brutally stabbed and left for dead. It was also true that Lewis had been forced to flee for his life.

Annie was overwhelmed by the lies that were being printed about her and she knew they would only stoke the fires of hostility that had started to burn out of control. With these reports circulating in the media it soon became known that Annie was recovering in the Seventh Day Adventist Hospital in Blantyre, and the villagers now started to throw stones on the top of the hospital roof to intimidate her further.

"The villagers and my stepchildren were hopping mad that they hadn't killed me," Annie says. "They obviously wanted to finish the job they had started, and I had to be smuggled out of the hospital in the middle of the night for my own protection, and go into hiding!"

After eight days in hospital Annie was taken to a friend's home in Blantyre where she knew she would be safe. The following morning the police came to interview her, but no charges were pressed even though her stepchildren and the villagers had made so many accusations against her.

The manager of South African Airways in Malawi was a personal friend of Annie and he took care of all the arrangements to get her back to Johannesburg, where she could receive further medical treatment.

Once the police had cleared Annie to leave Malawi, he laid her on the back seat of his car, to avoid any further media attention, and she was driven to the door of the plane, where she was taken aboard in a wheelchair

"The moment I got onto the plane, I felt I was back on South African terrain and I burst into tears," Annie recalls. "I hadn't cried up to that point. All the tension of the past weeks seemed to have dammed up inside me and the dam wall just burst. I was just so relieved to be alive. I will never forget how I cried and cried."

Annie arrived back in South Africa, her Malawian dream in tatters, her frail body in a wheelchair, her arms and legs black and blue, and her head still badly swollen.

"I was a real sight," she says. "My children were shocked to see me like that as they'd had no idea of what had been going on. I had wanted to protect them from worrying about me, but now they could plainly see what I'd been through, and it would take me a very long time to recover from the whole ordeal."

When she had been home in South Africa for a few days, Annie sent a letter to the editor of one of the newspapers that had published Lewis's children's lies about her. While she refuted some of the allegations made in the article, her main point was that she was not the ultimate victim of the attack – the real victims were all the people she had been helping:

> **Dear Sir, I was surprised that a newspaper of your calibre would print such outrageous lies about me on your front page... Mr Editor, do you really believe I would poison people or give orders to shoot others? Anyone who knows me is aware that my time is spent on the enrichment of the people of our country. Yet your newspaper prints insinuations and allegations of grave misdeeds.**
>
> **I am not the real victim of the savage attack on my life... The real victims of this attack are many, many Malawians. To begin with, forty little four-year-olds, from poor families, who a year ago were malnourished and who have become healthy little bundles of joy because they have been receiving medical care and two free meals**

a day. This, together with their pre-primary education, has come to a standstill.

Do you know, Mr Editor, how clever these little ones had become, how well equipped their school was? Did you know that someone who had no right at all closed that school, with threats that if it stayed open, I would be killed?

Annie mentioned the nine employees of the school who had lost their livelihood, and listed all the people participating in her community development projects, a total of close on one thousand people left without any prospect of an income.

Sir, are the perpetrators of this savage attack aware of the hardships they have caused to such a large group of people, and have they the ability to continue with the projects?

As for myself, I am recovering and capable of making a new life for myself in South Africa, but my heart grieves for my people who are left in hardship and confusion by a few individuals driven by evil forces.

(A copy of the letter was forwarded to the State President of Malawi, His Excellency Dr Bakili Muluzi; His Excellency Ambassador Jan P. Dykstra, Netherlands Embassy in Lusaka, and H. Munnik, Netherlands Consulate in Blantyre.)

Annie had never actually believed that the villagers would harm her because her life was spent helping them, but she now had to come to terms with the fact that she had been hated and reviled and her body disfigured.

She was sorrowful that she had to be separated from her loving husband, and devastated that a precious, innocent life had been lost, plus that of a helpless unborn baby; she grieved that people had been needlessly injured and was especially concerned for all those beloved African people who had lost their livelihood. Yet a real desire was being born in her heart to overturn these great injustices.

23

The serpent's back is broken

"LET NO UNKIND THOUGHTS OF ANY
DWELL IN YOUR HEART"

Annie's family were shocked to hear what had happened to her, to see the photographs, and to read the newspaper reports. Her brothers and sister wanted her to come home to Holland immediately. Her family and friends in South Africa felt it best for her to stay with them, and Lewis would have been quite happy for the two of them to relocate to Johannesburg permanently.

The ministry they had had in Malawi had been destroyed and there was nothing for Annie to go back there for. The windows of their home had been smashed; it was now just as exposed as the "derelict house" they had once lived in, and much of their furniture had been damaged.

The rented house lay dormant for about three months while Lewis was in hiding. Fortunately, the watchmen Lewis had hired were able to secure the property, and once things had calmed down with his children and the villagers, he returned to take charge of repairing the damage.

Annie felt that she had been banished and lost all her worldly possessions. These of course were replaceable, but the ministry they had built up seemed to be gone for ever.

The nursery school had been completely destroyed and all the community projects closed down. These could not simply be restarted, even if Annie went back, because she was still an outcast, hated by the Bvumbwe community, and they would have nothing to do with her work.

Annie was now also in a financial predicament. Her sewing business had come to an abrupt end and she had lost her only source of income. Fortunately, though she was still recovering, she was able to secure part-time work. By December she was able to move into a townhouse in Randburg where Lewis could come and spend Christmas with her and the children.

"After having the medical care I needed, I looked for part-time work," Annie recalls. "I had no choice; I had to pay my own way. Not for one moment, however, did I really consider forsaking the work in Malawi. I kept it buried in my heart."

Though her ministry would lie dormant for a season, this would be a time of healing and a period during which Annie could enjoy time with her children. Though it may have seemed that nothing was blossoming, nothing was happening, she is now sure that God was working behind the scenes.

Life was an uphill struggle, but Annie remembered Elisha Mashingwane's words: "If this is God's best, then this is God's best. Don't worry, Annie; you'll never be poor!" She also recalled a prophetic word she felt God had given her before she had even gone to Malawi, when she was still contemplating marrying "that man":

> You have entered now upon a mountain climb,
> steep steps lead upward;
> But your power to help others will be truly marvellous.
> Not alone will you arise.
> All to whom you now send loving thoughts
> Will be helped upward by you.
> Looking to Me, all your thoughts are God-inspired.
> Act on them, and you will be led on.
> They are not your own impulses,

But the movement of My Spirit,
And if obeyed they will bring the answers to your prayers.
Love and trust;
Let no unkind thoughts dwell in your heart,
Then I can act with all My Spirit and power,
With nothing to hinder Me.

Annie believed that God had called her to Malawi but warned her that it would be an uphill battle... that her life there wouldn't be easy, but if she was obedient to God's instructions nothing could hinder her and she would be empowered to help others in a significant way. She also knew that if she let unkind thoughts take root, God's power to shape her life would be held back.

Annie knew she had to forgive Lewis's children, but she didn't want to. Forgiving her first husband was easy in comparison with this insurmountable task.

But, in December 1996, God started speaking to Annie about not giving up on her vision, through an example from the life of the apostle Paul, as recorded in Acts 14:1–22:

Now it happened in Iconium that they went together
to the synagogue of the Jews, and so spoke that a great
multitude both of the Jews and of the Greeks believed.
But the unbelieving Jews stirred up the Gentiles and
poisoned their minds against the brethren...

And when a violent attempt was made by both the
Gentiles and Jews, with their rulers, to abuse and stone
them, they became aware of it and fled to Lystra...

Then Jews from Antioch and Iconium came there;
and having persuaded the multitudes, they stoned Paul
and dragged him out of the city, supposing him to be
dead. However, when the disciples gathered around him,
he rose up and went into the city. And the next day he

departed with Barnabas to Derbe.

And when they had preached the gospel to that
city and made many disciples, they returned to Lystra,
Iconium, and Antioch, strengthening the souls of the
disciples, exhorting them to continue in the faith, and
saying, "We must through many tribulations enter the
kingdom of God."

This biblical account had such clear parallels with Annie's story that she knew she would need to return to Malawi and ultimately to the ground where she had been left for dead, following the apostle's example.

Even though Paul had seen great miracles, the minds of many of the people he had helped were still poisoned against him. Like Annie, he was left for dead, but he recovered and returned to the very places where this had happened, to continue preaching the gospel regardless of the threat to his safety.

"I was struck by this story and knew God was talking to me; it meant I had to go back to the place where it had all happened," Annie shares. "I would have to forgive the perpetrators of the attack and put it behind me."

Annie knew God specialized in restoring broken relationships and making all things work together for good, and that He could even bring good from what Lewis's children had done to her, *if* she was able to forgive them.

She realized it was up to her how she responded to the circumstances that had befallen her. "God's word is true and He really does work everything together for good. I never lost my vision for Malawi; it was sometimes hard not knowing when I would be able to go back, and I'm glad that I didn't know at the time that it would be a year and a half before I could return."

Annie also never lost her love for her husband. She was encouraged to receive a beautiful birthday card from Lewis in May 1997:

> For my wife with love. It's your birthday and it makes it a special day for me too, because you mean so much to me as a dear wife. I find myself thinking of the many good memories we have shared, crazy times when we laughed our way through things, sentimental times that left us both a little misty, and troubled times when just having your love helped me to hang in there.
>
> My precious one, each memory is special and each one makes me look forward to spending many more wonderful years with you. Happy Birthday, your loving husband, Lewis.

During her time recovering in South Africa, Annie visited Lewis in Malawi twice, but on each occasion she knew the time was not yet right for her to stay. In the meantime she started looking after the Malawians in hospital in Johannesburg. She met a young university student from Blantyre who had been injured in a bus accident, and began to care for him.

He was so malnourished he was almost a skeleton, and when he was discharged from hospital Annie took him home to care for him. The Malawian government later paid for her to take him to Malawi, giving her an opportunity to be reunited with Lewis.

"I went to Malawi for just two weeks and found so much healing in going back to the place where the trauma had taken place. But forgiveness was a process I still had to work on, especially when I saw how everything was destroyed.

"The day I saw the wreck of the school, where those forty beautiful little ones' lives had been changed, I wanted to drown the whole of Malawi in Lake Malawi!"

Annie's parents: Harm and Maaike Terpstra on their wedding day, 25th August 1943.

Met dankbaarheid en blijdschap geven wij kennis
van de geboorte van onze dochter

H. Terpstra
M. Terpstra
— v. d. Wal

Antje Saakje

E.612

Burgwerd, 26 Mei 1944.

Annie's birth announcement

Annie at 18 months with baby brother

Nurse Annie Terpstra at 18, 1962

Annie aged 17 with a cousin in Amsterdam

Annie in white coat, leaving for the UK in 1965

Annie and her former husband, David, and their four children: (L to R) Samuel, Paul, Rebekah and Esther

Standing on beer crates preaching in Alexandra Township, Johannesburg

The house where Rhema Alexandra first began

Annie at about 35

Lewis and Annie on their wedding day, 7th August 1993

The derelict house where married life with
Lewis started

Annie, a week after the brutal
attack on her life

Right: Lewis and Annie on a visit to
Holland, in 1995, and the home
where she was brought up

Kondanani Children's Village, an oasis of beautiful gardens, shrubs and palm trees

Enjoying the outdoor trampoline and play area

Kegels Early Learning Centre

Preparing for the school day...

... and time out afterwards

Sports Field

Madalo Children's Village

Cattle Paddock

Head Office

Cheese Factory

Pig Pens

Fila Farm

Bio Gas Project

Banana Plantation

Lake Chikhwaza

Kegels Early
Learning Centre

Lewis
Chikhwaza
Learning
Academy

Kitchen
+ Hall

Kondanani
Children's
Village

Rory Alec
Clinic

Caring Hands
Infant Home

Proposed Site of
Conference Centre

Kondanani

Children's Houses
Missionary's Houses
School Buildings

Working together in perfect harmony: Annie and Lewis Chikhwaza in the Malawian bushveld.

Annie still had much work to do on her inner self, but the healing process had started. She had come to see that God's ways are the opposite of human ways. Was forgiving easy? No, but she had no wish to become a prisoner of unforgiveness. And every now and then God would encourage her with the brightest ray of hope.

Annie was heartsore after seeing there was nothing left of the nursery school, until Lewis told her he had been in contact with their former school gardener and that he desperately wanted to see her.

"*Amayi*, after you were attacked and could no longer look after the children, I carried on where you left off," he was delighted to tell her. "I now have three schools!"

Annie was amazed: this is what her vision for Africa was all about, being an example for others to follow. This was God's mathematics at work. She smiled when she thought of Reinhard Bonnke's message: "God can take a minus and turn it into a plus." This was even better: this was multiplication!

"I was overwhelmed by the gardener's beautiful story," Annie recalls with joy. "I was amazed, and after visiting one of the schools I was no longer angry. I thanked God! One school had to die for three more to be raised up."

This was such an encouragement to both Annie and Lewis, and they began to talk about her returning to Malawi. But Lewis wasn't convinced, because he knew the people of the surrounding villages had sworn to kill his wife if she ever came back

"Mommy darling, why don't we settle in South Africa permanently?" he had repeatedly suggested to Annie over the eighteen months she was away.

"God has a plan for us and it's not in South Africa," Annie would always answer. "I know it would be easier here, but we have been called to Malawi."

The time finally came when Annie felt she was well enough and in a sufficiently strong frame of mind to go back to Malawi for good – although she did not have the financial means to do so. In human terms it looked impossible, but she had two dear friends who were learning to specialize in the impossible. They would graciously step in to empower Annie to fulfil her vocation, at the right time... but more about that in the next chapter.

Annie could hardly wait to get back to Lewis and the African people she cared so much about, yet she cried and cried as she thought of her children and the grandchildren she had to leave behind. Tears flowed as she drove southward from Johannesburg, heading for Zimbabwe and on to Malawi.

About twenty miles from Harare, Annie saw something ahead that disturbed her. She dismissed it, thinking it must be the branch of a tree that had fallen across the road. But it was a huge python, as long as the road was wide.

Annie tried to slow down, but she was travelling at quite a speed and it was too late. She hit the massive snake and it smashed against both sides of her vehicle.

Then she felt she heard God speaking to her very clearly: "Don't look back. The back of the serpent has been broken."

Annie accelerated and kept driving forwards. She knew God had turned the situation around for her and Lewis and things would now be very different. Through her obedience in forgiving those who had harmed her, God had been able to intervene on her behalf.

She knew that when she got back to Malawi she would be stronger than ever. Thankfully, satan's plan to destroy her work had been averted. God's plan to empower her as a nation-builder was about to come to fruition. She felt a fresh boldness and a spiritual authority that meant she could return to Malawi with renewed confidence.

"Behold, I give you the authority to trample on serpents and scorpions, and over all the power of the enemy, and nothing shall by any means hurt you."

(Luke 10:19)

24

A miracle seed

"A HUNDREDFOLD RETURN"

From her early days as a believer, Annie had known the importance of sowing and reaping. She had learned to give sacrificially to Brother Andrew's ministry, sowing financial seeds in Open Doors that would bring future blessing in her life. It was also a principle she had been taught at Rhema Bible Church, and she had seen it in action in Alexandra Township. The more she gave to the people of Alex, the more God enabled her to do.

She and her fellow Rhema Bible school graduate, Wendy Alec, had seen God provide for them time and time again, in the unlikeliest of ways. Annie remembered the year and a half when Wendy had lived with her and her children. They had had nothing, yet they had been given all they needed.

It was now early 1998, eighteen months after the attack, and she felt God was calling her back to Malawi. She believed she had forgiven Lewis's children and she knew the time was right to return, but in human terms it seemed impossible. Annie had managed to get by living in Johannesburg, but she did not have the means to undertake the long journey back to Malawi or to restart her ministry when she got there.

She needed a miracle, and a seed she and Lewis had planted some years earlier was about to germinate and bring forth a miraculous harvest. Their overseas trip in 1995 seemed just a distant memory, but while in England they had done something significant, even historic. They were now to see vindication of their faith that when God's people "cast their bread upon the waters… it will return to them after many days" (Ecclesiastes 11:1).

During this visit, Annie had gone with Lewis to visit her spiritual daughter and her enterprising young husband. Still virtually unknown at the time, Rory and Wendy were living in a tiny house in East Molesey, Surrey, where the GOD Channel Europe was about to be born around a now-legendary kitchen table!

Colin Dye, the Senior Minster of Kensington Temple in London, would later write: "A young couple plan a major global television initiative from their kitchen table. The humble start of the GOD Channel, as the Christian Channel Europe, without finance, without recognition or institutional backing carries the hallmark of the Holy Spirit who inspired, encouraged and carried Rory and Wendy Alec through to one of the greatest Christian successes of Europe today."

As Lewis and Annie sat at that table, little did they know that a divine plan was unfolding, or how their futures would be intertwined to serve others. At the time they were sharing a simple Chinese takeaway, but God was working extravagantly behind the scenes.

"What's that beeping?" Lewis asked Rory.

"It's a fax…" he replied, as he saw an all-too-familiar logo begin to emerge. "It's from BSkyB!"

"What does it say?" Wendy asked excitedly.

"It says we've been granted a broadcasting slot on Sky!"

"That's incredible!" she said, as she hugged her husband.

"It's only two hours a day, from four until six o'clock in the morning, but it's a start."

"Our God is so faithful," Lewis said.

"I'm so happy to be here rejoicing with you," Annie said,

her face lighting up. "It reminds me of how much we laughed together in Bryanston!"

"But now we need get a broadcast licence, and that's going to cost money," said Rory.

The money would come from the unlikeliest source: a sixty-seven-year-old pastor from one of Africa's poorest countries. "This is for the licence," Lewis Chikhwaza whispered to Rory later, pressing eight hundred dollars into his hand. "Just don't say a word to Annie; it's all we have!"

Of course Annie was in full agreement with her husband when he told her what he had done. They were both filled with joy. This was the last of the money Lewis had received from the payout for his bus company, and she felt they couldn't have made a more worthwhile investment.

She thought it was wonderful that they had been able to help Rory and Wendy pay for the ten-year ITC licence that would secure the launch of the Christian Channel Europe, now the GOD Channel, and fulfil the legal requirement to keep it on air during its first decade of broadcasting.

At the time, Christian television was barely legal in the UK, and gaining this licence was a huge step forward. So many people had told Rory and Wendy that what they were doing was impossible, but Annie knew God was using them to break new ground.

She was excited and expectant, agreeing with them that God had told Rory to "launch Christian television in Europe" and that Dr Jonathan David had prophesied that he and Wendy would be used to "turn the destiny of the church".

Establishing Europe's first daily Christian television network seemed to them like David the shepherd boy taking on the giant Goliath. There were many obstacles in their way, and Annie felt privileged that she and Lewis could play a part in the beginning of it.

Annie believed that "what you make happen for others, God will make happen for you". She knew that as she helped someone else to achieve a breakthrough, it would somehow enable her to rise above the next set of challenges facing her. Like Rory and Wendy and their journey "Against All Odds", overcoming obstacles was becoming Annie's speciality, but now she was faced with a new one.

"One Saturday in February 1998, I began to despair," Annie recalls. "I knew I had to get back to Malawi, but how? We'd lost our income there and we couldn't go back to the village because of the death threats.

"I desperately wanted to be with my husband, but the only way we could be reunited was if we moved to Blantyre. That would mean a higher rent and we'd have to pay for six months in advance. We just didn't have the money, and, besides, I had no car to make the trip. I cried and prayed a lot that day!"

In the meantime Rory and Wendy's ministry with the Christian Channel was beginning to blossom, and programming had increased from two to seven hours per day. Wendy had come up with the bold idea of putting the word "GOD" as a logo in the corner of each screen, and the network had been rebranded "the GOD Channel".

Despite these breakthroughs Annie knew her friends were still facing daily battles in their vision to redeem the airwaves, and she thought she would phone and encourage them. She knew the best way to build herself up was to exhort others!

"Annie, you have to talk to Rory," Wendy exclaimed. "The Lord gave him a word for you just this morning!"

"Annie, why are you still in South Africa?" Rory asked. "I was praying for you earlier and God showed me that you need to get back to Malawi."

"Yes, Rory, I know, but it's taking a lot of planning. I just found out we will have to pay the rent for six months up front..."

"You're going back to Malawi, Annie," Rory interjected. "I'm coming to South Africa in a week's time and we're going to help you!"

It was another momentous phone call for Annie. Wendy wanted to know all about her future plans, and where she was being led to minister. "I think the Lord may be calling me to care for HIV/AIDS orphans," Annie admitted. "There's such a vast need. The population of Malawi is twelve million people and one million are orphans; I feel we've got to do something about this terrible crisis."

A week later, Annie met Rory at the Sandton Sun Hotel in Johannesburg and he promised her monthly support from the GOD Channel as part of the ministry's tithe. "That'll take care of the rent; now let's see if we can get you a bakkie!" he said, using the South African term for a small pick-up truck.

Shortly after this, Annie flew to Malawi to look for a house to rent, and she and Lewis managed to find one quickly. Things were beginning to fall into place, and when she got back to South Africa the vehicle she needed was waiting for her, provided by GOD TV.

Lewis and Annie had assisted at the birth of Rory and Wendy's ministry, and now the generosity of GOD TV's partners – people with a vision to fulfil the great commission to take the gospel into all the world – would in turn help them to reach out to widows and orphans with the love of God.

That eight hundred dollars had enabled Rory and Wendy to gain a licence from the Independent Television Commission to broadcast for ten years. The Christian Channel Europe launched on 1 October 1995, reaching thirty million homes in twenty-two nations. The Channel was dedicated to God by evangelist Benny Hinn at a service in Central Hall, Westminster on 24 April 1996. Annie and Lewis joined Pastor Benny, Rory and Wendy, Colin Dye, Ulf Ekman, and some three hundred other pastors and church leaders for the historic event.

"Rory and Wendy flew us over from Malawi for the dedication," Annie recalls. "It was a very powerful service and we felt really privileged to be there.

"I will never forget Benny Hinn praying for Rory and Wendy. He spoke about how the Israelites had prevailed in the battle against the Amalekites as long as Moses' hands were raised over them, but how, when his hands began to sag, they had started to lose, so Aaron and Hur had had to step in and hold his hands up.

"Pastor Benny exhorted us to support Rory and Wendy in the same way – holding their hands up continuously so they could be ever victorious as they waged war for the airwaves. That is what I believe God has called me to do as their loyal friend and as a partner in their ministry. This is what I believe He calls us to do for each other as we work together in the great commission."

Annie had learned some vital points about sowing and reaping. One was that the planting and the reaping took place in different seasons. Another was that you didn't always reap in the same place you had sown, although that might be part of God's strategy. Most important of all, she had a revelation that reaping a harvest always requires endurance. She could not afford to give up; she had to keep believing God would come through for her, no matter what.

And let us not grow weary while doing good, for in due season we shall reap if we do not lose heart.

(Galatians 6:9)

It was now the beginning of April 1998, and, looking back at her diary entry for 2 December the previous year, Annie saw that she had written that the time to return to Malawi was drawing near. That she had to go back to the place where she belonged. That she could never pull back from God's calling on her life. She had kept believing, kept trusting, and it looked as if God had now made a way where there had seemed to be none.

Overjoyed with her new "bakkie", but tearful at leaving many of her loved ones behind, Annie took to the road. The pick-up was filled to the brim with provisions and Annie was filled with hope. God had provided what she needed, and she knew this was the start of a brand new season in her life.

GOD TV has supported Annie's ministry faithfully since 1998 – far more than a hundredfold return on Lewis's gift towards the Christian Channel Europe's first broadcasting licence.

"Sowing and reaping definitely works," Annie concludes. "Lewis and I sowed a seed in the fertile soil of Christian media and God multiplied that back to us many times over. We also felt the joy of investing in the lives of those people who've come to know Jesus Christ through the power of Christian media.

"The word says to give honour where honour is due," says Annie, "and I want to acknowledge Rory and Wendy Alec for all they have accomplished. 'Against All Odds' is such an appropriate title for their story and I have watched in amazement how God has brought them through one challenge after another.

"I'm so proud that they never gave up; they never became weary in doing good, they pressed on to finish the race, and God still has such great plans for them. Their finish line is nowhere in sight! They are such a good example of what it means to be an 'overcomer'.

"I also want to commend them, as they are two of the most generous people I know; they have poured out their lives in so many ways, which is why we see God's blessing so evident on their lives and on GOD TV."

25

From one derelict house to another

A PARADISE IN THE MIDDLE OF BLANTYRE!

The serpent's back had indeed been broken, and God had provided a new home for Annie and Lewis in Blantyre. The door to yet another building was about to open for them, and with it would come much hope. There was nothing special about this door; in fact it would be attached to another dilapidated house! But it would become the threshold of a place of love, forgiveness, restoration, and refuge.

Annie was by now an expert at restoration projects. She had experienced God as the great restorer. She had watched Him remake broken vessels time after time. Now He was calling her to rebuild another broken building, and, more importantly, to restore broken little lives. She knew she had been asked to rebuild old waste places, raise up generations, and be a "repairer of the breach":

> If you extend your soul to the hungry
> And satisfy the afflicted soul,
> Then your light shall dawn in the darkness,
> And your darkness shall be as the noonday.
> The Lord will guide you continually,
> And satisfy your soul in drought,
> And strengthen your bones;
> You shall be like a watered garden,

> And like a spring of water, whose waters do not fail.
> Those from among you
> Shall build the old waste places;
> You shall raise up the foundations of many generations;
> And you shall be called the Repairer of the Breach,
> The Restorer of Streets to Dwell In.

(Isaiah 58:10–12)

Even before the attack on their lives, Annie had been thinking of how she might help to alleviate Malawi's most grievous crisis, the HIV / AIDS epidemic. So many Malawians had died, and she and Lewis had of course had first-hand experience of watching many dear ones fade away.

Now Annie was back in Malawi she knew the time would come, but first she and Lewis needed to get their lives and their vocation back on track.

They moved into their new rented home in Blantyre on 10 April 1998 and were able to unpack those of their belongings that had survived the attack. By May, Annie was itching to get back to work, and she went to visit an orphanage. As she stood holding a helpless AIDS-infected baby in her arms, she sensed God whisper to her: "This is how you will start rebuilding your ministry. You will begin with little babies like this."

"When God speaks, I jump." Annie says. "I just do it; it doesn't matter how impossible it looks, and He told me how I should go about things and where we would find the exact property to start our children's home."

Annie asked Lewis to go and look for a house in the area where she felt God had said they should start their work. He found a large property owned by the Presbyterian Church. For some reason they had let it stand vacant for years. When he told Annie about the abandoned house, she thought she had better go and see the place, even if wasn't ideal.

An estate agent took them to view the large colonial house and Annie knew at once that it was perfect. Yes, it was derelict. The hot-water storage tank was missing and many of the doors had been removed – it had in effect been gutted – but she could see the potential in a place others had completely rejected.

"I knew I needed a big house to accommodate the vision," Annie says, "so I wasn't put off by the fact that it had been vandalized and the garden was a junkyard of old cars. In my mind I could see it all beautifully restored, filled with little cots and precious babies!"

Annie knew that God would take care of the details if it was His will. By the end of June she had secured the house, but even though it was in a dire condition she still had to pay six months' rent in advance.

She was able to do this with GOD TV's support. The only problem was that the building was almost uninhabitable. Not that she would live there herself: it was to be used exclusively to house homeless children who had been left orphaned or abandoned.

"Isn't it funny how God took me to Malawi, put me in a derelict house, gave me a taste of it, and then, when I had to start again, gave me *another* derelict house, not to live in this time, but to start my ministry!" Annie exclaims.

Working with orphans would require a charitable trust, and Annie and Lewis set one up in the name of Kondanani. This was the name she had given the nursery school that had been destroyed; the name was all she had left of it.

With one in twelve Malawians being orphaned, she knew that even the largest house would soon be filled to overflowing, but she had to start with what she was able to afford.

"What are you going to do with this old house, Annie?" she was asked at the first meeting of Kondanani's trustees.

"It's wonderful that we have a property for the orphanage, but there's no money to fix it."

"I don't know how God is going to do it, but He will," Annie replied. "One thing I know about God is that money follows ministry, not the other way round. Otherwise we wouldn't need faith, and without faith it is impossible to please God."

"But you can't have babies in that old house..."

"With God's help I will be able to make this the most beautiful place, a paradise in the middle of Blantyre!"

Annie was all too aware that they had come to the end of their available funds, but she was convinced that God would complete what He had started. It was the beginning of a true walk of faith for Kondanani, as they learned to trust that God would provide what they needed every day, as He is "a father to the fatherless" (Psalm 68:5).

Annie thought back to her journey through Zimbabwe to Malawi and the word the Lord had given her: "Don't look back; the back of the serpent has been broken." Quoting Paul, she says: "I knew God was with me and I would be victorious. I was more than a conqueror through Him who strengthened me. I could do all things through Christ."

At the end of July, Annie returned to Johannesburg to speak at the Living Word Church. Pastors Andre and Josephine Canovas had invited her to take the Sunday-morning service and talk about her mission to Malawi. Annie had known Andre for many years and he had felt inspired to take up an offering for the work in Malawi, but he had forgotten she was coming!

When Annie arrived he was taken aback, as the arrangement for her to speak had quite slipped his mind. "The youth group have just returned from camp and they're taking the service this morning. I'm so sorry!" he apologized.

"What about giving me a few minutes?" Annie suggested.

She had come all the way from Malawi hoping the church would support the fledgling orphanage.

"OK, but just ten minutes!"

"Ten minutes... I'll hit the headlines!" Annie thought. "God can do great things in ten minutes."

When her turn came to speak, Annie quickly described how God had called her to Malawi and how all hell had broken loose to derail her ministry and she had been left for dead, but how God had helped her recover and sent her back to Malawi to make a difference. Her testimony immediately struck a chord with the congregation, and they were eager to hear more.

Annie spoke of the unbelievable poverty in Malawi and the plight of tens of thousands of children left without support because their parents had died of HIV/AIDS. "God is calling the church of Jesus Christ be His hands, His feet; we have a building, but we need your help to get it up and running, so please would you help me to get this orphanage started?" she appealed.

The response of the congregation was staggering. People started walking up to Annie and giving her whatever item of clothing they could take off. They started laying jackets and jerseys at her feet, even though it was the middle of winter, and some even gave her their shoes.

The pastor also took up a collection for Kondanani; it was the biggest mission offering the church had ever collected, and Annie was able to return to Malawi with more than enough money to get the building renovated and equipped.

"The cheque was substantial and the congregation were delighted by their own giving," Annie remembers. "They told me it was ten times the amount of their usual special offerings! What more can I say but that God is more than enough; He gives us beyond what we can think or imagine!"

The renovation work began as soon as Annie got back, and there was much to be done: The whole house had to be fumigated against termites, and closer inspection revealed that new beams would have to be installed in the roof and the ceilings replaced.

In addition to overseeing this complete overhaul of the building, Annie had to interview and appoint staff; nannies needed to be trained in baby care and a cook in preparing baby food. Baby products, clothing, and nappies had to be collected and they still needed cots and curtains! Annie knew it would all come in, as she trusted God.

> **Be anxious for nothing, but in everything by prayer and supplication, with thanksgiving, let your request be known to God.**
>
> (Philippians 4:6)

Annie was overjoyed to be back carrying out what she saw as God's plan. "It's in the centre of His will that you will find divine provision," she concludes.

God will often use the unlikeliest of people to meet a need, and Annie was not surprised when a Hindu group heard of what she was doing and proved keen to help her set up the orphanage. Thirty-four brand new cots were donated, plus all the curtains they required.

Gifts also kept flowing in from Living Word: Annie had to return to South Africa to pack all the goods that had piled up in a room at the church. It seemed to her as if heaven had opened and everything that the orphanage needed was raining down, and with Christmas coming up, there was an abundance of cuddly toys for the little ones.

"We also received many gifts from people in Malawi," says Annie. "When we didn't have enough kitchen utensils, I prayed about it and it was amazing how many we got: wooden spoons, kitchen knives, graters, ladles in abundance. It was like Moses and the tabernacle... I eventually had to say, 'Stop, Lord, we have too much!' He was supplying our every need."

Kondanani officially opened its doors on 4 November 1998, with Rory Alec as special guest. Before long the home for infants had become well known and the Welfare department started to bring needy babies. Lewis and Annie would become the guardians of many abandoned babies, who would come to call her "Mommy", while Lewis was simply "Daddy" or "Papa".

Some remain with Kondanani to this day; others lasted no more than a few weeks before succumbing to the HIV/ AIDS virus. Their little lives were cruelly snatched from them, but Annie and her team were always there to usher them into God's heavenly nursery, where there is no more pain, suffering, or sorrow.

26

You are forgiven

"REJOICE NOT WHEN YOUR ENEMY FALLS"

Annie had taken an abandoned house and restored it. In the same way she was rebuilding the lives of helpless orphaned babies. Out of the ruins of her once-blossoming nursery school, she had salvaged a name that exemplified the words of Jesus:

> "A new commandment I give to you, that you love one another, as I have loved you, that you also love one another. By this all will know that you are My disciples, if you have love for one another."

> (John 13:34–35)

A derelict house was now fit for purpose as a place of refuge – Kondanani, "Love one another", overflowing with God's mercy and compassion – and now she felt she had to show that love to the people who had reviled her the most.

At the time of the attack on her life in 1996 Annie had been filled with anger because nobody had been arrested for the assault and the police didn't do anything about it.

"I was furious," Annie confides. "I wanted the whole world to know about the injustice that had been done to me...

"I was going to inform Amnesty International. I had decided I would write to the UN Commission for Human Rights... and in short I was going to tell the whole world what had happened to me, and that justice had not been served."

But gradually Annie began to hear the voice of God asking her: "What would Jesus do in this situation?"

She began to see that hating Lewis's children was like poisoning herself and expecting them to be affected. She would end up only harming herself further.

She also realized that, whatever they had done, they were still his children, and nothing would ever change that. Continuing to resent them would only make things worse.

"I started taking the word of God and applying it to what had happened. I took every Scripture on forgiveness that I could find and I made it my own and I let the Lord do a deep work in my heart," she recalls.

One Bible verse that had a huge impact on Annie was the Amplified Bible version of Proverbs 24:17–18:

> **Rejoice not when your enemy falls, and let not your heart be glad when he stumbles or is overthrown, lest the Lord see it and it be evil in His eyes and displease Him, and He turn away His wrath from him [to expend it upon you, the worse offender].**

"To be honest, I wanted justice; I didn't want to let them off. But God's justice works differently. The life God wants us to have means an opposite Spirit; it's a different kind of life, and the Lord made it clear to me that *I* would become the worst offender if I didn't forgive them. I also realized that the wrath of what had happened would indeed be expended on *me* because I wanted human justice. It was a profound revelation."

Annie also remembered another word she believed had come from God: "Let no unkind thoughts dwell in your heart; then I can act with all My Spirit and power, with nothing to hinder Me." She knew that if she didn't manage to forgive them completely, her ministry and what she wanted to accomplish at Kondanani would be held back.

"So the day came when I could finally say that I had forgiven the children, but how could I know for sure? I knew I had to face them. I had to find out what would happen when I saw them again.

"If there were still feelings of hurt, then I wouldn't have truly forgiven them. Only when I was free from these feelings would I know God had done a miracle. Until then I needed to cling to my faith and keep walking in love."

Following Annie's return to Malawi, Lewis had to take part in a long legal battle with his children before his farm was returned to him. He had to go to court to prove he was the rightful owner of the property, and it was only once this was dealt with that Annie felt the time was right for them to go to visit the children.

She couldn't wait to see the proof of her forgiveness, but Lewis didn't want to risk any further confrontation with his children. "I have to do this, Daddy," she told her husband. "I've got to see what God has done. I want to experience His power of forgiveness!"

When Annie saw Lewis's son Jeremiah, there were no hard feelings. She was delighted. So she decided to visit all the children, one after the other. The last one was Dorothy, who had unfortunately become very ill, nobody knew then but she was in fact dying.

There was no doubt that God had enabled Annie to forgive Lewis's children from her heart and not just in her mind, but the greatest test would be for her to see Dorothy. After all, it was she who had led the mob.

The other children had watched while their father was chased with an axe and had witnessed Annie being assaulted. But Dorothy had participated actively in both situations, constantly shouting instructions to the villagers.

"We bought her several bags of groceries and went to her house," Annie recalls. "As we approached, she came slowly towards us. She did not look well, but wasn't yet bed-ridden. Of course, she didn't know how to respond to me; she obviously felt awkward, but I went and gave her a hug, which put her at ease.

"We went into her house and sat down. Lewis and I were on chairs and she sat on the floor, as is the tradition. And I looked at her and thought, 'I'm amazed', because there were no hard feelings. I was so excited, because this had to be supernatural!

"I should have wanted to throttle her, but that feeling wasn't there. It was gone, it was finished, it was over with. I was free from all the resentment, free from all the bitterness. God had done a great work.

"When I got back into the car I said to Lewis, 'Daddy this is amazing; this is supernatural. God has done it. I have truly forgiven her. There is no animosity!'"

"Our God reigns," Lewis responded, rejoicing with Annie over the reunion. It was just in time, because, barely a year later, Dorothy was dead.

Lewis and Annie helped to nurse Dorothy in her last days, caring for her until she passed away. As Annie sat next to her body in the middle of the night, minutes after she had died, she looked into Dorothy's face and softly said, "I'm so glad I forgave you.

"I thank God that, before you left, I was able to forgive you. You were forgiven. Only God could have helped me to do this."

God had removed the resentment, the pain, and the anguish and brought peace into a troubled relationship. And He had done it just in time, a great testimony to the power of forgiveness, but this was only the beginning...

Returning to Malawi also meant having to relive the horror of the death of the pregnant young mother, Eunice

Maliko. The prospect of this had bothered Annie all the time she was recuperating in South Africa, and now she was back and the court case against the watchman, Laison Bandula, was about to begin.

He had been arrested after the girl's death, when he went to the police station to surrender his rifle, but later released on bail. He had then been charged with murder and now, two years after the shooting, he was about to appear before the court.

Annie was concerned that Laison would be sentenced to life imprisonment for something that was not his fault. He had been trying to protect her and she didn't want to see him go to jail for that. He had also acted in self-defence, and fortunately the judge understood what had happened and gave him a suspended sentence for manslaughter. Laison was enormously relieved; he was free at last and could go back home.

Annie had always felt awful about Eunice's death and the loss of her unborn baby. "The wonderful thing is that today I have a good relationship with Eunice's family. They finally realized that I was not responsible for the death of their daughter and her baby, and they no longer hold it against me."

The Bible makes it clear that God's intention is that no one should perish, but that all should come to know Christ as their saviour. Annie's agrees, and, although she was once accused of killing an unborn child, she is now saving babies' lives every day.

Annie hadn't let her vision die; she had held on to her dream, and the obstacle race went on. Lack of forgiveness was never going to be a barrier that could not be overcome. She had stepped over it and was moving on.

It would take Lewis slightly longer than Annie to be able to forgive all his children fully. He felt betrayed by the way they had tried to kill him, dishonoured that they would stoop so low as to try to steal his land, and devastated by how they had attacked and ousted the woman he loved.

He had always meant the children to inherit the farm, but after the assault he decided he would sell it so there would be no more fighting over the land. "You were prepared to kill my wife and me over this land," he told them. "I can no longer bear this noose around my neck."

As soon as Lewis took occupation of the farm, he sold it to a cabinet minister he knew from his days as an MP. Unfortunately, the legal bills he had to pay to retrieve the land had been higher than he expected and there was not much money left after the sale. His children had ruined him financially and lost their inheritance, but they were forgiven and he was at peace with them.

"How can we talk about the children to the media or even in church?" Annie had asked Lewis after the attack. "We can't tell the story of what happened to anyone unless you are happy to do so. They are your children; how do you feel about it?

"It happened, didn't it?" he answered. "And you've got to testify. You have to share what God has done."

It was important to Annie that she and her husband should be in agreement over what they could share about the ordeal, and she tells the story only to show her gratitude to God for the way He saved her and her husband, and for how she was able to overcome bitterness and the right to revenge, with forgiveness, love, and reconciliation.

At the time of writing this book, five of Lewis's children have passed away. The surviving children have been to visit Annie but have yet to apologize. Despite this, there is no lack of forgiveness on her part. "They know Lewis and I hold nothing against them, and I pray for God's blessing on their lives," she insists.

27

Caring hands

"WE CRY AND THEN WE LAUGH AGAIN!"

Little Deborah was the first baby to arrive at the fledgling Kondanani orphanage in Blantyre. She was brought in on 7 November 1998 by her grandfather, an elderly gentleman who was enormously relieved to have found a place where she could be cared for her. He greeted Annie with a huge smile.

Deborah was HIV-positive and only eleven months old. Her whole family had died of the virus and her grandfather was her only surviving relative, but he was too old to look after her. He was deeply sad that all his children had died of AIDS and wanted to provide for his granddaughter in the best possible way, so he decided to bring her to Annie.

"She was such an adorable baby," Annie says. "I called her 'the Queen of Kondanani' because she was the first to come to us, and she was so regal. Tragically, she developed full-blown AIDS and her little body started to waste away. There was nothing we could do for her but love her. She passed away in June 1999."

Deborah had been in Annie's care for only seven months, but she had such an impact on her and all the staff. "I cried my heart out the day she died," Annie says, "but I knew she had gone to be with Jesus."

Annie wrapped the little body in the blanket Deborah's grandfather had brought her in and took her back to the old man for burial. He had visited her faithfully week after week, and he was devastated.

His usual smile had vanished and Annie did her best to console him. "We know little Deborah has gone to heaven and we want you to be certain of your salvation as well. Jesus Christ is the greatest comforter of all," she assured him.

Kondanani's doors had opened not a moment too soon. At last somebody was offering loving, caring hands, hope, and encouragement.

This was a country where there was no such thing as "social welfare", as it is known in developed countries. Innocent little lives were being devastated by the deaths of their parents from HIV/AIDS. Finally, something was being done to address this dreadful epidemic that was wrecking so many families.

With about one million orphans in Malawi it seemed an insurmountable task, but Annie and Lewis felt they had been called to make a difference, even if only to a few dozen lives, and even if it was just to care for little ones in their last days on earth.

Babies started to come via all sorts of routes. Some were brought by the police, others by social workers or family members. Many families had been almost obliterated by the HIV/AIDS virus and orphaned children would be brought to Annie by their last surviving relatives. Some were HIV-positive; others were not, but were still facing certain death from malnutrition.

Initially Annie went from village to village to see how she could help. She found little Stelia living with her grandmother, but malnourished and riddled with tuberculosis. She discovered baby Juma among some shacks, his feeble body covered in sores. Little Moses was found abandoned in a cemetery at about the same time as baby Miriam was discovered by the riverside, both victims of HIV/AIDS.

"I will never forget the day I met Stelia," Annie recalls, "because it was so typical of the situation of many families in Malawi. I stopped to talk to her grandmother, who had lost most of her children to HIV/AIDS and been left to care for ten orphans.

"My heart went out to her because she was so poor and she and the children had only rags to wear. Stelia was her youngest grandchild; she was just a few months old and was tiny. She had open sores on her body and was in desperate need of food.

"With the help of a local health worker and the support of the chief, we asked the grandmother if she'd agree to let the baby come with us so we could care for her. She agreed, and I gave her money to help her care for the other nine children. Unfortunately, she was later accused by the community of having sold Stelia to us, but that wasn't true!"

Back at the orphanage, Stelia was diagnosed with tuberculosis and Annie and her team fed her by tube and nurtured her back to health. Though children who have been malnourished are often affected mentally, Stelia was fortunate to escape this.

Stelia was later transferred to another facility, but Annie still sees her from time to time as she is friendly with the missionaries there. She remains in good health and is a bright young lady who is doing well at school.

Once babies were restored to health at Kondanani, it became possible that they could be adopted, especially if they had no relatives playing an active role in their lives. The first of Annie's orphans to be adopted was Juma.

"He was our miracle baby!" says Annie. "When I found him he was being suckled by his grandmother. But all she had for a breast was a piece of dry leather. He was skin and bone, with sores all over his body, just seventeen months old, and it was clear he wouldn't live another week like that.

"He wasn't HIV-positive but he was severely malnourished. I spoke to his uncle and begged him to bring the child to Kondanani so he could live. We received Juma the following day and he became such an adorable little boy. Fortunately we were able to save him; if we hadn't intervened he would most certainly have died. I was delighted when he was adopted by a wealthy local family who were able to give him a great life."

Years later Annie was visiting the Zomba Plateau, one of Malawi's tourist attractions, when she bumped into Juma, now aged six, and his adoptive mother. Annie started chatting to her.

"Who is this lady?" Juma asked his mother.

"Shall I tell him?" Annie asked. The woman nodded and Annie began to relay the story of how she had found this little boy among the mud huts and village shacks, how sick he was, and how she had nursed him back to health.

"And do you know who that little boy was?" Annie asked.

"Me!" he replied, with a knowing smile.

"Juma is now fourteen and very well indeed," says Annie. "He is a child of superior intelligence, which, considering his condition when I found him, is amazing!"

Juma's big grin, as he said goodbye to Annie and left with his new family, was the kind of outcome that made her heart glad, but she knew all too well that this was not always possible. While seemingly miraculous healings happened in some children's lives, in many other cases it was too late. HIV/AIDS had already taken its toll.

Little Moses was found to be HIV-positive soon after he arrived. It was only a matter of time before his condition deteriorated and, like Deborah, he died after being at the orphanage for a number of months. "All we could do for these precious ones was to guide them lovingly into God's presence, into the 'Kondanani Heavenly Nursery'!" Annie says.

These two little ones who died in the first year were gone but not forgotten. Annie named a feeding scheme for the villagers "Operation Deborah" and another community outreach programme was called "Operation Moses".

The work of Annie and her team involves many tears, but they are not without comfort. "The Holy Spirit is the Great Comforter and He helps us so much," says Annie. "I always think that, if Jesus wept, then it's OK for me to cry. We've seen so many babies suffer so much. At times I feel angry with the parents, because they've caused their offspring so much pain. Often the little ones can't even cry any more, they're so weak.

"This breaks my heart. It's so hard to watch HIV/AIDS babies become skeletons. Their faces start going grey and you know it's only a matter of time. We sometimes cry out to God and say, 'Lord, why does this innocent child have to die?' But we know there is no answer to this question.

"Of course we always pray for the children, and sometimes they are healed, which really builds up our faith, but then there are times when they aren't, and we go through the full range of emotions in the cycle of grief.

"The AIDS babies can die from the slightest infection – they get pneumonia, septicaemia, meningitis or something similar, and all we can do is hold them in our arms, love them, and usher them into heaven. We've seen many lives saved, but we've also seen many deaths.

"We cry and then we laugh again," Annie shares from her heart, "because we believe that every baby who dies goes straight to heaven. That is our personal conviction. The Bible doesn't say this specifically, but as they have not yet reached the age of accountability we believe it to be the case."

Mercifully, with today's antiretroviral treatment, HIV/

AIDS babies can live longer than ever before. One miracle case is that of Miriam, who was adopted by a French family in Malawi.

Miriam's mother had died of the virus and Annie and her team weren't sure whether it had been passed on to her. Annie had sent two blood samples to South Africa to be tested and both had come back negative. The adoption went ahead as planned; however, while on holiday in France Miriam became ill and was admitted to a Paris hospital, where it was found she was HIV-positive after all.

It was a great shock for the parents, but they continued to love and care for Miriam and, at the time of writing, she is still healthy. "Her family moved back to France, but they came to visit me last year," Annie says. "Miriam, now called Elise, has grown into a beautiful young woman, but we couldn't really communicate because she now speaks only French!"

With more and more children coming to Kondanani, Annie's emotions were being stretched daily, but that was not all that was being stretched. It was becoming a daily struggle to keep the doors of the orphanage open. Almost everything Annie needed for the babies had to be imported and the care of the growing number of children was beginning to cost an exorbitant amount of money.

"When I had about ten babies, I cried out to God, 'Lord, please hold off on any more for a while... I have to feed them, you know!' (As if our Father were unaware of this!) Needless to say, the babies didn't stop coming."

Another milestone for Annie was when she collected a set of twins from the hospital – orphans number thirty and thirty-one. Not that any of the babies at Kondanani are ever treated as numbers – this simply reflected the numerical sequence in which they came! However, it meant thirty-one mouths to be fed.

Annie wondered how on earth she had been able to cope with so many, but in reality God had provided for each one. "I'd asked the Lord to slow down when we reached ten babies, and now we had thirty-one. However, I no longer worried about how we were going to care for them. I knew that every need would be met, because I had experienced divine provision all along.

"There are plenty of times at Kondanani when I don't know how our needs are going to be met, but I never doubt that they will be. I just commit our needs to God in prayer. I say, 'Lord Jesus, You and I are in this boat together, and if it sinks we go down together'."

God's provision was evident daily, and every now and then He would do something so extravagant that Annie and her whole team would be amazed.

With the huge investment Kondanani had made in the orphanage in Blantyre, the board of trustees would often encourage Annie to purchase the facility outright and add to it, but the Presbyterian Church was not prepared to sell.

By this time the house had became too small for the forty-three orphans and Annie was forced to look for another property that could accommodate more babies. She went house-hunting and the first property she saw was ideal. But the price tag was four million kwacha.

"I didn't have a penny to put towards the house, but the owners said they would wait until I'd raised the finances. I sent a letter to Press Trust, a Malawian charity foundation, requesting their support, but they came back to me with some excuse for why they couldn't help. So I jumped into my car and drove the two hundred and fifty miles to their offices.

"You give millions away to football clubs each year," Annie told the head of the Press Trust. "I am asking you for just four million for the sake of your children, for the future of your country!"

It was a bold request, and he could see that this fiery Dutchwoman was not going to give up. Needless to say, Annie was given the money to buy the property!

The orphanage in Blantyre, the first phase of the much wider Kondanani ministry that exists today, would become known as the Caring Hands Infant Home. Annie knew that once the children reached three she would have to find a new place for them, and she was starting to get the vision for phase two: the Kondanani Children's Village.

28

Life is precious

"DON'T TAKE MY BABY!"

The Bible says that "when the enemy comes in like a flood, [God] will lift up a standard against him" (Isaiah 59:19), and Kondanani's Caring Hands Infant Home was to become a bright light in the darkness. It would pass a clear message to the children of Malawi: "You are valuable; you are precious; even if you are dying of AIDS, your life matters."

As we have seen, Annie had had a deep concern for others from childhood. She had always wanted and tried to "honour all people" (1 Peter 2:17). It didn't matter whether it was the so-called "dirty boat children" of the Netherlands in the 1950s, or the oppressed people of Alexandra, struggling against apartheid, or the HIV/AIDS-ravaged communities of Malawi.

She now found herself in a country where the average life expectancy was just thirty-seven years, where HIV/AIDS had doubled in the previous five years, and where life had become cheap. But Annie knew beyond a shadow of a doubt that each life was precious to God.

"God places a value on every life, no matter whose it is, and we must do the same," she urges. "While out walking in the villages of Malawi, I have seen so many hopeless cases. I'll never forget the plight of one young man I met who was HIV-positive. He was so weak; his face was covered with flies, but he didn't have the strength to brush them away.

"He'd been left for dead, but he still mattered to God. Jesus had died for him, and God expected me to honour him and to honour his memory by caring for victims of this dreaded disease. I began to realize I'd been called to be a defender of those who couldn't defend themselves."

**Open your mouth for the speechless,
In the cause of all who are appointed to die.
Open your mouth, judge righteously,
And plead the cause of the poor and needy.**

(Proverbs 31:8–9)

This verse is always on Annie's mind because she believes it is what God wants for those who are suffering. "It is the very heartbeat of God," she says. "There's so much injustice in the world, but we can defend the voiceless. We are instructed by God's word to honour all people, and to honour life itself."

Kondanani therefore presents a viable alternative to abortion – that of adoption – because Annie believes that the lives of those who are still in the womb are just as precious as those who have been born. She has arranged over twenty adoptions to date. Little Juma was the first, but today children from Kondanani are living with their adoptive families in several different parts of the world, including Holland and Australia.

"Adoption is the answer to abandoned babies," Annie firmly believes. "Adoption is also the answer to abortion."

Annie sees abortion as a terrible tragedy. She mourns the deaths of millions of babies who have been killed in the name of "freedom of choice". She regards it as similar to the child sacrifices of ancient times, when children were slaughtered to appease the Ammonite deity Moloch.

"The Lord is the protector of the innocent, those who cannot fight for themselves, the unborn – and so must we be!" she declares.

Although abortion is illegal in Malawi, it is available in certain circumstances and many women's lives have been put at risk through unsafe backstreet abortions. Having experienced the trauma of being forced to terminate a pregnancy, Annie feels great compassion for women who have found themselves with an unwanted pregnancy, or who have had an abortion and can't forgive themselves.

"Don't take my baby. Don't take my baby!" This is the cry of a mother's heart. It's a cry Annie knows well. 'Abortion is never the answer, but there is forgiveness for it," she maintains.

When she hears the word "abortion", there is always a flashback to 1972, when her first husband forced her to terminate a pregnancy because he was having an affair and planning to leave her, and didn't want "to be burdened with another child".

Every March she thinks about how old her baby would be, and wonders whether it would have been a boy or a girl and what he or she would have accomplished in life. She has forgiven herself for what happened, but it took a long time.

For a woman who has devoted her life to protecting babies, abortion is one of the worst things she could imagine. "I've always believed that life begins at conception and I would never have considered killing my own child, but I wasn't given the choice. I was sedated and confused, and it all took place so quickly that, when I awoke, I wasn't even sure what had happened. All I knew was that my breasts were full and there was no baby to take the milk.

"The whole system forced me to have an abortion," Annie says, "because David told the medical authorities I was not of sound mind. He persuaded the doctors that my body could not cope with having a new baby so soon after my last one, and he resorted to blackmail to ensure I didn't put up a fight with the doctors. He threatened to send the children to a home if I didn't do exactly as I was told."

Annie is a fighter, but she did not have the strength to resist David at that point. She was in a fragile emotional state, in which she felt manipulated and unable to make her own decisions. "I had hit rock bottom and the system didn't give me authority over myself and my own body. I didn't want that abortion, but I had no control. I was in a sanatorium and it had been decided between the father of my children and the doctors that it would be far better for my medical health for me not to have another baby.

"My son Paul was only eight and a half months old and I was four and a half months pregnant. I will never forget going into that operating theatre where they were going to do the D&C. I remember our family doctor putting his hand on mine, a small act of kindness, but it made David very angry.

"He robbed me of our child, but even if I had made the decision myself, I would have still robbed myself of a child. It doesn't matter which way it happened; it was a very hurtful situation. I have peace about it now but I still often think about it, even decades later."

Annie was moved to tears when she read this anonymous story that illustrates the sanctity of life:

> A worried woman went to her gynaecologist and said,
> "Doctor, I have a serious problem and I need your help!
> My baby is not even one year old and I'm pregnant again.
> I don't want kids so close together."
>
> "OK," said the doctor. "But what do you want me to do?"
>
> "I want you to end my pregnancy," she said. "I'm counting on your help."
>
> The doctor thought for a while, and then he said to the lady, "I think I've a better solution to your problem. It's less dangerous for you too."
>
> She smiled, thinking that the doctor was going to accede to her request.

Then he continued, "So that you don't have to take care of two babies at the same time, let's kill the one in your arms. This way, you can get some rest before the other one is born. If we're going to kill one of them, it doesn't matter which one it is. There would be no risk to your body if you chose the one in your arms."

The lady was horrified and said, "No, doctor! How terrible! It's a crime to kill a child!"

"I agree," the doctor replied. "But you seemed to be OK with it, so I thought maybe that was the best solution."

The doctor smiled, realizing he had made his point. He had convinced the mother that there's no difference between killing a child that's already been born and one that's still in the womb. The crime is the same.

Love says, "I sacrifice myself for the good of the other person." Abortion says, "I sacrifice the other person for the good of myself..."

Jesus sacrificed Himself for the good of sinners! That's perfect love!

(Writer unknown)

Although there are some parallels to Annie's situation in this story, she would never have made such a choice; nevertheless, she still had to find the strength to forgive herself for what had happened.

"Forgiving myself was the hardest thing. I sat with Pastor Joe Peter in his office at Rhema for many hours. The guilt continued to play its part over the years and it added to my growing despair with my first husband. Even long after my divorce it was still a huge problem in my life."

"Have you asked God to forgive you, Annie? Pastor Joe asked her one day.

"Yes, I have!" she answered.

"Well, who do you think you are? Are you bigger than God, that you cannot forgive yourself? If He has forgiven you, then who are you to not forgive yourself?"

The words finally hit home. Annie realized that God had truly forgiven her, and she could no longer hold it against herself.

"The memory of that abortion will always be there," she admits, "because the consequences of it are always there, but God has made it bearable. If you've been involved in an abortion, ask Him to forgive you and make a decision to start protecting life from now on.

"And if you had a baby that was aborted, be assured that your child is in that wonderful heavenly nursery, where you will one day meet again, just as I believe I will meet my unborn child and all the little darlings that have passed away at Kondanani from HIV / AIDS."

Annie and her team are moved to tears when babies pass from their arms into those of Jesus, but they are sure that they have gone to a better place. "Their lives are so precious to us," she says. "We see Jesus in them when we feed them, we see Jesus in them when we give them something to drink, and we see Jesus in them when we dress them. The babies become part of us; we love them, and when they slip away we mourn the loss of a loved one."

The deaths may not affect the Malawian staff as much as they do Annie and her missionary workers, as there is so much death in Africa and they are more used to it. But Annie feels that she will never get used to it. She often reads her staff stories about missionaries such as Robert Moffat, who lost many of his children on the missionfield but who persevered with his work because he felt God had called him.

The growing number of babies at Kondanani's Caring Hands Infant Home, whether HIV-positive or not, was a clear indication to Annie of what her next ministry step should be. She had initially planned to nurture malnourished and ailing toddlers from the age of one to three and then return them to their families when they were healthy enough, but the reality was that if she did this they would die.

Annie believed that God did not want this to happen, but she wondered how she would obtain the land for phase two of the orphanage. Once again the answer would come in a way that would bring personal healing to Annie and her family and show her how much God loved each and every precious life in her care.

29

Life out of death

"I WILL REDEEM THE LAND WHERE
YOU WERE LEFT FOR DEAD"

Annie Chikhwaza knew that she would have to return to the place where she was mercilessly attacked and almost killed. This is what the apostle Paul had done after he had been stoned, with extraordinary results, and this was what she sensed God was challenging her to do. Like Paul, she would have to defy the threats against her life and continue to do her ministry work regardless of the trials she faced.

It had also been revealed to her that the land where she had been left for dead would be used to give new life to others. A place of hatred would become a place of love. Annie trusted that God would keep His word, but knew she would have to be patient and wait for the appointed time.

The seven-acre plot where Annie had been stoned, beaten, and stabbed had been defiled by this appalling crime. For a time it seemed that the work there was at an end, but God had not given up on His plan. He had been working behind the scenes all the while to create the refuge He had promised for the children of Malawi.

Most assuredly, I say to you, unless a grain of wheat falls into the ground and dies, it remains alone; but if it dies, it produces much grain.

(John 12:24)

"The attack was awful, but look at the good that came out of it!" Annie says today, looking back on it all. She was brutally assaulted and her blood fell to the ground like that grain of wheat. But, four years later, new life was about to spring from this near-death experience. The place where her blood had spilled would become a life-giving sanctuary for many children who would otherwise have perished.

Annie's ministry had all but died after the attack in 1996, but it had been resurrected at the orphanage in Blantyre, and was now about to expand and be multiplied beyond her wildest dreams.

> **If My people who are called by My name will humble**
> **themselves, and pray and seek My face, and turn from**
> **their wicked ways, then I will hear from heaven, and will**
> **forgive their sin and heal their land.**

(2 Chronicles 7:14)

Thanks to Annie and Lewis's obedience, forgiveness, and perseverance, God was going to heal their land and make it fruitful once again.

The first part of this healing came in 1999, when Kondanani was able to purchase the seven-acre plot where Annie and Lewis had once lived to start building the Kondanani Children's Village.

Back in 1994, when they had moved into the rented house, Annie had felt God telling her that it would one day be theirs. She had shared this with Lewis, adding that the house would be auctioned and they would be able to buy it.

But after the attack this promise seemed all but dashed, especially when the property was put up for auction while Annie was far away in South Africa. All she could do was pray and trust, because they had lost their income, and there was no reason to buy a house they had fled from even if they had

had the funds to do so.

She did however remind Lewis of what God had promised them. "Daddy, do you remember how the Lord showed me that the landlord is going to get into financial difficulty and the house will be auctioned?

"The house won't sell to anybody else, because God wants us to have it, and when the time is right, we will be able to buy it!" she assured him, and, she continued to remind God of His promise.

In 1997 the house was put up for auction, exactly as Annie had said. Lewis went to the auction and successfully bid for the property, but he didn't have the money to complete the deal.

When Annie returned to Malawi in 1998 she phoned the building society to find out the situation with the property. She was concerned that Lewis would be sued for the money, but they had somehow forgotten about the sale and she was told that another auction would have to take place.

Annie's diary for 10 July 1998 reads: "'Expect not one but many miracles' is God's word for me today! Noah built that great big ark… why? Because God told him to. God has promised us we will expand, but He can't do anything until we move forward in faith."

On 13 April 1999 Lewis went to the second auction for the property and managed to secure it once again, but this time for far less than he had bid the first time! In fact, he was able to buy it for a quarter of the previous price.

Even so, he and Annie didn't have the resources to secure the deal, but they felt reassured that, as they set out faithfully to build Kondanani Children's Village, God would supply the finances and every need would be met.

Once again GOD TV empowered the Chikhwazas' vision of ministering to widows and orphans, and Annie was bowled over by a phone call from the UK.

She was on a trip to South Africa at the time and was having a meal on the Randburg Waterfront with her elder daughter. Rebekah's mobile phone rang and she looked at her mother, wondering if she should take the call. "It's for you," she exclaimed.

"Annie, Annie, is that you?" a woman with a British accent asked excitedly. Annie realized it was Vivian, Rory Alec's personal assistant.

"Rory's been trying to get hold of you to tell you that we've received your proposal for the Kondanani Children's Village," she said. "He and Wendy have been praying about it and they want you to know that the Lord has instructed GOD TV to buy the property you need for Kondanani!"

"That's wonderful news!" Annie could hardly contain her delight. It was a dream come true, and she wanted to start ululating at the top of her voice, as could be expected from an African woman. She was in fact now very much an African woman, but she felt she had to behave with Western-style decorum, seeing that she was in a restaurant!

"You know GOD TV has a heart for widows and orphans," Vivian continued, "and we want to be part of this next stage, so you can restart your nursery school and have a place for the orphans once they're no longer babies."

"Thank you, Vivian. I appreciate Rory and Wendy's help so much. This is amazing. How can I ever thank the partners of GOD TV enough?"

And so Kondanani Children's Village was started in Bvumbwe. Acting with humility and forgiveness had eased the family tensions and Annie was finally able to return to the house she had been chased from, to bring new life out of that deathly situation.

"It was wonderful to think I could start again. We still had the orphanage in Blantyre and now we would also have a nursery school for three-year-olds. I had previously had the school on the neighbouring farm, which was destroyed, and now I would have a brand new school right next door. What's more, we had the space to build houses for the three-year-old children!

"This was not something I'd achieved. This was God's doing. If we give Him our brokenness, our patience, and our humility, He can make us channels of His love and care."

"I wonder if I'm worthy to be so blessed..." Annie wrote in her diary on 12 November 1999.

"This answer to prayer is not to meet your needs, Annie, but the needs of the orphans of Malawi, and they are worth it, each and every one," she felt God respond.

Once the land was paid for, Annie and Lewis relocated from Blantyre to their old home, and work started on transforming the seven acres into the Children's Village. Of course Rory wanted to be there for the ground-breaking ceremony, and this time he brought a camera crew from the UK with him.

It was now the year 2000 and Annie and Lewis were delighted to have him with them, especially as he made a series of programmes on what God was doing in Malawi through Kondanani. Rory interviewed Lewis and Annie on the lawn of their home, asking how God had brought them together and observing that the Lord had done extraordinary things.

"It's amazing to think that a lady born in Holland went to South Africa and then to Malawi and married a man of God, and how God is now using them to run an orphanage, and we are going to show you everything in great detail," he told GOD Channel viewers...

"What you are going to see will make your heart sore," he said, referring to the HIV/AIDS babies, "but this series will also bring your heart so much joy as you see what your giving is achieving in this desperate situation."

Rory visited the orphanage in Blantyre and was moved by seeing the little ones in their cots at Caring Hands. He was impressed by the staff, dressed smartly in their green uniforms and singing a song of welcome in Chichewa. He spent time interacting with the babies on camera and was visibly touched to meet little Winston, a skeleton of a baby suffering from HIV/ AIDS who passed away the very next day.

The GOD TV crew went out to film the Operation Deborah and the Operation Moses initiatives – feeding schemes Annie had set up which involved a team of people taking food and milk formula into the villages to feed malnourished children and their mothers, and weighing the babies to gauge their progress.

They filmed an innovative construction system for prefab houses that would be used to build several homes at the Children's Village for the children and their housemothers. The whole front of a house was built during one of the fifteen-minute programmes to demonstrate how fast these homes could be put up if the finances were available.

"The Lord has called GOD TV as a media ministry to be a servant to those who are ministering to widows and orphans," Rory said, "and we are privileged to be here to film what God is doing in Malawi through the work started by an amazing woman of God and her very fine husband."

Finally the crew filmed the ground-breaking ceremony that represented the official start of the building of the Children's Village. Rory, Lewis, Annie, and the Deputy Minister of Social Welfare each took a spade and dug out a little earth as a symbolic gesture towards the many sets of building foundations that would follow.

Life had indeed come from death. As a poster in Annie's office reads: "I have held many things in my hands and have lost them all, but whatever I have placed in God's hands, that I still possess."

Before long, Annie and Lewis were overjoyed to be back in their old home, her life was no longer in danger, reconciliation had come to the community, and there would be a new start for them and the surrounding villages. Lewis's former farm next door was no longer a problem because it was now owned by somebody else. In their eyes, God had worked a miracle.

30

Love one another

> "THE KINGDOM OF GOD BELONGS TO
> SUCH AS THESE."
>
> (Mark 10:14, NIV)

The wonderful thing about healthy babies is that they keep on growing! By the year 2000, Annie and Lewis had over forty toddlers nearing the age of three and needing to move from Caring Hands in Blantyre into a family home of their own.

The acquisition of the seven-acre property in Bvumbwe came just in time for the first houses to be built to accommodate the three-year-olds. There was great excitement as Annie and Lewis trusted God for the funds to come in and gradually, house by house, Kondanani Children's Village was established.

This is the dream they had had all along: "Kondanani, Love one another!" Here they could live among the children, showing them the love of God in action and building a new community that would overturn the hatred of the attack on their lives.

Annie took charge of project managing the building of each home and fitting them out to make the children as comfortable as possible. She designed the homes to accommodate twelve children each, four to a room, with a resident housemother, nanny, and cleaner. As the children grew they would need to build more houses, and so the village expanded year by year.

Lewis continued to lead the pastors at Bible Faith Ministries and Annie would accompany him to the Sunday services. Thanks to his pastoral care and hard-earned wisdom in dealing with cultural sensitivities, and Annie's creative and leadership capabilities, Kondanani went from strength to strength.

Running two "campuses" was enormously challenging for Annie, as it involved travelling back and forth along the fifteen miles between Caring Hands in Blantyre and the Kondanani Village in Bvumbwe, and she called out to God to send people to help her. Little did she know that He would bring her someone from as far away as Australia.

As a Bible school student at Hillsong Church in Sydney, Cherie Martin had always had a passion for Africa. She stumbled across Caring Hands in 1999 while leading a backpacking tour through Africa. The Infant Home in Blantyre was situated right in front of a hostel for backpackers, and they would sometimes come to see the babies.

Cherie fell in love with Malawi and after she returned to Sydney she felt called to return to Kondanani as a volunteer. At the beginning of 2002, She e-mailed Annie who quickly responded, "Come back to Malawi; we can definitely use you!"

A single mother with a two-year-old daughter, Cherie joined Kondanani in June 2002. She has been with the Children's Village for ten years now, and her daughter, Tandazi, has grown up with the other children.

An outgoing, bubbly person with exceptional organizational skills, Cherie soon began to ease the load on Annie and became her executive assistant. Tandazi is now twelve and can speak fluent Chichewa. In her own unique way she has been used by God to bridge the gap between black and white!

Cherie and Tandazi live in their own house on the property and Tandazi attends school with her friends from the Children's Village. She also has a room in Annie's home, where she brings friends to play. Tandazi sees Annie as a grandmother and calls her "Nana". She is also a bold witness to her granny in Australia!

"Tandazi is an adorable child," says Annie. "She spends a lot of time at my house, where she comes to watch television and play video games with her friends. She has been at school with our children since nursery age and is a clever, bright girl. She's also very respectful and obedient, and not in an 'I have to' sort of way but because she wants to, which is very encouraging."

Caring for children to the degree Annie and Lewis had in mind was always going to take an exceptional, dedicated team, and they began to accept other missionary volunteers who could help them achieve their vision. In addition, many local people were employed, and Kondanani started to make a difference not only in the children's lives but also through bringing economic empowerment to the neighbouring villages.

A central kitchen was built to prepare the children's meals, overseen by several busy cooks and with a very large pantry. Each day Annie, Cherie or one of the team members would have to allocate the food for the day, which would be prepared by the kitchen staff and collected by each housemother so that the children could eat together as a family in their own home.

Clothing the children was another challenge, so a sewing room was built where a tailor could work full-time making everything from shirts and trousers for the boys, and dresses for the girls, to towels for their bathrooms, and sheets for their beds. A huge storeroom was also built to house the clothes donated for the children, with Cherie acting as a benevolent quartermaster dishing out supplies and provisions to the troops!

Some orphanages in Malawi expect their children to sleep on mats, as they do in the villages, but not at Kondanani: each child has his or her own bed, complete with comfortable mattress and clean bedding.

Education is also a priority, and Annie and Lewis's next step was to build a nursery school. This was funded by the Kegels Family Trust in Holland and named the Kegels Early Learning Centre. The school has ten classrooms, including a computer room, plus a principal's office, staffroom, storeroom, and washroom facilities for the boys and girls. It currently accommodates about fifty-five children.

The school is U-shaped, with a central courtyard filled with brightly coloured children's playground equipment, where one can often see toddlers racing around on their tricycles or toy motor bikes; there is a slide and swings and best of all a trampoline! The kids also love visiting their rabbit hutch.

The principal of the Kegels Centre, Lystra Tingle, is a positive, resourceful person with infinite patience and a great big smile. A missionary to Malawi from Trinidad and Tobago, Lystra is also a qualified teacher with a genuine love for children and an obvious passion for God's work. She is a volunteer at the school, as are all the missionaries at Kondanani, each being supported by their home church or individual sponsors.

In addition to overseeing five Malawian nursery school teachers, Lystra also coaches teachers from other schools, as there is currently no training facility in the country for nursery school teachers.

After the move back to "their old rented property", Annie and Lewis were happy to be in the house they had shared as newlyweds. Annie named it "Mphatso House" ("Mphatso" meaning "gift" in Chichewa). She still lives there today, next door to the houses of the Children's Village, the Kegels Nursery

School, and the homes of the volunteer missionaries who do such wonderful work.

All the buildings at Kondanani are set in landscaped gardens, with towering palm trees creating the perfect backdrop to a natural oasis. There are flowering shrubs, all kinds of indigenous trees, and expansive lawns.

Frangipani blossoms exude a rich fragrance across the village. Orange and purple bougainvillea plants transform wire fences, and hibiscus bushes flaunt magnificent red and pink blooms. Walkways are neatly lined with zigzag bricks alongside rockeries containing various flowers, rose bushes, and carefully placed arrangements of pot plants.

These gardens have been lovingly created by a visionary and her band of hard-working gardeners, and the views are breathtaking. Tall blue gum trees stand upright in a straight line against the clear African skyline, punctuated here and there by sprawling palm fronds. The sun blazes down on a lake in the distance, water glistens, and you can see the hazy blur of faraway mountains. Rocky outcrops in the distance lead to Malawi's famous Mount Mulanje, which is a potential future world heritage site.

The Chikhwazas had certainly been given serene surroundings in which to bring up children, helping young boys and girls to appreciate the wonders of creation.

Annie and Lewis were full of joy as they looked out from the *khonde* of their home, beyond Annie's beautiful hanging baskets to the green lawn where some of the children were playing volleyball. It was a wonderful sight, and they loved hearing the sound of little voices having fun, enjoying life and each other. "This is truly an oasis of love!" Lewis observed.

In between building homes for the children, Annie and Lewis also built several homes for the missionaries, each one attractively furnished by Annie with its own African décor.

Altogether ten have been built, including a guest house that can be rented by parents seeking to adopt a baby.

One of the missionaries who has lived in these houses is Linda Ford, a volunteer from England who came to the Children's Village after seeing a programme about it on the GOD Channel. She was watching the special broadcasts on Kondanani in 2000 when she heard Annie appeal for people to come and join her. She had felt called to Africa for quite some time but it crystallized while Annie was speaking, and she decided to relocate from Birmingham to Malawi.

She arrived in Bvumbwe in 2004 and stayed for five years. She continues to visit regularly, coming for about three months at the end of each year in order to help with the children's concert at Christmas.

"Malawi is a beautiful country," Linda says. "Yes, it's poor, and it took me a while to get used to the bush, the thatched huts, and the poverty, but I believe that with the right kind of help there is potential for it to be different. Kondanani has made a big impact on my life. I was an insecure person when I arrived, but through Annie's love and teaching I grew so much as a Christian."

With all its various buildings, gardens, pathways, and driveways, Kondanani is like a little town. It even had its own clinic at one time. This was housed in one of the largest buildings in the village and named after GOD TV's co-founder. The Rory Alec Clinic was initially built to house babies needing intensive care, complete with a room full of incubators and many other rooms filled with little cots and baby equipment.

When Annie decided to relocate Caring Hands from Blantyre to Bvumbwe it became the infant care facility until a new Caring Hands building could be completed. It is now being transformed into a community rehabilitation centre for children in the surrounding villages, offering physiotherapy, speech training, and other much-needed treatments.

Of course Rory's wife, Wendy, also has a building named after her: the orphanage's hall, where school assemblies and other gatherings are held alongside the central kitchen. It is called "Wendy's Place". Apparently Annie called it after her spiritual daughter because of her legendary cooking skills (or lack of, depending on whom you ask, and Annie's not telling)! It seems to be a private joke between them that goes way back...

"She cooked pasta and put sugar in it. But, shush... don't tell!" Annie whispers with a smile!

Since the Kondanani Village was established in 2000, Annie has found increasing favour with the surrounding community. She sees this as proof that "in all things God works for the good of those who love Him, who have been called according to His purpose" (Romans 8:28, NIV).

"People now realize that we never intended any harm. The villagers come to visit and there are no hard feelings. We recently invited a group of fifteen leading chiefs to come and see an example of a Christian orphanage at work, and they were so encouraged to see what was happening."

"I wish I could be at Kondanani," said one chief. "I actually wish I could be an orphan! These children are much better off than they would be outside."

"That's the plan!" Annie concludes with a huge grin.

31

Redeeming the land

"WE KNOW WHAT YOU'RE GOING TO DO WITH IT!"

Ever since Lewis Chikhwaza had bought his farm in 1971, he had planned to use it for God's work. But it had become the focus of a bitter family feud, fuelled by his children's selfish ambition, and it had been lost.

This was despite all the wonderful things Lewis and Annie had seen happen at many revival meetings held on the property, and the dozens of people who had been baptized in the dam, which Annie fondly refers to as "Lake Chikhwaza"! Losing the farm made no sense to Lewis or Annie, who always believed that God would somehow give the farm back to them.

If the first part of the redemption of their land had been glorious, they could not have expected what God did next. He had restored the land on which Annie had been left for dead, and now He was going to give them the land for which she had been supposed to die, and Lewis would be blessed by seeing the restoration of his farm for God's purposes while he was still alive.

After the attack it had taken Lewis ten months to get his farm back. The court battle was lengthy, and once it was over he was determined to sell the property to ensure that the family feud came to a complete end. A Member of Parliament bought the forty-three acres and took them over from Lewis. But he later lost his job and was unable to repay his loan to the Malawi Development Corporation (MDC), so they took it back.

The MDC tried to make a go of the property, running it as a farm and initiating various projects, but eventually they decided to put it up for auction.

In the meantime, while Annie was out walking around the Children's Village she would talk to God about the neighbouring land. She never wanted it for herself, but she had seen great things happen on the farm and she didn't think it was right for it to be in the hands of unbelievers.

"There were so many prophecies spoken over that land, of what a blessing it would be, and I just wanted to see these fulfilled," Annie says. "Then, in May 2000, God gave me a word: 'This land shall also come to Kondanani!' He spoke right into my spirit."

Annie was overjoyed, but in human terms it seemed impossible. Even so, she knew God could find a way where there was no way, if she kept her faith strong and continued with the vision of expanding the Children's Village.

She realized she would have to come up with a comprehensive proposal for Kondanani to take over the farm, and she went about putting this together. She also watched any new developments on the farm with a keen interest.

She was amazed when the MDC started making alterations to the ten-bedroomed house that she had long considered. Then they put in an entire banana plantation and an irrigation system, a sizable investment.

Annie would update Lewis regularly on any improvements being made. "Daddy, do you know what they have done now? They've planted bananas! They have done it for us, and they don't even know!" This was her faith talking, but the time would come for action.

In May 2003 Annie felt inspired to start raising funds for the land. Again GOD TV made a significant contribution, along with the Goshen Trust, run by Albert Dicken. "Rory and Wendy and Albert were quick to come to my rescue," says Annie. "They must have had great faith in what we were doing to provide the funds!"

Then, in August 2003, Lewis was reading the newspaper and discovered that his old farm was up for sale. "Mommy darling, they are inviting people to submit bids for the farm..."

Annie knew the time she had been waiting so patiently for had come. "We've got to put in a bid!" she replied, wondering whether the seven and a half million kwacha the Trust had saved to buy the property would be sufficient.

"I may not have enough," she cried out to God.

"Just bid what you have and I will take care of the rest!" she felt was His answer.

Then, in October 2003, God gave her another clear instruction: "I want you to walk around the perimeter of the farm seven times, just as the Children of Israel did before the walls of Jericho fell..."

It may have seemed a silly idea to some, but Annie took it seriously. She and her staff started walking around the forty-three acres and they did it every Friday, praying for and blessing the land as they went and anointing it with oil. They stuck faithfully to this routine for six weeks, but then heard the disappointing news that the farm had been sold to somebody else.

"This can't be," Annie said. "The Father has been so clear that this land is coming to Kondanani, so we are going to go round it a seventh time. We're going to be obedient to what He has told us to do."

So they walked around the perimeter of the land for the last time and then they just sat and waited.

God had spoken, and Annie and her team now expected to see the results. It was as simple as that. But, for several months, it seemed as though she had completely lost the bid. During that time nothing happened on the farm; nobody moved in, and it stood empty. But all that was about to change.

On 13 February 2004 Annie finally got the phone call from the MDC that she had been waiting for.

"Mrs Chikhwaza, could you come and see us, please? We want to talk to you about the land."

Needless to say, Annie and Lewis got there in no time! She was immediately encouraged when she was shown into the MDC official's office, because he had the word "Jesus" as a screensaver on his computer.

"We can't find the man who won the bid for the farm," he confided.

"I'm not surprised, because the Lord has told me this land belongs to Kondanani..."

"Well... we have studied your proposal, and we would like you to have it, because we know what you're going to do with it!

"However, the seven and a half million kwacha is not enough. We need nine and a half million, and we must have it by Wednesday."

This was two million kwacha more than Kondanani had in the bank. It converted to twenty thousand American dollars. It was a small fortune, but Annie knew she had to take another step of faith.

"Fine, no problem" she said, with no idea where she was going to find twenty thousand dollars. It was Friday, and she would have to secure this additional amount over the weekend.

Annie went home and drafted an e-mail to update her supporters. She had some American visitors staying with her at the Children's Village and they asked what her strategy was.

"Hasn't the Lord spoken, hasn't the Lord said?" she replied boldly. "This is what the Lord promised Lewis and me. My strategy is that He is gong to supply the finances!"

Annie had sent out e-mails, but she had only a few days. There was nothing she could do apart from trust God and pray.

"By Tuesday afternoon, I hadn't received a penny!" Annie recalls. "The following morning I needed to have the additional twenty thousand dollars. Worse still, I was scheduled to do an interview with Malawi Television on my plans for the future of Kondanani!"

She went ahead with the interview and spoke about the miracles God had already done to provide for the orphanage, and she told some of the children's stories, how they had arrived with nothing and now had everything.

"Now, Mrs Chikhwaza, what are your plans for the future?"

Annie felt she had to prophetically declare what God was going to do and that this would bring about a breakthrough in the spirit realm.

"We have bought the land next door, and we are going to expand Kondanani into its next phase, with a new primary school and several new houses," she said on national television, as Lewis watched in shock! "We are also going to relocate Caring Hands and build a brand new facility for our babies!"

It had been a long day, and Annie and Lewis went to bed hoping there would be some good news in the morning, before the deadline for paying the money.

They were sound asleep when the phone rang at ten past ten. It was a lady calling from Southampton in England. Annie had never met her or spoken to her before, although she was a sponsor of one of the children.

"Annie, if I give you that money for the land, are you certain you will secure it?" she asked politely.

"Yes, definitely!" Annie answered.

"Well, then, you've got it!"

Annie and Lewis were overjoyed. They jumped out of bed and walked around the house with their hands held high, praising and glorifying God because He had done it again.

"He is the Great Restorer. He is the Great Redeemer," says Annie. "By His resurrection power He can bring life out of death, turn sorrow into joy, water into wine and provide a home for those who have none."

The miraculous provision for the purchase of the forty-three-acre farm provided the space urgently needed to relocate the original orphanage from Blantyre to Bvumbwe. Annie had been keen to do this for a long time, as it was impractical to travel between the two campuses, and the original orphanage in Blantyre that had been financed by Press Trust was sold.

Owing to various complications it took several months for Annie to obtain the money from the sale, but this was just one more of the obstacles she has had to overcome.

The funds from the Blantyre home were finally reinvested in building the new Caring Hands Infant Home on its own piece of ground on the other side of the road to the Kondanani Village.

Because of the delay in payment the little ones initially had to be transferred to the Rory Alec Clinic, but in January 2010 came the historic day when the new Caring Hands building was opened by Press Trust, the Malawian donor organization which had provided half of the funds required to build it.

This facility now accommodates approximately sixty babies under three years old, cared for by a matron assisted by thirty-one full-time nannies, who have been specially trained to care for young babies.

Caring Hands is an impressive L-shaped building, designed by Annie to provide care for babies and toddlers.

From the moment you walk through the gates to the reception area, parents' lounge, and matron's office, you have a sense that everything runs like clockwork in this orderly facility, with its neatly manicured front lawn and flowerbeds.

This of course changes when you get to the large play area, where a dozen little ones are playing on brightly coloured baby blankets with soft toys strewn everywhere! You are overwhelmed by the cuteness of these precious bundles, some crying, some laughing, some needing a nappy change, and others gazing up at you with beautiful big brown eyes.

It breaks your heart to think that someone could abandon these precious children, each with their own sad history. But that no longer matters: they are safe now, and loved and cared for by the matron, Stella Gama, with a full complement of staff working on shifts around the clock, overseen by Annie and Cherie.

Of course Caring Hands operates an orderly schedule to keep the babies secure in their routine. There are feeding times, nap times, bath times, and so on, with what seems like an army of carers, cleaners, and laundry staff. You only have to look at the clothes lines to know what a huge task running an infants' home is. In addition to what seems like miles of white nappies flapping in the wind, there are endless rows of pastel Babygros™!

If you think visiting the playroom is an emotional experience, your heartstrings are tugged even more when you venture into the nursery, with its rows of miniature white cots and pastel letters of the alphabet on the wall. Some of the cots contain sleeping babies, some hold tiny newborns – most flourishing, a few fighting for survival against HIV/AIDS. There is also an intensive care room with incubators for tiny infants.

The matron ensures that the weight of each baby is checked every week and they are inoculated against childhood diseases. Children who are HIV-positive also receive their antiretroviral drugs here.

It's a joy to see the babies sleeping peacefully, and to know they are receiving expert care. Then you wander through to the toddlers' quarters, with its much larger cots and children's tables and chairs. Here you are mobbed as the two-year-olds come running to hug you!

They grab you around your legs and don't want to let go. You run your palm over their little heads and tell them how special they are. Then their nannies guide them into a joyful, energetic huddle and they begin to sing. You can't help getting misty-eyed as you look into their smiling faces and tell them how clever they are. They don't sing nursery rhymes but Sunday school songs: "Yes, Jesus loves me," they belt out at the tops of their voices, "the Bible tells me so!"

This is what Kondanani's Caring Hands Infant Home is all about: children leaving a place of desperation behind them and coming to know the love of God. They have entered a place of hope, nurture, and redemption.

Lewis Chikhwaza had always intended his own children to inherit his farm, but because of their prodigal behaviour the land was sadly lost to them. But by God's grace it would still be his legacy to the children now under his guardianship, the orphaned children of Malawi.

32

A place of blessing

MADALO VILLAGE AND FILA FARM

Following the purchase of the forty-three-acre farm from the Malawi Development Corporation in 2004, Annie and Lewis had all the land they would ever need to expand Kondanani for the next age group and beyond. They and the children in their care felt blessed beyond measure!

The Chikhwazas had started in 1998 with babies who were now about six years old and growing out of their homes at the Kondanani Children's Village. It was time for them to move into bigger houses with larger rooms, and the Madalo Children's Village would be their new home.

While there were both boys and girls in each home in the Kondanani Village, Madalo would provide the space for separate homes for the two sexes and would become an ongoing building project.

Each house was built with a cavernous central lounge/dining-room area, a bathroom, and three bedrooms, where the children could sleep four to a room on two sets of bunk beds. Each house also has a lounge and bedroom for the housemother and a bedroom for the nanny. And, of course, each home has its own *khonde*!

The houses are named after the much-appreciated person or family that contributed to their construction. These include House of David, Martha's Cabana, Angela's Cottage, Heinrich

237

House, Christina's Place, Brielle House, Broekers Cottage, and Bata House.

Madalo was, of course, Lewis's youngest son, and it is also the Chichewa word for "blessing". How fitting that the new village should be named after the young man whose death was a catalyst for the attack on Lewis and Annie's lives.

It is tragic that he lost his life so unexpectedly, as he had tremendous potential, and Annie says that Madalo Village is a place where destiny and potential will never again be short-lived. How wonderful for the children to live in "a village of blessing"!

"Our children have tremendous potential and we want to ensure they all fulfil their God-given destiny," says Annie. "We want to teach them that they were born to be a blessing as well as to be blessed."

On their third visit to Malawi in 2004 Annie was delighted to show Rory Alec and Albert Dicken around the new farm property and take them through one of the children's homes, showing them all the rooms where the children eat and sleep, their bathroom, and the housemother's room.

Albert, who runs the Goshen Trust, has been a faithful supporter of Kondanani and, together with GOD TV, helped Annie and Lewis to buy the farm. "It is amazing to me what faith and vision are accomplishing here at Kondanani!" he observed during a special *Behind the Screens* report on the GOD Channel.

During this broadcast Rory Alec announced that GOD TV would commit a further thirty-seven thousand pounds to Kondanani to cover the cost of several building projects, including the refurbishment of the ten-bedroomed house and its reroofing! Annie finally had her chance to ululate in true African fashion as she expressed her joy.

"Right now my heart is beating very, very hard because I am so very grateful. I am just overwhelmed by the generosity of the GOD TV family. Thank you so much for being such a tremendous support to our children's lives."

Annie also announced on camera to GOD TV viewers that Kondanani had reached the milestone of its hundredth baby, "but then we have lost the same number of babies to HIV/ AIDS," she added sadly. Running an orphanage was always going to be a bittersweet experience, however rewarding.

"We thank God for the opportunity to get the gospel out through media," Rory said, "and to support this work here on the ground in Africa, where I am amazed at the level of excellence of Annie and her workers. They are doing a great job and I look forward to seeing these buildings complete on my next trip!"

As the children started moving into their new homes in the Madalo Village, Annie was overwhelmed to think of all the extraordinary things God had done to provide for these precious ones. That fateful day when she had gazed with horror upon her wrecked nursery school was now a distant memory. God had brought them something much, much greater!

Back then she had joked grimly about drowning the whole of Malawi in Lake Malawi, and now they had their own little dam back, where new converts could be baptized in "Lake Chikhwaza". She recalled the bricklaying project, the apple seedlings, the sewing projects, and the self-help initiative for pastor's wives, all of which had come to an abrupt end. But now they had a banana plantation, an irrigation system, and enough land to keep cows, bulls, goats, pigs, and chickens.

Fila Farm, as it would come to be known, would offer many income-generating opportunities that would help make all facets of the ministry more self-sufficient. It truly is a place of unending blessing.

Named after Felix Starker, Kondanani's first missionary farmer, whose nickname is "Fila", Fila Farm is a place the children love to visit to see the animals.

With about fourteen hundred banana trees and orchards containing apples, guavas, and mangos, there is no shortage of fruit for the children and Annie and Lewis soon bought several cows to provide milk and Annie's favourite: cheese!

The farm now has nine bulls as well as the twenty-two cows that provide milk for the children every day. A farm kitchen enables workers to use some of this to make butter and cheese and there is also a drying room for the cheese.

Malawi is a long way from Friesland, where Annie was born, but her love of cheese and her Dutch connections have paved the way for the cheese-making project to flourish, with special machinery being delivered from the Netherlands in 2009. Cream is also sold to private individuals and companies, and Annie tithes a portion of the milk to another orphanage.

To complete Fila Farm's selection of livestock it also has two hundred pigs, which are sold for pork. Annie hopes to add goats and chickens to complete the ideal picture of an African farm. She also has plans to breed tilapia fish in the two-acre dam.

An innovative bio-gas project has recently been built on the farm, recycling animal waste to provide gas for Kondanani's cooking needs. There are several boreholes for the provision of water to the houses, and for the irrigation of the land and the banana plantation.

Of course there was one particular building on the farm that brought back many memories for Annie – the derelict house. Though Lewis had done all he could to repair this ten-bedroomed house, it was God who would ultimately make good on Lewis's promise to Annie.

Lewis had started the renovations in 1996, but the attack had put them on hold. The MDC made some improvements in 2003 and the large colonial home was finally restored to Annie's satisfaction in 2005 with funds supplied by GOD TV and others.

It now houses Kondanani's headquarters, and she has an office there. Who would have thought the day would come when she would be able to work in the building without wearing socks to ensure that her toes did not get nibbled by rats? Having said that, perhaps she secretly misses her portable stove...

Probably not, because she is still living in Mphatso House, that same three-bedroomed house that she and Lewis once rented, but thankfully she has just had her kitchen refurbished. After fourteen years of faithful service she finally has the kitchen she always wanted!

It is here that the missionaries often gather at the weekend around a bowl of soup and a game of Scrabble, but more about "the Scrabble wars" in a later chapter...

In addition to Kondanani's head office, the ten-roomed house now contains the classroom for the ABCs. This is where the six-year-olds spend their first year of "big school". As soon as they are seven they move to the "Lewis Chikhwaza Christian Academy", named after Annie's husband, the co-founder of Kondanani.

The refurbished house also has a recreation room, a music room, a computer room, and a library for the children. And at the back of the house a large veranda has been added, plus an office for the farm manager.

"Not only are Kondanani's farmers essential to making us self-sustaining, but they are also wonderful father figures to the children," says Annie.

The Lewis Chikhwaza Christian Academy was set up in 2009 and now comprises three large buildings on its own four-acre site opposite the Caring Hands Infant Care home. These are the Vlaming, Melanie, and Nocolien Learning Centres, and they accommodate about eighty students at present. The school is completed fenced off and has its own gardens and a well-equipped playground with complex jungle gyms. Here the children have everything they need to ensure a first-class education.

Every effort is made to educate them to the highest standard, and they are keen to learn. The educational syllabus used is the Accelerated Christian Education system (ACE), which keeps the students motivated, and they are able to work at their own pace. If a child is very bright, he or she can finish high school by the age of fifteen. Kondanani has children who are already two years ahead.

The children speak English well, although their first language is Chichewa, and their development is remarkable. Their final exams before college or university will take place at the American Embassy in Lilongwe, as the ACE programme follows an American curriculum.

As all the children at Kondanani are educated using the ACE system, their entire education can be done on site, including high school, trade school, and university. This does not mean that it is cheap. Annie's annual ACE education bill is over one hundred and fifty thousand rand per year.

Each day at the Lewis Chikhwaza Academy starts with the pledge to the Bible:

> **I pledge allegiance to the Bible, God's holy word. I will make it a lamp unto my feet, and a light unto my path. I will hide its words in my heart, that I might not sin against God.**

The students also make a pledge to the Malawian flag and the Christian flag, a white banner displaying a small red cross in a navy block, which is used in ACE education. During special assemblies, currently held in the hall at "Wendy's Place", the children often sing the Kondanani Anthem, an inspirational song written by one of the missionaries and included at the end of this book.

During these assemblies the teachers reinforce the message that each student is highly valued. To illustrate this, in one assembly a teacher gave some of the children a card with a number on it and told them to pretend they now had a number instead of a name.

He called them up to the front one by one, calling only their number. "Imagine not having a name," he said. "Imagine being treated like a number..."

The children were horrified, but they played along. They could soon see that it was an awful prospect being a number rather than being called by their name.

"It makes you feel that people don't really know you," one girl said.

"It's even worse when someone points at you and says, 'Hey you!' I don't like that," one of the boys observed.

The message came through to the children loud and clear – our names identify us as individuals. The Bible teaches that God writes our name on His hands (Isaiah 49:15–16). He knows all about us and He cares for each of us. In Isaiah 43:1 God says, "Fear not, for I have redeemed you; I have called you by your name; You are Mine."

No child at Kondanani, whether at Caring Hands, the Kondanani Village, or the Madalo Village, is ever a mere number. Each is treated as unique, with their own special gifts and calling and destiny.

> For You formed my inward parts;
> You covered me in my mother's womb.
> I will praise You, for I am fearfully and wonderfully made;
> Marvellous are Your works, and that my soul knows very well.
> My frame was not hidden from You,
> When I was made in secret,

And skilfully wrought in the lowest parts of the earth.
Your eyes saw my substance, being yet unformed.
And in Your book they all were written,
The days fashioned for me,
When as yet there were none of them.
How precious also are Your thoughts to me, O God!
How great is the sum of them!
If I should count them, they would be more in number
than the sand;
When I awake, I am still with You.

(Psalm 139:13–18)

33

The door of hope

Every parent knows the commitment it takes to bring up a child. It's no easy task even in developed countries, where support is available should things go wrong, but imagine being a parent in one of Africa's poorest countries, where there is no such support.

It's a challenge millions of Africans rise to each day, trying to make ends meet, one way or another, and there are those who just can't cope any longer. All hope seems lost, as if God has abandoned them and their newborns, but the truth is that God has not forgotten them.

Imagine the despair of a poverty-stricken young woman in Malawi. She can hardly fend for herself and now she has a baby to care for. Picture her shuffling her way along a muddy village pathway as the sun goes down and all hope fades.

She is awkwardly carrying an unhappy little bundle in her arms, trying to cover it from the eyes of passers-by. For other women this unexpected gift would be cause for celebration, but for her it is just more desperation, echoed each time the baby cries.

She hasn't eaten a proper meal in days and is still trying to get her strength back after the ordeal of childbirth. There is no food and no family.

Still grieving the death of her own parents from the deadly scourge of HIV/AIDS, she is barely more than a child, an orphan, and now a mother at the age of fourteen. Can you fathom the depths of despair that would drive this young girl to abandon her baby and somehow manage to walk away?

Thoughts like these have gone through her mind all day long, and she has almost given in, but then she hears there is hope. "There is a woman named Annie", the villagers tell her, "who will help you, as she has helped many others."

Shrouded by the shadows, the young mother edges towards the place she has been told will not turn her baby away. Her heart is breaking; she doesn't want anyone to know what she is doing – the shame is too great – but there is no other way. Her poverty is just too overwhelming.

Imagine the tears rolling down her cheeks as she quickly places the baby on the threshold of a specially built doorway. Without hesitating she gives her child's hand a last squeeze before disappearing into the night. Picture the helpless little soul lying there, abandoned and alone.

You can almost hear him or her start to cry, but there is no need. An electronic device has alerted the dedicated team of missionaries inside. Moments later a door on the other side opens and the infant is taken up into a pair of loving hands.

A brightly coloured sign above the opening says "THE DOOR OF HOPE". This is the vision God gave Annie and Lewis Chikhwaza and their team at Kondanani to offer hope for the abandoned children of Malawi.

With twelve million people and one million orphans in the country, Kondanani obviously cannot take every child, but the Children's Village is making a huge difference in the lives of close on two hundred children. The organization is a brilliant example of how an orphanage should function, challenging other such institutions to follow its lead.

With such a vast number of orphans in Malawi, Annie believes that an anonymous drop-off point is essential. She is all too aware of countless babies abandoned in toilets and rubbish bins in the poorest areas of this developing country, and it is her aim to offer desperate woman an alternative that has some dignity.

In an interview with David Aldous on *In Depth* on the GOD Channel in 2005, Annie shared the horrific story of a baby who had been thrown down a pit latrine by a young mother to hide her shame. She even took a stick and pushed it down the "bush toilet" to ensure the baby had drowned. But the grandfather heard the baby's cries and came to the rescue. By a miracle the little one had survived, and the old man brought the baby to Kondanani.

"If only that young girl had known about our Door of Hope," Annie says. "Of course this is not the ideal way for a baby to come to an orphanage, but there *is* no ideal way, and I'd rather they came anonymously through a hole in the wall than half-dead after being dumped in a toilet.

"Most of our children are brought in by a helpless family member, often the last surviving adult in a family. All the others have died of HIV/AIDS and they are all the baby has left, and they cannot cope. Others are brought by the Malawian Department of Social Welfare."

In one way or another, Annie has been and is still mother to hundreds of children, providing an oasis of love for many, many families in distress. If you ever visit Kondanani, you will meet this band of happy faces from babies to teens. You will also find an actual "Door of Hope", easily accessible from the communal dirt road that runs through the village.

It's more of a window really, an opening in the wall, but this is Kondanani's place of sanctuary for new mothers or family members who for some desperate reason are unable to keep their babies – a heavenly drop-off point for newborns who would otherwise be cruelly discarded and in some cases killed.

The newspapers are full of stories of African babies who have been found dead or abandoned in dustbins or pit latrines, and Kondanani's "Door of Hope" is a desperate measure to prevent such tragedies.

"We are trusting God for things to be different in Malawi," says Annie. "But until we overcome the scourges of HIV/ AIDS and poverty in our country, we have to provide a way for mothers to bring their babies anonymously and know they will be well looked after.

"We've yet to receive a baby in this way, but people are reassured by the fact that the Door of Hope is there," she says. "The reality is that people don't have to go to such extreme measures; they can simply knock on Kondanani's door and we will help them care for their baby.

"We believe God has 'set before us an open door that no man can shut', as the Bible says in Revelation 3:8, and we have seen hundreds of babies come through our gates. In this way we are providing hope each day for the hurting children of Africa."

"God loves these children," adds Annie. "He has a plan for each one. His eyes are on the sparrow, His heart is that not even one would perish – but we live in a fallen world, which has turned its back on God, and daily we are faced with the consequences of sin.

"Our heart at Kondanani is to share the love of God with all, to share the hope we have, which is Jesus, believing that He can turn around even the worst situation, and cause all things to work together for good.

"Jesus is our great redeemer; He can take a life that nobody cares about and use it for His glory. This is what we believe He will do for each child He has placed in our care. The children of Kondanani are nurtured and loved, not just looked after."

The first thing Annie and her team do when they receive a new child is dedicate them to God, praying that He would undo any harm done by the circumstances surrounding their birth and let them grow up strong and healthy to accomplish all He intends for their lives.

Witchcraft is common in African countries, and Annie is quick to counter any curses that may have been uttered over the children, by praying for them in the name of Jesus, and where a child has been given an inappropriate name, a new one is given.

For example, one of the children brought to Kondanani had been given a Chichewa name that translated as "Should Have Been Dead Long Ago". Annie immediately changed this to Zoë, a Greek name which means "life".

"What on earth makes a woman abandon her newborn baby?" Annie asks. "Have you ever asked yourself that question? I've stopped asking. Instead, I try to understand the circumstances some women find themselves in.

"Without condoning such an act of desperation, I realize that there is terrible poverty within a culture where children are considered a status symbol, especially among the uneducated, and where many women are still forced to have as many babies as possible.

"With another mouth to feed, and often with no support from a husband, some women don't know what to do, and they abandon their baby in the hope that, when he or she is found, they will have a better future somewhere else. Others lose their husbands to HIV/AIDS while they are pregnant and know that HIV/AIDS is going to take their lives too.

"Abandoning one's baby is not something that is entered into lightly, or an act which can be judged without knowing the background, but that will never be known in most cases."

Kondanani often receives calls from the Malawian Department of Welfare. One of these concerned a baby abandoned in the forest. The Welfare people called to ask if Annie would take the baby.

The three-week-old was discovered under a bush wrapped in a tattered T-shirt (fortunately it was warm at the time so she wasn't too cold), and she was found before she became dehydrated.

Kondanani received her with open arms, seeing it as a privilege to be part of her life. The team gave her love and care and called her Lystra, after the principal at Kegels Early Learning Centre. Little Lystra has now been adopted and is living in the Netherlands.

In another situation, Annie was heartbroken to meet a grandmother at the gate of Kondanani's Caring Hands facility, who had brought a set of orphaned twins. Both children have now been adopted and also live in the Netherlands.

They were two boys, one named Blessings and the other Hastings. They were fourteen months old, a little older than the babies Kondanani usually takes in, but their condition was so appalling that Annie did not have the heart to turn them away.

Blessings weighed only four kilograms and his brother seven kilograms. Blessings had a large open wound on his body and they both looked like skeletons. They had no hair on their heads, only a bit of fluff.

Neither of them could sit or stand, but after just two weeks at Kondanani both babies had put on quite a bit of weight and their skin had changed from pale grey to a healthy chocolate brown. Their hair had started to grow and Blessings's wound soon healed.

"We rejoice at the way things have improved for these precious little twins," says Annie. "We're so grateful to our Father God that He sees fit to have us take care of them and all the precious lives in our hands."

Some doors open easily and lead nowhere. Others are stuck and need to be forced open but take you to places you never dreamed possible. The story of Annie Chikhwaza is one of forsaking life's easiest options to beat down all the obstacles in her way. And, in so doing, she has opened a door of hope for many people.

It seems as if God looked down on Malawi and saw the desperate plight of its people, and sent them a woman who was no stranger to pain or suffering. He knew that she was ideally equipped to comfort others with the comfort she herself had received through many heartbreaking experiences.

34

God is a faithful God

A TRIBUTE TO LEWIS CHIKHWAZA

Kondanani had indeed proved to be an oasis of love for the people of Malawi, but such a cross-cultural, multifaceted ministry would never have been possible without Lewis Chikhwaza. When he died in December 2005, Annie was heartbroken.

She had lost the love of her life and her "beautiful African love story" had come to an end. She would now have to carry on with their vision alone, safeguarding Lewis's legacy and staying faithful to the call to transform African lives.

"Half of me has been torn away," Annie wrote at the time, "and I will need healing to be made whole again. However, I'm fortunate that I'm not left without hope. Father God is my comforter and a defender of the widows."

Looking back over Lewis's life, Annie remembers what a great man of God he was. "He was a gentle servant leader who loved God and His word. He often preached about overcoming obstacles and would always take time to exhort people who were struggling.

"He was an exceptionally wise man and he revered the Bible. He used to say that he would eat God's word: 'It's as the psalmist says, sweeter than honey to me', and he would often quote Scripture."

How sweet are Your words to my taste,
Sweeter than honey to my mouth!

(Psalm 119:103)

"Even in his last days Lewis would sit outside or on the *khonde* and listen to his favourite preachers on his tape recorder. He loved Kenneth Hagin, Kenneth Copeland, and Ray McCauley from Bible school days!

"Lewis was also such a positive, energetic person, and a real character. I'll never forget his great big smile, which would always light up my day!" Annie says. "If anybody asked him how he was, he would invariably reply: "I'm full of faith, full of hope, and full of life!"

Annie and Lewis had been married for twelve years when he died after a brief illness at the age of seventy-seven. Annie nursed him lovingly to the end. She knew the time was coming when they would have to say goodbye, and that somehow seemed to make things bearable for her.

"Lewis was a wonderful husband because he knew how to love his wife as Christ loved the church, and I was more than happy to submit to him because I felt his protection. He was a very strong man, although he came across as gentle. I was given such love and care by him that it was easy for me to submit!

"He also never felt threatened by me, so there was never any competition between us. He recognized what God was doing in my life and he had such confidence in himself that he never felt insecure. He would praise me and I would praise him. We truly valued each other. This is why we had such a successful marriage."

Lewis Chikhwaza was a humble man of God who was quick to give others the credit when things went well and had no problem taking the blame when things went badly. A straightforward, uncomplicated man from an impoverished nation, he was also a great visionary in his own right.

He was able to see past his own limitations and the huge challenges facing his country and believe that God could turn even the most abysmal situation around. He had the foresight and dedication to look outside his culture, traditions, and country for revelation of the word of God and to bring this back to share with his people.

He was a leader Malawi could look up to: a politician at one time and an MP and friend of Malawi's long-standing president, the late Hastings Banda; he was an emerging businessman in 1964 when Malawi was finding its feet after Nyasaland had gained independence from Great Britain, and the first Malawian to own a transport company.

Lewis was also the founder of two Christian ministries, Holy Cross and Bible Faith, a pastor to pastors, and the overseer of a network of churches. He was the co-founder of an orphanage, a nursery school, and a children's village; the husband of his first wife, Elizabeth, and father of ten children, and the husband of his second wife, Annie, and "Papa" to a multitude of grateful, smiling faces.

It is not surprising, therefore, that when he died he was given a state funeral by the government of Malawi attended by the Malawian President, Bingu Wa Mutharika. There were four thousand people at the sombre event and it was covered on Malawi state television and radio.

"It was an amazing day and I was delighted that Lewis was honoured in this way," Annie says, "but for me personally it was a very tearful, stressful time. Not only was I grieving but I had to take care of so many things and of course it was going to be difficult dealing with the family."

Lewis's death released a flood of deep-seated anguish among his children and grandchildren. Five of Lewis's children had passed away and now he too had died, and Annie was aware that many people in Malawi still saw death as the result of witchcraft or poisoning. She had forgiven Lewis's surviving children but she wondered how they would treat her now that their father was gone.

Annie and Lewis had bought back the farm only the year before he died and she was so grateful that Lewis had lived to see that day. She knew they had legally purchased the land from the Malawi Development Corporation in Kondanani's name, but she was still concerned that there might be trouble.

The Chikhwaza children and the grandchildren would all be visiting the property for the funeral, and she would have to manage the situation very carefully. Fortunately the government stepped in and took care of the arrangements, but despite this there would still be the odd skirmish.

"Some of the family members, probably a handful of the grandchildren, attacked two of our missionaries, and I was devastated. I couldn't believe that, after the nine years that had passed since the attack, some of them still thought I had stolen their land and wanted to take revenge. Cherie and Linda were both beaten, which was awful, because they had absolutely nothing to do with the situation."

Lewis died on a Friday morning, and on the Sunday morning before his burial Annie just wanted to be on her own with him one last time. She asked his sister, who was mourning next to the coffin, if she could have a few moments alone with her late husband. This made the old lady angry and she went to call some of the family members to come and chase Annie out.

They didn't want her to be left alone to mourn privately in the room, and Annie couldn't believe she had been sent away from her own husband's coffin.

"It wasn't a time to start putting up a fight," she recalls with tears in her eyes. "I had to leave it. I went to my bedroom and wept. It was heartbreaking for me to think that certain members of Lewis's family still saw me as having had something to do with the deaths in their family."

After the funeral, one of the grandchildren nevertheless asked Annie for money to start her own business, and she gladly gave it. "Sadly, there isn't much contact between the children and me, but often, when they have a need, they still come to me and say, 'Mommy, I can't afford this, or I can't afford that' and I try to help them when I can because I want them to know they've been forgiven."

> **Don't repay evil for evil. Don't retaliate when people say unkind things about you. Instead, pay them back with a blessing. That is what God wants you to do and He will bless you for it... Now who will want to harm you if you are eager to do good? But even if you suffer for doing what is right, God will reward you for it. So don't be afraid and don't worry.**
>
> (1 Peter 3:9, 13, 14, NLT)

Annie had been introduced to President Banda by Lewis and had met President Bakili Muluzi several times because Lewis had served with him in parliament. She had even called on his support days before she was attacked. Now Malawi's latest president, Bingu wa Mutharika (who died in 2012), was coming to preside over her husband's funeral, but it nearly didn't happen. Why? Because Annie nearly chased away the President's aides!

Once Lewis had died, people started arriving to pay their respects. "The African grapevine is excellent!" Annie observes. "Soon we had several people on the property, including three men who looked quite shabby to me." She was reluctant to let them inside her home.

"Thankfully it came to the ears of one of the pastors in Lewis's network that these were the President's men. 'Mommy, I know they don't look very smart,' he said, 'but the President has sent them.' I nearly chased away the President's aides! I learned that day never to turn a person away because of what they are wearing."

"The President had sent an envelope with enough money to buy a decent coffin, which I couldn't have afforded. Then I was told my husband would have a state funeral and that the President was going to be there. The whole funeral was suddenly taken out of my hands and I had no say in the arrangements.

"Within an hour there were four hundred policemen on the property. They started erecting gazebos where the dignitaries would sit: there would be one for the President and the Chief Justice, government ministers, and high-ranking officials.

"Another one for all the pastors from the Bible Faith Ministries network and the many other pastors from all over Malawi, and another gazebo where I would sit with the first lady, women government ministers, and the principal female mourners."

Lewis was obviously highly regarded by his countrymen and his state funeral was a fitting tribute to a great Malawian. His legacy lives on through the work of Bible Faith Ministries, which Lewis handed over to his son Jeremiah, whom he always considered a great preacher. His memory also lives in the hearts of all at Kondanani, and especially those children who are privileged to attend the Lewis Chikhwaza Academy.

In an interview shown on the GOD Channel, Rory Alec once asked Lewis to share his favourite expression with viewers. "God is a faithful God and He cares," Lewis said, in effect summing up his life. Despite hardship and sorrow the Lord had always been faithful to Lewis, and his life is a testimony to God's grace. The GOD TV Guide published a tribute to Lewis in its February issue of 2006:

> The GOD TV family sends our love and condolences to Annie Chikhwaza and all at Kondanani on the death of her husband Lewis, who co-founded the Children's Village with her in 1998.
>
> GOD TV has been closely aligned to Kondanani as part of our vision to support widows and orphans and the charity has been featured on the GOD Channel regularly.
>
> Most recently, Annie was interviewed on *In Depth*, where she shared the amazing story of how God led her to marry Lewis and move to his home country of Malawi, where the Lord raised them up to provide a sanctuary for many homeless children orphaned through the HIV/AIDS epidemic in Africa.
>
> Now Lewis, or "Papa" as he was known to many, has gone to his eternal home at the age of seventy-seven years. He was laid to rest at Kondanani, close to the Christian Academy named after him.
>
> Lewis was a well-known businessman, politician, and in the last years of his life, a minister of the gospel. More than four thousand people, including the President of Malawi, Dr Bingu wa Mutharika, attended his funeral, which was carried live on state radio and television.
>
> Both Lewis and Annie have sowed generously into the lives of Rory and Wendy and the mission of GOD TV; we would not be here as a ministry today without their love, generosity, and care. GOD TV has sowed a love offering into Kondanani in Lewis's memory and we encourage our viewers to pray for Annie and the work of this groundbreaking ministry.

As you drive in through the gates of the Madalo Children's Village, you can look across the sprawling green lawn to the white marble memorial to Lewis Chikhwaza in the middle of the front garden. It's a simple but elegant grave, edged by white chains and flowering shrubs – an ideal resting place beneath indigenous trees and surrounded by the bountiful lives of hundreds of contented children:

LEWIS MONTFORD DANIEL CHIKHWAZA

Born 15th March 1928

Promoted to Glory 2nd December 2005

You were full of life, the God kind of life.

I miss your love and care.

You left a memorial which has eternal value.

Your wife, Annie Chikhwaza

35

An oasis of love

THE HAPPY CHILDREN OF KONDANANI

Kondanani is an oasis of love in a struggling, developing nation. There is no place quite like it. From the brightly coloured signs on the gates of the various facilities to the myriad of smiling faces that greet you, there is nothing dull and depressing to be seen. Yes, it's the home of over one hundred and eighty orphans, but these children lack for nothing.

This is a place of immense hope, where God is glorified, the Bible is honoured, and miracles of provision keep flowing. This is a haven where a future generation of Malawians is being raised that does not know poverty, fear, superstition, witchcraft, or hatred. These are young people who love God and each other, who are receiving a first-class education, and who will no doubt shape the Malawi of tomorrow.

What Annie and her team have accomplished since 1998 is to turn many sets of dire circumstances around, saving the lives of many, many children who would never have survived if they had been left to fend for themselves in the villages.

"It is all about placing a value on children whom others would discard because they are seen as worthless," Annie says. "But we get our children as babies and nobody sees them as worthless, nor do they grow up with that label. Instead, they are taught who they are in Christ.

"They are loved, cuddled, cared for, and kissed. Though some of them have come to us malnourished, this hasn't been a huge setback because they have been nurtured and fed well here, so they are now bright, intelligent kids.

"They are normal, happy children. They have never been looked down on, and there is no reason whatsoever to feel sorry for them."

The children of Kondanani have a busy life at home and at school. In addition to this, their free time is packed full of afternoon sporting activities, Friday-night movies, and youth clubs, plus the opportunity to learn musical instruments, read in the library, and attend children's church on Sundays, monthly birthday celebrations, concerts, prizegivings, and, best of all, the annual Christmas party, where they receive their gifts.

One of the housemothers dresses up as Father Christmas and the children ask questions such as, "Why does Father Christmas have the same shoes as my housemother?"

The Lewis Chikhwaza Christian Academy is planning to start taking a group of children to the ACE convention in South Africa and the older children are hoping to be picked. Kondanani has it's own music group, "The SuperKids" which often performs in public and the orphanage has many budding athletes. The Kondanani team have won a local mini-marathon race a number of times, though the village people still can't quite understand this. They see the run as a punishment!

As part of the Kondanani vision to bring up a generation of children with a sound Christian-based background of care and education, Annie and her extensive team have built up a far-reaching community with every facility to provide for the needs of the children and to be as self-sufficient as possible.

Situated on a total of fifty acres, all the different elements of Kondanani work together to provide a paradise for children that is filled with love. But this does not mean that there have been no problems. Feeding so many is always a challenge, and there are times when Annie has not known where the next meal was coming from, yet the children have never gone hungry. They get three nutritious meals a day as well as snacks.

The orphanage has been broken into several times, requiring electric fences to be put up for the security of the staff and children and creating separate contained units for the two villages, Caring Hands, and the Christian Academy.

1n 2012 Annie came to the conclusion that, with the children becoming teenagers, the boys and girls needed to live in separate villages. A visionary with an ability to be flexible, she saw that the best solution was to have all the boys live at the Madalo Village, which is a separate entity, and house all the girls along with the younger children at the Kondanani Village.

The boys and girls will continue to go to school together at the Lewis Chikhwaza Christian Academy, although there are separate learning centres for the boys and girls. Annie has taken the onset of teenage years in her stride and provided for it as part of her overall strategy.

Her hope for each child in her care is that they will grow from babyhood to childhood to adulthood at Kondanani.

"We have our own nursery school, we have our own primary school, we will have our own high school, and we will ultimately provide university-level ACE education and a trade school, so the children will have all their education at Kondanani!

"As the children get older, so I keep on building," she says. "I'm building all the time. I'm never free from building something. Fortunately we have plenty of land to expand onto, and I have a whole team of contractors to assist me!

"I'm sure some of the children will want to stay and learn a trade and work for Kondanani as farmers, carpenters, plumbers, electricians, welders, or whatever they want to be. The children will stay with us until they get married and set up their own homes, or find employment elsewhere."

Looking back at all that has been accomplished, Annie is relieved that the days of the angry villagers who reviled her are long gone. In fact, her neighbours now bring fruit for the children and she in turn blesses them with milk!

Giving is an enormous part of everything Annie does and, much to many people's surprise, the orphanage is committed to tithing to other orphanages. "Giving is one of the most important things a Christian can do," Annie says. "Do you know, if you are a servant, it means you are a *doulos* (slave). This means your will has been swallowed up by the will of another; you are no longer your own, and at Kondanani we give.

"Now you are going to say, 'You are an orphanage, an African orphanage; how can you give?' We give because we know it unleashes a harvest of blessing!"

During a financial audit by Stewardship Services, which handles Kondanani's child sponsorship, an accountant expressed surprise when he went through the orphanage's books.

"Everything is fine," he said. "Just one thing: you have so many entries that say 'gifts'. What do you mean by that?"

"That is our tithing, our giving," Annie replied.

"But you are an orphanage; what do you mean?"

"Well, we give!"

"But so much?" he questioned.

"Yes, because we *need* so much! So we've got to give!"

"OK, then; I am happy with that."

Annie is constantly exemplifying a lifestyle of giving, something which the missionaries she mentors have picked up on. Each Sunday, while one of the missionaries remains at the orphanage on duty, the others go to church in Blantyre. Annie takes them in the microbus along with a group of the older children. Afterwards they have lunch in town and often one of the missionaries will disappear for a few moments while they secretly settle the bill!

Annie also models a lifestyle of giving to the children, encouraging them to care for each other. Her years of giving to the ministry of Brother Andrew have served her well and the thousands of rand she poured into Rhema Alexandra have brought about an ongoing harvest. The seed Annie and Lewis sowed in GOD TV has eternal value and Annie continues to sow into other ministries all the time.

When she visited another orphanage in Malawi and saw that they had no mattresses, instead of criticizing them she had a truckload of mattresses delivered.

"You can't build an oasis of love without giving," Annie insists. "As the saying goes: you can give without loving, but you can't love without giving!"

Annie has an impact on the lives of children every day, but she also empowers her staff. Over the years she has nurtured several "spiritual daughters" whom she encourages to have a dream within her dream. These include Cherie, Linda, Fiona, and Amy.

Annie is the first to admit that she could not do what she does without the support of her volunteer missionaries. "We have been through so much together" she says. "I am so grateful to each and every one of them as we maintain a standard of excellence."

"I could not do what I do today without the missionaries," she says. "They have been called by God to stand alongside me in this great vision. They also understand my commitment to excellence in all we do, as we dedicate our work to the Lord."

> **And whatever you do in word or deed, do all in the Name of the Lord Jesus, giving thanks to God the Father through Him... And whatever you do, do it heartily, as to the Lord and not to men, knowing that from the Lord you will receive the reward of the inheritance.**
>
> (Colossians 3:17, 23)

As executive director, Annie leads by example. Everything she does, she does to the highest possible standard, and she looks only to God for her reward. She is not paid a salary and has to obtain her own support. "I thank God for His provision every day, both at Kondanani and in my personal life. It's an ongoing testimony of His faithfulness, day after day!"

She is grateful to each of the missionaries who have helped her over the years, including Alice, whom she met on a tour of Israel with GOD TV. Alice came for a few months and ending up devoting four years of her life to the work of Kondanani.

"It is impossible to acknowledge all the missionaries, but they have stored up a great reward in heaven," Annie says, "and we continue to trust God for new missionaries to join us and minister to our children, especially men and women who will stay for a number of years because the children get so attached to them and we hate to see them go after just a short while."

Annie and her team continue to build, build, and build without stopping. A pastor at Rhema once said to her, "Annie, there are twenty-four hours in a day; you are already using forty-eight hours, and now you want to work seventy-two?" It was a joke, of course, but she is a hard worker and an inspiration to her team.

It doesn't seem as if anybody retires at Kondanani, especially not Annie, who has already passed the usual milestone of sixty-five. She is inspired by Rita, a seventy-five-year-old woman who came to volunteer at the orphanage for six weeks.

Rita's father was a missionary in Malawi for twenty-five years and her mother for fifteen, and she came to follow in their footsteps. Once a major in the South African Defence Force, she was still very fit and healthy and an example to the other missionaries.

Though they work hard, the missionaries also have fun, sharing laughs at Annie's home each afternoon as they come together for fellowship and when they sometimes play games at the weekends. Scrabble is very popular, but it can get quite heated.

"It's only the clever ones who can play Scrabble," Annie says with a grin. "But imagine this... the school principal, the teacher, and the executive director are left with only a few letters to get out at the end of the game. One of us has an H, another an O, and the third person an E. We agreed 'ho' was a word but what about 'he'? Can you believe it? We even looked it up in the dictionary. We have never laughed so much at our own stupidity, and we will forever be teased about it!"

Another amusing story is of the day Linda sent Annie a text to ask if she could use her room while she was away, but she abbreviated it to "rum". Annie was concerned, as she doesn't allow alcohol on the property; however, she did have a small bottle of rum for cooking. She instructed Cherie to hide it immediately and keep an eye on Linda! Days later when the misunderstanding was cleared up they fell about laughing.

Whenever Annie speaks in public she has a gift for weaving humour into her message, whether it's sharing funny things the children have said or done or talking about her travels. She once got on a train in England and was most impressed by the excellent standard of service as she sipped tea in a luxury coach. "It's amazing how well they treat passengers in this country," she thought to herself, until the conductor pointed out that she was incorrectly seated in first class! She laughed so much that he let her stay where she was for the rest of the journey.

Then there was the time Annie and Cherie visited Chipata in Zambia, where they are looking to start a new orphanage.

As part of gaining government support for the future project, the District Commissioner and the Head of Welfare took them to meet a Zambian king.

"We were surprised that, when we got to 'the Royal Kraal', it was actually a township house and the king was in his overalls!" Annie says with a smile. "Once he had changed and we had been given instructions in royal protocol, we went in to meet him...

"Cherie and I had to bow down on one knee and say '*Bayete, Nkosi*', the traditional salute to an African chief, made famous by Shaka Zulu.

"In simple terms it translates as 'Greetings Great King', but we got it all wrong and it came out as '*Majerie, majerie*' and who knows what that means!"

According to African tradition, they should have taken a live chicken, but Annie was not going to risk having a chicken make a mess of her car, so they stopped at a supermarket and bought a frozen one! Unfortunately, by the time they got to meet "his royal highness", the package had started to defrost.

So there was Cherie, on one knee, presenting the king with a package that was dripping all over the place. He looked at it questioningly. "Oh, it's a chicken!" he finally deduced.

Annie and Cherie had made two cultural blunders in one day, and all they could do was laugh about it.

"The king turned out to be a very nice man who had been to Amsterdam, so we struck up an immediate rapport," says Annie. "He welcomed the idea of Kondanani coming to Zambia, which was great, but I'll never forget that dripping chicken!"

Annie regards Cherie as her successor, the one who will ultimately take over the running of Kondanani. In the meantime she continues to mentor the younger woman, and is grateful she is able to leave the Children's Village in Cherie's capable hands when she visits her children in South Africa or goes overseas on fund-raising trips.

They are always on the lookout for new missionaries who will join the orphanage, people who have a vocation and are self-supporting or funded by a church. ACE teachers are especially in demand.

Cherie has been instrumental in helping Annie deal with adoptions and was a pillar of strength throughout the orphanage's most high-profile adoption, which has been widely publicized in the media, often giving incorrect information. Finally, Annie is able to set the record straight...

36

Mercy for Madonna

MERCY, OUR LITTLE "MOSES"

Kondanani has received its fair share of high-profile visitors over the years, including the State President, but nothing prepared Annie and her team for the media attention surrounding the visit of the world-famous pop diva Madonna, and her adoption of one of the children.

Controversial singer, songwriter, and actress Madonna and her husband at the time, film producer Guy Ritchie, visited Kondanani in 2006. It was a meeting that was facilitated by the government, who were eager to put Malawi on the world map, but to Annie she was simply a mother seeking to adopt a child.

"I knew Madonna was the focus of immense media attention, but I've never been one to be overwhelmed by celebrity. Behind all the hype and the bodyguards, she seemed pretty normal to me. I think she's a different person off stage. One thing I saw for myself: she's a loving mother and her children are well behaved."

Much has been reported in the media about Madonna's adoption of Mercy, some of it inaccurate where Kondanani was concerned, so what actually took place? Annie is one of the few people who really knows.

Adoptions are confidential and Annie never speaks about them in a way that will expose a child or family; however, in this case the media have already covered every last detail.

Annie doesn't disclose anything that isn't public knowledge; she simply shares her perspectives on what happened, to set the record straight.

"Madonna's plan was to adopt two children in 2006, a boy and a girl," Annie says, "but this proved to be difficult because of the criticism levelled against her, fuelled by the world's media."

Looking back at the media coverage, many people were concerned at the time about foreigners taking Malawian children away from their country of birth, and the authorities seemed to be divided on the issue.

Madonna's adoption of little David Banda from an orphanage in Mchinji and her application to adopt Mercy James from Kondanani became the focus of wrangles with the children's extended families and legal proceedings against Mercy's adoption, which absorbed the world's media.

"Madonna soon realized she needed to adopt the children one at a time, and seeing that David was in such poor health she decided to adopt him first," says Annie. "Mercy of course was in very good condition at Kondanani, and Madonna decided she would leave her in our care and come back for her another time."

But how did Madonna come to meet Mercy in the first place?

"In July 2006 I had visitors from the USA, a single man and a couple who seemed interested in adopting a baby," Annie says. "I advised them of the procedure they would have to follow to meet our government's requirements, and they said they would return in October.

"In late September I got a phone call from the Welfare, who told me that an important visitor was coming and that I was to ensure that no strangers were on the property.

"I was unaware at first of who this could be, but I'd seen

a newspaper article and thought it had to be Madonna. Then the media descended on us!

"Mrs Chikhwaza, when is Madonna coming?" This was all the journalists gathering at the gate wanted to know.

"What makes you think Madonna is coming?" Annie asked. "You know more than I do!"

With the growing media interest in Kondanani, Annie realized she would have to be careful how she handled things. "You get the media on your doorstep and they can be vultures," she maintains, "especially when they don't research things properly and their reports carry inaccuracies." She had learned this from bitter experience of all the newspaper articles covering her attack.

One of the journalists, a BBC reporter from South Africa, told Annie that he had waited twenty-seven years for Nelson Mandela to get out of prison so he could easily wait a few days for Madonna to arrive! He didn't have to wait long.

Madonna and Guy Ritchie arrived in a convoy of four-by-four vehicles, accompanied by an entourage of bodyguards. Annie was surprised to see that she had come with the American couple and the man she had met previously.

After brief introductions, Annie took the group to Caring Hands to see the infants. Madonna was thrilled to see the babies and sat down in the play area to cuddle them. Little Mercy James caught her eye.

Newspaper articles correctly reported that Mercy had been brought to Kondanani by the Welfare after her fourteen-year-old mother had died in childbirth and her eighteen-year-old father had fled the village. Her grandmother and uncles were too poor to cope with another mouth to feed, and Annie and her team had cared for her from just a few days old.

It soon became apparent to Annie that it was Madonna who wanted to adopt a child and not the other couple, and that she had set her heart on Mercy. Annie was asked by the Welfare authorities to take the baby girl to the Kumbali Lodge, where Madonna and Guy Ritchie were staying, for a medical check-up.

Annie and Cherie flew with Mercy to the Lodge near Lilongwe, two hundred and fifty miles away. It was a two-thousand-acre private game reserve, where Madonna felt she could be free from media intrusion, and Annie and Cherie were each given a luxurious room for the night, with a little cot especially prepared for the one-year-old girl.

"I can't stop talking about Kondanani!" Guy Ritchie said to Annie. "There is no place like it in Malawi, and I've seen quite a few orphanages. What is it that motivates you?" he asked.

"What an opportunity to share the gospel," Annie thought to herself. She says: "I had about eight people listening to me: Madonna, Guy, their bodyguards, and others. I spent a couple of hours telling them my story and of course intertwining it with the Christian message.

"I shared how God had called me to start Kondanani and all the things that had happened to deter me. I told them how the Lord had saved me from the attack on my life and how I'd overcome many obstacles by His grace.

"I testified to how God had called me as a teenager but how I didn't understand what it meant to be a Christian, and how I finally realized I didn't have to become a nun to serve God. Finally, I shared how I'd given my life to Jesus at nineteen and how He had transformed my life.

"Each one of those people sitting at that table was given the gospel message loud and clear, as I spoke about our need for a saviour and that salvation is found only in Jesus. So none of them can ever say they didn't hear the good news!"

In 2008 the Minister of Social Welfare phoned Annie to

inform her that Madonna was returning to Malawi to adopt Mercy. Annie was once again instructed to take her to the Lodge while they awaited the outcome of the appeal.

Annie had shown Mercy a newspaper article with a picture of Madonna and her children, and the three-year-old girl recognized her immediately. "Mommy, mommy!" she cried, which pleased Madonna no end.

Of course Guy Ritchie was not with Madonna this time, as the couple had divorced. "I missed him," Annie says. "He is such a nice man!" However, she was introduced to Madonna's children, Lourdes (eleven at the time), Rocco (eight), and her newly adopted Malawian son, David (also three).

"David and Mercy took an instant liking to each other; they were great friends from the beginning," says Annie. "They played together so well, it was as if they had known each other all their lives."

Annie left Mercy, Madonna, and the children to spend the afternoon together, and when she came back, the world-famous recording artist was in Annie's room singing to Mercy. She had given her a bath and was putting her to sleep with a lullaby. "Madonna is very sweet as a mother and I could see it wasn't an act."

Though the Malawian Social Welfare had facilitated the adoption, the courts were not happy about another high-profile adoption by a foreigner, and they initially refused Madonna's application. They ruled that she hadn't been in the country for long enough and Mercy had to remain at Kondanani.

Madonna finally won the appeal case and was free to adopt Mercy and whisk her away in her private jet to a new life. It was an adoption that Annie would be criticized for, on account of Madonna's lifestyle and beliefs, but Annie sees it as an opportunity for God to work in the pop star's family.

"You know what, Mercy is our little Moses," she asserts. "She was dedicated to the Lord, and just wait and see... I believe with all my heart that God will use that child in the life of Madonna."

> So the woman conceived and bore a son. And when she saw that he was a beautiful child, she hid him three months. But when she could no longer hide him, she took an ark of bulrushes... put the child in it, and laid it in the reeds by the river's bank.
>
> And his sister stood afar off, to know what would be done to him. Then the daughter of Pharaoh came down to bathe at the river ... and when she saw the ark among the reeds, she sent her maid to get it. And when she opened it, she saw the child, and behold, the baby wept. So she had compassion on him, and said, "This is one of the Hebrews' children."
>
> ...So the woman took the child and nursed him. And the child grew, and she brought him to Pharaoh's daughter, and he became her son. So she called his name Moses...
>
> (Exodus 2:1–11)

Annie was concerned about allowing Mercy to go to a non-Christian home and she wrestled with the situation in prayer. Ultimately she had to comply with the Malawian authorities, and she was inspired by the story of Moses. He had been brought up by the daughter of Pharaoh in all the ways of Egypt, but he still became the deliverer of his people.

"Just as the children of Christians can turn their backs on God, so the children of unbelievers can turn their faces towards God," Annie believes. "Many Christians have come out of ungodly homes; Mercy is dedicated to the Lord and I am convinced she will make a difference in Madonna's life and in the lives of her Malawian relatives."

Madonna's appeal concerning Mercy's adoption was the focus of a documentary by Britain's Channel 4 television station. Entitled *Madonna and Mercy: What Really Happened*, it was presented by Jacques Peretti, an investigative reporter who questioned Madonna's motives for adopting children in Malawi. He also probed into her links to Kabbalah, a cultish philosophy based on Jewish mysticism.

The documentary presented Kondanani in a positive light; however, the well-spoken reporter got his wires crossed as he incorrectly attributed the orphanage's success to Madonna's support.

"Although the orphanage was founded and is currently run by Christians, Madonna's Kabbalah charity is an important donor of influence here," he erroneously stated.

"Kondanani is five-star orphanage; what they are doing here is extraordinary. It's a centre of excellence. A fantastic level of care is been given to these children.

"If this could be rolled out across the whole of Malawi you can see why the government are prepared for Madonna to carpet-bomb the country with aid because this could be in every village across Malawi. The government can't afford it. Maybe the price they will have to pay is to buy into Madonna's loony religion as well."

While Annie was pleased that Kondanani was seen as an example of how an orphanage should be run, she was furious that the documentary had linked its funding to Kabbalah, and understandably Konandani's true supporters were equally upset.

"This documentary led some people mistakenly to believe Kondanani is what it is because of Madonna, but that's so obviously not true. Especially when people hear how God has provided so miraculously for this ministry.

"I was also criticized for allowing the adoption to go through, but ultimately I had no say in the matter and I would never accept money from any donor that came with strings attached.

"I made this very clear to Channel 4 when they grilled me about it. I told them we weren't receiving funding from Madonna or her charitable organization in Malawi, but they chose to broadcast their own conclusions because it fitted their storyline.

"They couldn't believe that an orphanage could be as successful as Kondanani without celebrity backing. But they completely missed the point: Kondanani has succeeded purely by God's grace and His provision."

Despite his one major error, Jacques did capture some insightful glimpses into life at Kondanani and the adoption process. This is an extract from a piece he wrote in the *Guardian* newspaper of 12 June 2009:

As far as I know, since the Madonna story blew up, no Western journalist has ever been allowed in Mercy's orphanage; I guess I am lucky. Inside, I am taken to Mercy's large communal nursery room, freshly painted and hanging with kids' pictures and messages about God's love. Children run hysterically up to the white Westerner, and I find myself subconsciously deciding which would be cutest to adopt...

I am directed round the immaculate dormitories and play areas and dining hall and crèche, walking down pristine paths bordered with stones and flowers, and intermittently nodding to enthusiastic volunteers. It is all absolutely and undeniably fantastic.

Everywhere across Malawi, children sit quietly by the roadside, waiting for life to do something terrible to them. Here, they run up to you speaking perfect English, each more impossibly charming and clever and funny and take-home-able than the last.

I ask a group of children a little older than Mercy where she is. "She's gone," a little boy in glasses says. "We are sad, because she was our friend." Would these children also like to be adopted? "We would like to leave and come back as a nurse," they say. One girl says she would like to be a presenter "on GOD TV".

Annie wonders how Mercy's life will turn out. What will she become? She and her brother David are growing up in the limelight, with the world's press watching their every move. They now speak English, Italian, and French but still have a tutor to retain their Chichewa. This is a positive sign, and Annie is convinced Mercy will not forsake God or her Malawian people.

"Mercy's family still see her as their next hope," Annie confides. "They told me that her mother was a bright student and how they joined together financially to send her to high school. She was their hope for the future, but she fell pregnant and died in childbirth. They agreed to allow Mercy to be adopted so she could have the chances her mother lost. They are still counting on her.

"For me she will always be our little Moses. We let her go into the world, but we are trusting that all things will work together for good."

During the *Madonna and Mercy* documentary, Jacques also showed "The Door of Hope": "Outside the orphanage I see something that stopped me dead, a hole in the wall where babies can be left anonymously.

"You put your baby in and the buzzer goes off; they hear it and come and fetch your baby. It is a portal to survival. Do you keep your child with you in a life of poverty? Or do you put them through the hatch, lose them for ever, but give them a chance for a better life?"

Ultimately Annie hopes to give every child a better life, whether it is through adoption or whether they stay at Kondanani until they are adults.

37

My African dream

From her time spent caring for the people of Alexandra Township in South Africa to becoming the executive director of Kondanani, Annie Chikhwaza has been committed to eradicating poverty.

"I have a dream of an Africa where people are flourishing," she says, "because poverty is a curse. I want to see the African continent come to a different way of thinking, where communities are not dependent on handouts, but where people are empowered. We need to envision the people of Africa with a new mindset, helping them to live beyond the cultural traditions that keep them ensnared."

Annie hopes to achieve this by raising a new generation of African leaders from among the children of Kondanani, whom she expects to help transform the nation of Malawi, whether they remain at the orphanage or are adopted. She also dedicates herself to her staff members, mentoring and encouraging them so that they are equipped to influence this new generation of leaders.

Annie also travels internationally, speaking at charity events and in churches, challenging people to think differently about aid to Africa. She wants to see donors who are committed to working alongside the African people by investing in projects that are not throwing money at a need, but teaching local communities to find their own way of meeting that need.

"The world is pouring money into Africa to develop the continent, yet many of the traditions and cultural practices of the African people keep them underdeveloped," she observes. "We have to address the cultural issues that do not promote health and well-being.

"We need to come up with solutions for inadequate shelter, unhealthy sanitation, subsistence living, alcoholism, and fear of witchcraft and revenge. We need to lead the way, humbly showing people a better way of life, and encouraging them to become more entrepreneurial, not existing purely for themselves but making a greater contribution to society."

Annie believes the church has a vital role to play in the development of Africa, by helping to overturn cultural apprehension. "Many Africans are fearful of their ancestors and live lives that are steeped in witchcraft. We need spirit-filled pastors who will demonstrate that the power of God is greater than the power of evil."

She also questions the logic of Western aid organizations which, in their political correctness, encourage cultural tradition even when it is detrimental to social development. "Why send medical doctors if witch doctors are able to cure diseases and why build schools if children don't need to be educated?" she asks.

"Why should orphans sleep on a mat because the poor do? And yet we get into a bed with sheets and blankets. We need to do to others what we expect should be done to us!" she insists.

"I think it's critically important to make an investment in the lives of our children. The investment I make is my life, as do the others who work at Kondanani and the donors who give money. When one invests in something, there has to be a return on that investment – a worthwhile return from a worthwhile investment.

"The media cannot understand that we as an orphanage can have such high standards. Because we're an orphanage, they think we're meant to be poor. But poverty is not what God wants for our children.

"Unfortunately, begging is still the mindset of many Malawians. 'Give me, give me, give me' is definitely not my mindset! I believe in trusting that God will provide, and doing everything with excellence, 'as if for the Lord'. We are also committed to sowing and reaping, which is why we continue to see God's blessing."

Kondanani now has an increasing annual turnover, as the orphanage takes on more and more children. "I run it like a business," Annie admits, "but I don't run the children like a business!" she adds emphatically.

The orphanage employs a full-time accountant to ensure its financial affairs are in order. "Anybody can come at any moment and check the books," Annie assures her critics. "We make sure that everything is done according to the laws of Malawi, and everything is above board."

Once a successful group credit manager in South Africa and the owner of her own credit management company, Annie knows how to manage money, and Kondanani has no debt whatsoever. Everything is paid for in cash, otherwise it doesn't happen. Annie has certainly made good use of the business skills she picked up in Johannesburg while working to help finance her ministry in Alexandra.

On the one hand she is a loving mother to more children than an average mother could imagine, and on the other hand she sees things in practical business terms. "I want to see a return on my investment!" she declares.

"When we receive a child at Kondanani I hold that child in my arms and I think to myself, what do I want to be the outcome of that child's life? If I'm going to pour my energies into the life of that child, if our missionaries are going to invest their skills in that child, and if our donors are going to spend their money contributing to his or her well-being, then what do we want back?

"We expect a good return. When that child grows up, I want to hear them say, 'Mommy, I had a happy childhood; I know Jesus Christ as my saviour and I had a good education.' When we hear that from each child in our care, then we will have achieved our objective."

Annie believes this return will come from each of the children in her care, and also from those who have been adopted. "Adoption is the answer to abortion," she reiterates. "By going through with her pregnancy, a mother is at least making some investment in that child's life, and adoption takes this further."

Annie explains that if a child is never visited by family members, or has none, then Kondanani can apply to the Malawian authorities for an adoption to take place.

"We work closely with the Malawian Ministry of Social Welfare and all our adoptions are done through the courts, with the legal consent of surviving family members," she insists.

Even though Kondanani offers to cover the travel costs of the children's relatives to allow them to visit them, the majority are ultimately abandoned, clearing the way for adoption, but most adoptive parents want to adopt babies.

With regard to the media furore over Mercy's adoption, and the wider issue of foreigners adopting Malawian children, Annie believes no child should be denied a loving home if that option is available; however, this should be done within the framework of the laws of the nation.

She works closely with a reputable Dutch adoption agency that carefully screens prospective parents, who, if they are successful in adopting a child from Kondanani, pay nothing but the necessary administrative costs. Even so, the number of adoptions Kondanani has arranged is very small in comparison with the number of children the orphanage cares for.

When *Sunday Times* journalist Dan McDougall gatecrashed a staff breakfast at Annie's home one Saturday morning, she was reluctant to talk to him, as she did not want any more publicity concerning Madonna. But he insisted he was investigating good and bad aid to Africa, and Annie agreed to talk to him if he would wait until the breakfast was over.

His article in *The Sunday Times* of 19 June 2011 was entitled "Ambition Impossible" and was critical of Madonna's adoption of Mercy and the termination of her project to build a school in the country, while acknowledging that "there are successful orphanages in Malawi" and referring to "Annie Chikhwaza, who operates the highly regarded Kondanani Children's Village orphanage".

An extract from Dan McDougall's report reads:

With fundraising comes accountability, this raises a number of concerns, which are the concerns of the NGO workers on the ground, including a woman called Annie Chikhwaza, who runs a wonderful orphanage, a fantastic orphanage called Kondanani, which in fact was an inspiration for Madonna. Annie told me on camera that she was very concerned about celebrities starting charities and then spreading themselves very thin and therefore losing control.

Annie's orphanage is successful because she controls it with a rod of iron, every single penny is accounted for. That is why it is a successful charity because in Africa you have to keep a tight watch on things, you have to be constantly vigilant... Donors who give money need to know exactly what has happened to it, that such projects come with accountability.

Annie does not need an internationally acclaimed newspaper to vouch for Kondanani's credibility, although this is a bonus; the fruit of her labour speaks for itself, backed up by the orphanage's accounts.

Kondanani has also received Malawian government recognition. In a nation that has about a million orphans in a population of twelve million, the authorities look to Kondanani as an example of how to run a children's home. "The Welfare see us as a model orphanage and often send social workers to us to see how we operate, so they can learn from our example," Annie says.

Annie also shares this example overseas, inspiring international audiences with her down-to-earth, no-nonsense approach, her extraordinary testimony of what God has done in her life, and her humorous delivery.

When she spoke at the River Church in Exeter in the UK, her message had a similar effect on the congregation as the time when she was given only ten minutes at Living Word Church in Johannesburg. The pastor, Michael Meyers, was moved to take up an offering for Annie at the end of the service and the church has been supporting the orphanage ever since, through its "Africa Night" fund-raisers.

"Annie's story is like dynamite as you hear miracle after miracle," said Pastor Michael. "She was left for dead, bleeding from the wounds of a machete, and it's a miracle she is here with us today.

"I believe that this is the time for African people to rise up and that ministry that is a friend of Africa will be blessed. This offering is the oil from our alabaster box, which we are pouring on the children of Africa that Annie is caring for.

"We pray God's blessing on this awesome work. To think that Annie has built what is really a small town – we thank God that we can have the privilege of participating in this ministry."

Annie truly believes that Africa is ripe for revival and that the next major revival in the church is going to come from there. Africa is a continent with huge resources, not least of which are its people. There may be many challenges and many obstacles to be overcome, but Annie testifies that God can turn even the most desperate situations around. What He has done in her life He can surely do in the lives of others.

"We may not be able to solve every problem," Annie acknowledges, "but by bringing up a new generation of leaders we can make a positive contribution to the future of Africa, a worthwhile investment, and there is no doubt that the lives of our children will have a ripple effect and we will see a great return on all we have invested."

Annie and Cherie and the team at Kondanani see Africa as a continent with untapped potential, but most of all they recognize that it needs the life-changing message of Jesus Christ, and the transformation that only prayer can bring. The missionaries have a prayer meeting every Friday morning at six o'clock, when they pray for the children and their needs as well as for all the orphanage's donors, from Cross International to GOD TV to personal sponsors.

"Father, I pray that you will help us to meet the many needs of our children," is Annie's constant prayer. "Help us to be the arms of a father and of a mother, that we may embrace each child in the name of Jesus. Show us the talents each child has, that we may train them up in the way they should go.

"Thank you for providing for each child beyond just having their basic needs met. Thank you for seeing our desire to do the best for our children. We're investing in the lives of these children, in this country, so that leaders will arise to take this country in a godly direction. We're going to see great things in the lives of our children!"

Cherie echoes Annie's commitment to this cause. "As a team, we want always to feel and act as parents towards our children, and to do the very best for each one. Not as an institution, not even as a ministry, but as parents, loving and nurturing each child individually, and it is our prayer that all who support us would share this approach."

38

A dream within a dream

DWELLING TOGETHER IN UNITY!

Annie Chikhwaza is a born leader, but she has also worked hard to develop her leadership skills and overcome the insecurity of her youth. God has given her a talent for breaking new ground. She established a thriving church in Alexandra Township and, together with Lewis, built up the ministry of Kondanani, which is touching so many lives in so many ways today.

She is an ordained minister of the church through Faith Christian Fellowship (FCF) in Tulsa, Oklahoma, USA. She and Lewis visited the United States in 2001, where she was ordained by Reverend Buddy Harrison, and she has attended the annual FCF Conference in Europe.

In addition to bringing up her own four children single-handedly, Annie's career in credit management equipped her perfectly to fulfil her lifelong dream of helping others. She has been responsible for helping to start many entrepreneurial ventures and is an insatiable builder!

The architect of the buildings at Kondanani, she has indeed built a small town, with herself as mayor! Will she run for parliament? She has been asked to consider becoming an MP, like her late husband, but her heart is not in politics. She is committed to nurturing a future generation of Malawian leaders who will shape the destiny of the country.

Running such a large organization, with approximately one hundred and fifty paid staff and several volunteers, is an enormous responsibility. Annie is committed to building this team of faithful men and women and fostering efficient managers who still need her direction and support, but whom she expects to use their own initiative.

"For a vision to be successful, it's so important to have other leaders who will live out their vision within your wider one. This is like having a dream of your own, to achieve something significant within someone else's wider dream!" she says.

"I don't want to sit down with every missionary every day and tell them what to do. I want them to function like a visionary within their own department as well – in line with my vision, but at the same time adding their own ideas and bringing their unique talents, abilities, and gifts.

"As a leader I see the need to give others the freedom to contribute in this way and to encourage them as they step out and say, 'Go for it!' This instils confidence in the team. Cherie is my right-hand woman and I rely on her completely to make the correct decisions that affect her areas of responsibility; the same with our farmer who needs to make on-the-spot decisions regarding the livestock.

"Linda and Fiona are examples of women who came to Kondanani with feelings of insecurity, and I've seen such a transformation in both of them. They are now confident women who can achieve things they never thought possible.

"Fiona has moved on after seven years of faithful service, and Linda was with us for five years and still helps me with Kondanani in the UK, and she comes out to the orphanage every now and then to help us when needed. It's wonderful to be able to leave her to her own devices and stand back expectantly and see what she's able to deliver.

"I was amazed when Fiona devised a system to track the progress of our school monitors. I couldn't have come up with that, but Fiona did! It's amazing how people can surprise you when you give them the flexibility and authority to be creative and find their own solutions."

"Annie is good at building people up and I grew so much in my faith and became far more confident in myself during my time at Kondanani," says Linda. "She is a great team-builder who helps people maximize their talents and abilities. She inspired me to study the word of God and taught me how to take a Bible study. This has enabled me to stand up for my faith a lot more!"

Annie has reached peaks in her life she would never have dreamed possible as a teenager. Given the rejection and the abuse she faced, how did she ever develop her own self-confidence? How did her leadership skills develop?

"I think that leadership is something you are born with, to an extent... Going back to my childhood, I kind of knew how to be in charge, but leadership is also something that can be developed as we begin to see ourselves the way God sees us.

"I had such low self-esteem at one time, but I trained myself to look at how God sees me and today I am constantly mentoring others to do the same. It doesn't matter so much how you see yourself or how others see you. What is important is knowing how God sees you."

During her time at Rhema Bible Church Annie learned the value of finding Bible verses that are relevant to her life, and affirming the promises of God in every situation facing her:

I'm the head and not the tail,
I'm above and not beneath...

I am seated in heavenly places with Christ Jesus...
Greater is He that is within me
than he who is in the world...
I am more than a conqueror...

I am blessed coming in and blessed going out...

I haven't been given a spirit of fear, but a spirit of love and
of power and of a sound mind... I have the mind of Christ!

These were just some of the scriptural themes that would circulate in Annie's head from day to day as she renewed her mind from the Bible and built up her faith so she could set out and do new things for the kingdom.

"Approval addiction is a huge problem in our society," Annie observes. "People want to be liked, so they just go with the flow. You can never build your self-esteem that way because you always hold back, to avoid confrontation. You have to develop the courage to stand for what you believe in and inspire others to do so as well.

"So I teach all the time on seeing yourself the way God sees you. And it is amazing how He sees us as believers. He sees us as forgiven, cleansed, with a unique purpose in life. We look at ourselves and say, 'I'm such a bad person; I don't have much value; I'm no good.' Who says so? You may say that, but does God say that? Definitely not!

"Every morning at Kondanani we take God's word to pieces and it is the best time of our lives because it really invigorates us. We find out who we are in Christ, and this causes the life of God to come alive in us. The 'God kind of life' is what we need in our lives."

When fostering missionary leaders at Kondanani, Annie first and foremost wants to know that they truly are "sent ones", called by God, that they have a hunger to go deeper in their faith, and that they have a genuine love for the children. "Commitment to the vision and leadership capabilities are also important," she says.

Leadership is not without its challenges, and Annie has had to overcome many, from the loss of key members of staff who have moved on to occasionally dealing with workers who have been caught stealing. She is also committed to ensuring that a Christian moral code is followed by all, according to the perimeters set out in the Bible.

"When you lose a valued staff member it can feel like a betrayal, but if their heart wasn't truly in what they were doing, then they weren't the right person for the job, so I bless them and move on," says Annie. "It is also very difficult to deal with workers who have been dishonest; sometimes there is mercy, but unfortunately I also have to dismiss people. That comes with being a leader.

"One of the problems we face is women volunteers coming from abroad and falling in love with Malawian men. They think that, because I had a successful cross-cultural marriage, it will work just as well for them, but my situation with Lewis was exceptional because he was older and not governed by culture. God was also clearly in our relationship.

"Some people think cross-cultural marriages never really work and can't be what God wants, but I have proved that is not true; yet often they *don't* work – we see couples getting married and then getting divorced because the cultural differences are so great, so I always encourage the women that I mentor to be very careful in choosing a husband.

"I feel responsible for the missionaries at Kondanani and I keep telling them that. I know what it's like to have a good marriage and I know what it's like to have a bad one. And when it's bad, it's awful. So I urge the single girls to be cautious, and the same with the single men: they have to know that the woman they marry is God's choice to be their wife.

"I am very aware that, if the enemy can't get you one way, he will often send you a partner who will cause you to fall from grace, and I don't want to see that happen to our staff, especially our missionaries, who are called by God."

Annie believes that being a leader is all about setting an example. "You can only lead by example," she maintains. "I cannot expect others to do things that I'm not prepared to do myself! I'm also committed to bringing the team together in unity; this is very important, this is why we meet together often and we sometimes go away for 'team-building weekends' where we relax together and have fun."

> **Behold, how good and how pleasant it is**
> **for brethren to dwell together in unity!**
>
> (Psalm 133:1)

Annie's typical day is jam-packed! She gets up at quarter to five each morning for a time of prayer, followed by a Bible study with the missionaries at six; then it's a shower at seven and breakfast at half past seven and the day unfolds with one thing after another, from management meetings to overseeing building sites.

Whether sitting talking to her project manager Mr Mediane on the *khonde* of her home or going over the cash flow with her accountant, Stoney, at head office in the Madalo Village, Annie exemplifies a dedicated work ethic.

There are endless trips to the market to bargain for fruit and vegetables or into town to buy everything from children's clothes to building materials. Annie and Cherie and the other missionaries enjoy these excursions, especially when they have time to grab a bite to eat. A favourite destination is the rustic outdoor buffet known as "The Tent", which serves a variety of local dishes, including spicy chicken and *nsima*.

Lunch in Malawi is at noon and is the main meal of the day. Annie often cooks meals for all the missionaries, especially at the weekend. "My house is everyone's house!" she says. She and the missionaries get together on her *khonde* each afternoon at five o'clock to have tea and cake and to share fellowship and discuss the events of the day, especially amusing stories of what the children have said or done.

Annie is able to access the GOD Channel by satellite in her sitting room and she and the missionaries often watch the live events, helping them to keep up to date with what God is doing across the world. She also loves music, and Classic FM can often be heard playing in the background, bringing Western orchestral sounds into a remote African setting. You would never think it was remote, sitting in Annie's comfortable lounge, but it is.

It is here where she likes to relax in her favourite navy-blue armchair, surrounded by photographs of her children's weddings and her ten grandchildren. Lewis's photo is positioned in the centre of the mantelpiece, and, although his elegant upright chair is sadly empty, his influence remains everywhere.

It's early to bed for all at Kondanani, because there are new dreams to be dreamed and more busy days on the horizon, with fresh challenges to face as Annie and her team forge ahead with their far-reaching vision.

What Annie has created here is a little bit of heaven on earth. Like Moses, she has led the children of Kondanani out of the desert into an oasis of love – where miraculous provision does indeed seem like manna from heaven. A "possibility thinker", like Joshua and Caleb, she has fearlessly brought them into a promised land.

"With God all things are possible," Annie teaches, knowing that this is invariably dependent on teamwork. She is grateful that, just as Moses had Aaron and Hur to hold up his hands, she has a dedicated team beside her to fulfil the dream God gave her to build a refuge for children, where people truly love one another.

39

Our fight for Africa's children

In February 2008 the Dutch television station *Evangelische Omroep* (EO) broadcast a documentary on Annie's life entitled *Mem in Malawi* ("Mother of Malawi"). The film is a remarkable dramatization of her life story, highlighting her transition from rebellious teenager, through suicidal young nurse smoking a cigarette, to an enterprising young woman, transformed by her relationship with Jesus Christ.

Annie grew tearful when she recalled the moment Jesus became real to her in that service with Brother Andrew some fifty years ago. "I never looked back from that day on," she sobbed, as the video showed a black and white photograph of the famous evangelist preaching in Holland. "Jesus completely changed my life!"

The documentary also recreates the turmoil of the attack on her life – the shattering of glass, the knives, and the axes – and shows her lying in hospital with a black eye and a swollen face, but it also shows the immense good that can be done by the power of forgiveness.

God took a self-harming teenager and made her life count in ways she could never have imagined. Annie's fight to die was turned into a fight to live and a fight to let others live. It became a struggle first for her own children, then to reach out to Lewis's children, and ultimately a fight for a better life for Africa's children. "Will you join me in this quest today?" she asks.

Mem in Malawi shows Annie bathing a baby boy named Earnest, singing a lullaby to him in Dutch, dressing his little body, and combing his air. There is joy and laughter as she kisses the little boy, but more tears when she relates how his mother passed away.

Annie anoints the child's head with oil as she dedicates him to God: "Jesus says, 'Whoever receives a little one like this, in My name, receives Me!'" she quotes, as missionaries sing gently in the background. "Lord, your beautiful face is all I seek; when Your eyes are on this child, Your grace abounds to me..."

Annie starts to pray: "We thank you, Father, that you have brought Earnest to us, that he does not have to suffer hunger, poverty, and sickness because he has come into our arms and we have received him as we would receive You. Thank you for this precious gift you have given into our lives."

The documentary records that Earnest is Kondanani's one hundred and twenty-seventh child. Yet he is not a number; he is called by name, but the reality is that in a nation of one million orphans there are thousands just like Earnest who need to be cared for. Might you be able to help them?

How can you join Annie's fight for the children of Africa? You can share her wider vision within your own vision in several practical ways. Please tell your family and friends about the plight of the children of Malawi; share this book with them; consider making a financial investment in Kondanani to see a return that has eternal value. Maybe you could sponsor one of the children monthly. If you have a missionary vocation, you might consider becoming a volunteer at the orphanage, or, if you are able and feel led, even think about adopting one of the babies.

Adoption is a long, involved process but it is immensely rewarding. In November 2008, an episode of EO's *A Good Start* focused on a young couple, Jan and Esther Ekkel, who had been waiting for a baby for several years. Through the efforts of a Dutch adoption agency and Kondanani in Malawi, the big day finally came and they were told they had been assigned a son, Chimwemwe, in Africa.

A camera crew followed them to Kondanani, where they met their child for the first time. It was a joyful, emotional experience as the Ekkels experienced life at the orphanage and waited for the legalities of the adoption procedure to be finalized. This took several weeks, but they got to take their son, renamed Thomas Chimwemwe Ekkel, on a holiday to the beautiful shores of Lake Malawi.

They also made a moving visit to Thomas's grandmother, to see his birthplace and visit the grave of his mother, before saying goodbye. They were overwhelmed by the poverty of the village – the tin plates, pots and pans on the dusty floor. It was a sad day, but also a day filled with hope for Thomas's future.

"Your painful years of waiting are over; your dream has become a reality," Annie told the parents as they left. "God has blessed you with a beautiful little boy with a lovely nature. It's amazing that he has become a part of you so quickly. We have to say goodbye but it's not a painful goodbye. We thank your for being a part of us while you were here."

Not everybody can adopt a child, but everybody can help in some way. Annie's heart and the vision of Kondanani are powerfully illustrated by these words from the book of Job:

> I delivered the poor who cried out,
> The fatherless and the one who had no helper.
> The blessing of a perishing man came upon me,
> And I caused the widow's heart to sing for joy...
> I was eyes to the blind,

And I was feet to the lame.
I was a father to the poor,
And I searched out the case that I did not know.
I broke the fangs of the wicked,
And plucked the victim from his teeth.

(Job 29:12–17)

Will you become eyes to the blind, feet to the lame, and a father or mother to the poor? Will you cause a widow's heart to sing for joy, and help those who have no help? Together we can pluck the victim from the teeth of death as we fight for precious African lives.

Fighting poverty is not easy; there are many obstacles to be overcome. In a very poor country there are always those who will break in and steal. Kondanani has had several robberies in which various items have been stolen, but thankfully only two where the lives of the missionaries were put in jeopardy and some of the women were tied up and threatened with rape.

Annie was thrown onto a bed with a gun pressed to her head, but was rescued just in time. Linda was pushed against a wall at gunpoint but the perpetrator was disturbed when she cried out to God for help and he disappeared into the night. Cherie's clothing was ripped to shreds, but when she told her attackers they would have to deal with her God if they hurt her, they stopped.

God has protected the missionaries of Kondanani, and in the most serious of incidents Cherie was able to get away by actually driving through the locked gates and calling the police. Later that night the same burglars murdered an elderly couple in the neighbourhood, a horrific tragedy that showed what these men were capable of.

It was after this that Annie had the Kondanani Village, Madalo Village, Caring Hands, and the Christian Academy fenced off separately, with electric fences. She still trusts in the power of Psalm 91 as the best possible insurance policy, but she is also aware of the need to provide practical protection for her staff and the children.

One can hardly imagine who would steal from orphans. Just as it is hard to understand how anybody could destroy a nursery school. When you are feeding the poor, and praying for people, and ministering to their needs, and seeing miracles, you would think that people would assist you rather than try to drive you away.

Annie has had to overcome being reviled and put it behind her. One of the hardest things she has had to deal with is being falsely accused, but the same thing happened to Jesus. How does she overcome false accusation? "I have the word of God so firmly planted inside me," she says. "That has always been my only weapon."

> **"No weapon formed against you shall prosper, And every tongue which rises against you in judgment You shall condemn.**
> **This is the heritage of the servants of the Lord,**
> **And their righteousness is from Me," says the Lord.**
>
> (Isaiah 54:17)

"We have to be humble before God, so when I am accused of something, I think about it and ask if there is any truth in it. If there isn't, I condemn every word that has been spoken against me, because it is the devil who is the father of lies and I trust that God will vindicate me."

Widowhood is another burden Annie has to bear. She remembers how Lewis would bring her coffee at five o'clock each morning and how each day he would tell her, "I love you, Mommy". She misses his voice calling her in the house, "Where are you, Mommy?" There are still tears sometimes, so how does she cope with them? My joy is replenished in giving," Annie shares.

Sometimes a leader has to walk alone, especially when it comes to cash flow, and there are times when Annie feels she is up against the wall financially. "I have nearly two hundred mouths to feed, so please don't ever let me hear you complain about how much it costs to feed a family of four!"

Seriously, God always provides, but there are times when Annie's faith is tested. "I never tell the staff if there is a financial problem because I don't want them to have to worry; that is not their responsibility.

"One day we had less than thirty pounds left in our account and I thought to myself, 'What are we going to do?' But I stopped and prayed. I said to God, 'This is not my project; this is Your project, Lord', and I could feel the faith welling up inside me.

"Ten minutes later I had a phone call saying that some visitors had come to Caring Hands and donated clothes for the babies and left a cheque. Later that day an American group came to the Village unexpectedly, with bags of food and clothes, and they gave me an envelope of cash. When I told them what an answer to prayer this was, they insisted on giving me even more funds!"

Annie is grateful for God's continual provision. "Air Malawi put an article about Kondanani in their in-flight magazine and a wealthy American businessman saw it and sent us twenty-five thousand dollars, which was exceptional. A church in the Netherlands later gave me a cheque for thirty thousand euros. We thank God for these great gifts, but we're also grateful for the charities that support us regularly, such as GOD TV, and the churches who give to us so faithfully – not to mention every individual who sponsors a child."

So much has happened since Annie stood with that first HIV/AIDS baby in her arms. So many lives have been saved since Rory Alec had a vision of Annie caring for the children of Africa and heard God telling him to help her. What does the future now hold for Annie and Kondanani?

Rory believes Kondanani will continue to expand. "I see this extraordinary work having a major influence in Africa," he says. Rory last visited the orphanage in December 2011 as part of a series of *Behind the Screens* specials to celebrate GOD TV's tenth anniversary of broadcasting to Africa.

"Thirteen years ago I was privileged to join with Lewis and Annie Chikhwaza in breaking ground here at Kondanani, and we now see the most incredible progress. There was nothing built then; now look at all the children's homes and the schools – it's amazing. There is everything here that a child needs to grow and flourish.

"What Annie has achieved is extraordinary, and it has been a joy for Wendy and me and GOD TV to support this phenomenal work, enabling these children to thrive. Kondanani is an oasis of love and tranquillity, a place of nurturing for children from newborns to teenagers. It's a place of great blessing, fruitfulness, and divine provision. I'm moved as I see such ingenuity, entrepreneurship, and the favour of God."

GOD TV's Head of Production, Graeme Spencer, was deeply moved as he directed the *Behind the Screens* shoot. "I first met Shepherd, Maggie, and Junior eleven years ago, when they were babies; now look what incredible people they have become," he said. "Shepherd wants to be a cameraman, Maggie a teacher, and Junior a news reporter!

"I remember the ground-breaking ceremony; now there is a new nursery, new schools, a clinic, and so much else. I broke down and cried as I had not been back since then and was emotionally wrecked by what God has done."

Annie will be seventy on 26 May 2014, yet she has plans to build further homes at Kondanani and her next major project is to build a conference centre overlooking "Lake Chikhwaza" that will accommodate five hundred people for various functions and thus generate income for the charity, as well as doubling up as a school hall for the children.

She and Cherie are also looking to start again from scratch in Zambia! They have visited the central African nation and everything is in place if they can find the right couple to run it. They met the local chief and he has given permission for them to set up a new Kondanani modelled on the existing village. Whatever the next step is for Kondanani in Africa, it's clear that Annie will not be retiring in the foreseeable future...

"I know God has a lot more in store for us; my spiritual ears are open to hear what the Spirit has to say," says Annie. "I have His divine instruction, so what else do I need?"

> **"And I was hungry and you gave Me food, I was thirsty and you gave Me drink, I was a stranger and you took Me in, I was naked and you clothed Me, I was sick and you visited Me, I was in prison and you came to Me."**
>
> (Matthew 25:35–37)

This is God's challenge to every believer...

40

Victory: My story

THANKS BE TO GOD, WHO CAUSES US

TO TRIUMPH

Throughout this book you have read about challenges, obstacles, and seemingly insurmountable problems. These have ranged from overcoming guilt and shame to surviving the hopelessness of abusive relationships. You have read about the heartache of false accusations and the threat of having one's life snatched away.

There have been times of immense grief as loved ones have passed away, causing many tears of sorrow. There have also been practical examples of the trials of everyday life. These are some of the hurdles that most people face at one time or another, barriers that stand in their way, hindering their progress, and, in the worst cases, extinguishing all hope.

It's clear that there can be no victory in life if there is nothing to overcome. Remember Annie's words: "Life is an obstacle race; sometimes you have to go over, sometimes you have to go through the obstacle, and sometimes you need to find your way around it. Whatever the case, just because you are faced with an obstacle does not mean you should stop or give up!"

Annie has spoken frankly about how she has found light in the darkest of situations of her life and how she was able to persevere because of her faith in God. "Victory is my story," she says, "and it can be your story too."

Every person can find a measure of success through their natural abilities, but real victory, genuine triumph, lies in only one place... in God. He has called us to be "more than conquerors" through His Son, Jesus Christ, and it is He who can give you the inner resilience to keep on going.

The Bible says that Jesus stands at the door of our heart and knocks. He promises that if we just open that door He will come into our lives – if we let Him. This is the greatest "Door of Hope" you could imagine!

God loves you and has a plan for your life. If you open the door of your heart today, He will make your life an oasis of love for others, equipping them to find solutions to their immediate problems as well as eternal salvation.

> Behold, I stand at the door and knock. If anyone hears
> My voice and opens the door, I will come in to him and
> dine with him, and he with Me. To him who overcomes I
> will grant to sit with Me on My throne, as I also overcame
> and sat down with My Father on His throne.
>
> (Revelation 3:20–21)

If you would like to open your heart's door to Jesus, if you would like to experience the transformation Annie experienced at Brother Andrew's gospel crusade, then you can say this simple prayer:

> Father God, I believe that Jesus Christ is your Son and
> that He died to pay the price for my sin. Thank you
> for forgiving me. Lord Jesus, I accept your free gift of
> salvation. I pray this in Jesus' name, Amen.

This prayer is taken from GOD TV's "Existence" web page, which answers questions about sin and salvation and provides video testimonies from others who have come to know God (see www.god.tv/ex – Jesus is the core of our existence!).

The message of this book is one of finding victory in the face of defeat, and hope in the face of despair, and replacing hatred with love. As you have seen from Annie Chikhwaza's example, you can trust God to rebuild your life from scratch if need be, and He will also empower you to help others.

> Blessed is the man who fears the Lord,
> Who delights greatly in His commandments.
> His descendants will be mighty on earth;
> The generation of the upright will be blessed ...
> He will not be afraid of evil tidings;
> His heart is steadfast, trusting in the Lord.
> His heart is established;
> He will not be afraid...
> He has dispersed abroad,
> He has given to the poor;
> His righteousness endures forever;
> His horn will be exalted with honour.
>
> (Psalm 112:1–9)

Annie believes that God gave her a prophetic word in 1998, encouraging her to embrace Him, and all would be won:

> You will conquer. The conquering spirit is never crushed.
> Keep a brave and trusting heart. Face all your difficulties
> in the spirit of conquest. Rise to greater heights than you
> have known before. Forces of evil within and without you
> flee at My presence.
> Win Me and all is won. All.

Annie has treasured these words as she has seen the power of God at work in her life, time and time again. She has overcome molestation, divorce, abuse, abortion, carjacking, a broken back, false accusation, attempted murder, losing everything she had built, burglary, attempted rape, and the death of her beloved husband, and she has had her heart broken by seeing so many children die of HIV / AIDS.

Considering everything she has been through, does she think it has been worthwhile? As she looks back over her life, would she do it all again?

"The word of God says to count it as joy when you go through trials. It is not the trials and temptations that are the joy, of course, but the outcome – all you have accomplished – which is why you would do it again!" Annie answers.

"Would I want to go through all those situations again? No, not really! But if I had to, I would, because look at the results. All that heartache has borne incredible fruit.

"With hindsight I see it was all God's plan, but I had to suffer in order for the Father to build in my life, for the future of our children. I believe now that it had to be this way. My blood had to flow in order for God to work."

Annie is an example of a life redeemed from destruction (Psalm 103:4), and she knows well the promise of Psalm 116: "I was facing death, and He saved me!" Take courage from her extraordinary testimony and be assured that what God has done in her life, He can and will do for you, as you trust Him. An anonymous quotation sums this up perfectly:

Only God can turn a MESS into a MESSage;
a TEST into a TESTimony;
a TRIal into a TRIumph
and a VICTim into a VICTory!

"We have got to finish that obstacle race!" Annie stresses. "We can't afford to lose our vision or give up, or become bogged down by sin. This is not the time to give in to temptation but to overcome all the works of the flesh. We have to keep running with endurance as we look to Jesus.

Therefore we also, since we are surrounded by so great a cloud of witnesses, let us lay aside every weight, and the sin which so easily ensnares us, and let us run with endurance the race that is set before us, looking unto Jesus, the author and finisher of our faith, who for the joy that was set before Him endured the cross...

(Hebrews 12:1)

"Keep looking to Jesus because He is the one who will keep your vision afloat," Annie advises. "I'm so glad today that I never lost my vision for Malawi."

She insists that having problems is not an excuse to quit. "God did a strange thing in my life. He took me to a new country to marry a man who was from a different culture, without any disposable income. He told me that this was where He wanted me to be, and He wasn't going to change His mind because things got tough. He wasn't going to say, 'Annie, your obstacle race is too difficult; you'd better go home to South Africa'.

"The devil always tries to stop God's plan from succeeding, and we must never allow that to happen. He has tried to destroy me so often: being left for dead in front of my house was not the first time he tried to kill me. Remember how many times I tried to commit suicide as a young woman, when the doctor said to me, 'Annie, God has a plan for your life'?

"I couldn't see it then, but now I see just how that plan for my life has unfolded, so I want to encourage others, because God has a plan for their lives too. So when thing gets difficult you cannot give up; you have to rise to the challenge!

"If I'd lost my vision, there would be no Kondanani today. Never even consider giving up on what you feel God is asking you to do: don't take the easy way out. The attack on my life was not the end; it was the beginning of something good. My friend Wendy understands this well and that's why I have asked her to write a few final words at the end of this book.

"We have to understand who we are in Christ, that we've been given everything we need to live as He wants us to. Not just a little bit, not a half measure – it is all there, and that includes God's protection. That doesn't mean we will never be in danger: I've been attacked, nearly raped, and burgled at Kondanani. Why? Because following God *is* an obstacle race. But if you give up at the first hurdle, you'll never become the person God wants you to be.

"Some people think that overcoming obstacles strengthens our character, but it isn't about our character; we want to become like Jesus – that is what changes our lives and helps us to face the next obstacle.

"Believers should do things in faith and trust God for His protection. Don't be put off by the risks of your calling, because it may bring many dangers, but God will see you through them, there is no doubt about that.

"The Lord has given me many significant verses over the years but Psalm 91 is my core Scripture. It is my insurance policy! That doesn't mean that I am never going to be in danger, but this is the promise of God to me, and He is faithful and keeps His promises."

Annie Chikhwaza has always been one to push the boundaries of possibility. She knows she serves the God of the impossible, who can redeem even the direst circumstances.

Abandoned by a man who tried to thwart her ministry, she was called to marry one who would empower it, but it was not an easy choice to give up everything and go to Malawi. "But I was so happy," she says, "because I was doing what the Father wanted."

Even so, her back was broken in a horrendous car accident and later she was attacked and severely beaten up. For a time the future looked bleak, yet God was always in control. Annie and Lewis Chikhwaza and their team at Kondanani have transformed the lives of so many children and the work they started is set to carry on from strength to strength in the years ahead.

God has clearly anointed Annie to "bind up the wounds of the broken-hearted and proclaim liberty to the captives" (Isaiah 61), but we must not allow her to do it alone. It is time for the church to be the hands and feet of our Lord Jesus.

"The church of today can no longer reach out on a spiritual level alone," Annie affirms. "Salvation is for spirit, soul, and body. We have to feed the hungry and bring water to the thirsty. The tears may flow, but nothing makes me happier than the task set before me."

"So often Christians see the need and say they'll pray about it, but do nothing," said Don Botham, producer of *In Depth with Annie Chikhwaza*. "Annie saw the need and responded to it and, despite many difficult days, the lack of resources, and the pain of seeing little children dying, she has endured to make a difference in the lives of many who would otherwise have perished.

"This is the gospel at work in a powerful way, a testimony of God's grace and one woman's fortitude in the face of enormous odds. I urge people to follow her example and reach out to their communities in a similar way."

"Sometimes I stand in front of my house and look at everything around me and think to myself, 'Only God could have done this!'" Annie concludes.

God has opened door after door for Annie Chikhwaza, and He can also open a door for you. If you walk through it, and never give up on your personal obstacle race, your life too can become a Door of Hope for others.

Allow the love of God to fill you so that you too can create an oasis of love wherever you go, for:

Who shall separate us from the love of Christ?
Shall tribulation, or distress, or persecution, or famine,
or nakedness, or peril, or sword...? Yet in all these things
we are more than conquerors through Him who loved
us. For I am persuaded that neither death nor life, nor
angels nor principalities nor powers, nor things present
nor things to come, nor height nor depth, nor any other
created thing, shall be able to separate us from the love of
God which is in Christ Jesus our Lord.

(Romans 8:35–39)

Kondanani Anthem

We were the forgotten children,
Unwanted and lost.
Just another mouth to feed,
A promise of great cost.
Our beginning laced with rejection,
Poverty and despair,
Without hope and a future;
Life was empty, cold and bare.
One day the answer found us,
A helping hand from on high
Who reached into our situation
And didn't pass us by.
We arrived at Kondanani,
A village full of love
For the unwanted and rejected,
Governed by God above.

We are the children of destiny,
Hand-picked by the King.
Chosen as His precious gems.
That is why we sing.
That is why we sing.

There began our new life
In this special place;
The life we knew has long gone,
Disappeared without a trace.
We're the leaders of tomorrow;
Our destiny is sure:

Teachers, lawyers, doctors,
Whose motives and thoughts are pure.

We are the children of destiny,
Hand-picked by the King.
Chosen as His precious gems.
That is why we sing.
That is why we sing.

We will change our nation;
From nothing we have come.
We'll transform our generation
Until our work is done.

We are the children of destiny,
Hand-picked by the King.
Chosen as His precious gems.
That is why we sing.
That is why we sing.
We'll bring glory to our King!

Afterword

WENDY ALEC

An epic battle for the Last Days is upon us. The evil one is furious with what God is doing in the lives of believers, and so many have been propelled into traumatic situations.

They may be in a pit, like Joseph, or in the lions' den, like Daniel, or in a fiery furnace. But when Peter was "sifted as wheat", how did Jesus respond to him? "I have prayed for you, that your faith should not fail," He said (Luke 22:32).

My dear friend Annie Chikhwaza is an excellent example of a woman whose faith has not failed her. She has been in the pit, knows the lions' den well, and has often been sifted. Her life has been threatened many times and she was even left for dead, but by God's grace she has prevailed.

Annie is an overcomer, and I know your faith will have been strengthened as you have read her testimony of what God can do in the most hopeless of situations. I want to encourage you today – what God has done for Annie He can and will do in your life, if you just trust Him.

And if you feel you have been sifted as wheat, I believe the Lord wants to respond to you in the same way as He spoke to Peter. "I have prayed for you," He says, "that your faith wouldn't fail you."

It's my prayer that reading this book will not just have strengthened your faith but that you will have experienced the love of God in a new way, and that your hope in God has increased. I believe the Lord wants the church to achieve new breakthroughs, and that's why stories like Annie's are so inspiring, because they prove what can be done by the power of God working through His faithful people.

I regard Annie as a spiritual mother. She took me into her home and helped disciple me when I was young. Now she is doing the same for countless others! We have shared many tears of joy and laughter as we have experienced God's provision together and been enabled to overcome the opposition we have faced. We thank God that He has sustained us all these years and that our faith has not failed us. May your faith never fail you.

I trust that Annie's story will continue to give you hope, but if you feel hopeless for any reason today, be assured that God is on your side and that His plan for you will come to fruition.

The promises of the Bible offer such hope for people who, like the "woman with the issue of blood", have been from doctor to doctor and done all they can to find healing. Some have been weighed down with feelings of depression and anxiety, not wanting to live any longer, saying, "Father, I can't go on like this; I'd rather go home to be with You."

As the chapters of this book have unfolded you will have discovered how Annie dealt with such challenges, and seen how God came through for her – and He will most certainly come through for you too.

The Father wants His children to see His power at work, to see the Holy Spirit bring the answers to our prayers. He is not a vague, distant spiritual entity. He is close to the broken-hearted; He is moved by the tears of the innocent victims of HIV/AIDS in Africa, whom Annie so lovingly cares for, and, if you are hurting today, I hope you know that He is close to you.

God will not forsake you, and Jesus will not forget you. The Father sent His Son into the world so that you might have eternal life. If you are a believer, your name is written in the Book of Life and God knows the very number of hairs on your head.

But Jesus did not come just to secure your eternity, but so that you might also overcome all the troubles of this life. He is the Author and the Finisher of our faith, and He will finish what He has started.

And be assured that God's blessing is not just for heaven; He wants you to experience it right here on earth:

> **I would have lost heart, unless I had believed**
> **That I would see the goodness of the Lord in the land of**
> **the living.**
> **Wait on the Lord;**
> **Be of good courage,**
> **And He shall strengthen your heart.**

> (Psalm 27:13–14)

Annie sees life as an obstacle race, and I hope that her story has inspired you to climb over each obstacle you encounter, and continue the race.

The Lord wants to reveal His mercy, His compassion, and His loving-kindness to the world, and it's our heartfelt desire at GOD TV, in partnership with the many charities we support worldwide, including Kondanani, to be part of this work. Together we can indeed be an oasis of love for those in need.

Wendy Alec
GOD TV Co-founder and Director of Television

Kondanani Children's Village contact details

Annie Chikhwaza
Founder and Executive Director
e-mail: annie@kondanani.org

Cherie Martin
Executive Assistant
e-mail: cherie@kondanani.org

Kondanani Children's Village
PO Box 30871
Chichiri, Blantyre 3
Malawi
Telephone:
Mobile: +265 (0) 999 299 151
E-mail: annie@kondanani.org
Web: www.kondanani.org

Bank account details:

UK

Bank name: Co-operative Bank
PO Box 250, Delf House, Southway,
Skelmersdale, WN8 6WT.
Account name: Kondanani
Account number: 65111057.
Branch sort code: 08 92 99

Netherlands

Bank name: ABNAMRO
PO Box 11034, 230 IEA Leiden.
Account name: Stichting Kondanani Nederland
IBAN: NL33ABNA0623246597
BIC code (SWIFT address): ABNANL2a

Malawi

Bank name: Standard Bank of Malawi
Victoria Avenue, Blantyre. Limbe Branch
Account name: Kondanani
Type of account: Savers Plus
SWIFT code: SBIC MW MX
Forex account numbers:
USD: 0240055839700
GBP: 0340055839700
EUR: 7040055839700

South Africa

Bank name: Standard Bank, Tyger Manor Branch
Account name: Kondanani, Malawi
Account number: 076381005
Branch sort code: 050410
International SWIFT no.: SBZAZAJJ
Type of account: Market Link

Other books by Al Gibson

Life on the Line

Also published by Monarch Books, Lion Hudson

Touching heaven, changing earth – the amazing account of how an ordinary man died and went to heaven.

When you put your life on the line for God, it will become a lifeline for others.

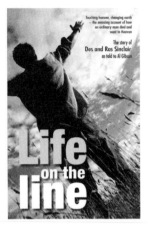

As he lay dying in a hospital bed in New Zealand, evangelist Des Sinclair was caught up into heaven, where he experienced a startling glimpse into the world of the supernatural. Des may have been pronounced "dead" but his life's calling was far from complete, and God sent him back to have an impact on the world. Since then he and his wife Ros have travelled around the globe witnessing remarkable miracles, including seeing three people raised from the dead.

The Sinclairs have preached the gospel in the face of fierce opposition. Des was thrown out by his father when he was just eleven years old; he has been abused, imprisoned, tortured, and sentenced to death, yet delivered time and time again in the most extraordinary circumstances. Their conviction, shared through story after story, miracle after miracle, is that when you put your life on the line for God, it will become a lifeline for others to hold on to.

www.life-on-the-line.com